THE GEORGIA HISTORY BOOK

THE GEORGIA HISTORY BOOK

By Lawrence R. Hepburn

 INSTITUTE OF GOVERNMENT
THE UNIVERSITY OF GEORGIA

THE GEORGIA HISTORY BOOK

Editor: Emily Honigberg

Design and production: Reid McCallister
  Production assistant: Linda Layson

Typesetting: Debra Peters

Proofreading: Dorothy Paul

Institute publications editor: Ann Blum

Fourth Printing

Library of Congress Cataloging in Publication Data

Hepburn, Lawrence R., 1940-
    The Georgia history book.

    Includes index.
    SUMMARY: A textbook of Georgia history from the first Indian inhabitants to the industrial and political developments in the 1980's.
    1. Georgia—History—Juvenile literature. [1. Georgia—History] I. Title.
F286.3.H46   975.8   82-9183
ISBN 0-89854-080-1   AACR2

FOREWORD

The Georgia History Book is the result of several years of research and writing initiated at the request of social science educators. When the Georgia Studies course, including a history component, was mandated for the public schools, no text then available could meet the multiple objectives of the social science curriculum. With these objectives in sight, and in consultation with teachers and curriculum coordinators, the research and writing of this book began.

The first purpose is to instruct students about Georgia's past. Major happenings are described. The major focus, however, is on *people*. Ordinary Georgians as well as some well-known ones are included.

As the Georgia Studies program is an integral part of the social science curriculum, the text addresses the methods of historical and social scientific inquiry. What questions do historians ask? What sources of information do they use? To teach students to *do* history (much as they might do mathematics or science), requires that they work with historical materials, not merely consume conclusions. To meet this requirement, the textbook includes documents from the past.

Of related concern is the nature of the learners—young people beginning to consider who they are and what they wish to become. Thus, the textbook includes material that might help students identify with worthy persons who lived in other times but who faced life situations similar to those the students are facing. A final aim, then, was to stimulate learning and, at the same time, help students make the history of Georgia's people their own.

The author is Lawrence R. Hepburn, educational research associate at the Institute of Government. As a high school teacher and college professor, Dr. Hepburn has for over 15 years been developing instructional materials and teaching teachers. He is the author of another volume in this series, *State Government in Georgia*.

Delmer D. Dunn
Director
Institute of Government

April 1982

ACKNOWLEDGEMENTS

Map credits: James D. Ingram, Dolores V. Holt, Cartographic Services, University of Georgia, 10, 13, 21, 22, 26, 29, 52, 65, 66, 70, 72, 91, 92, 95, 102, 104, 109, 142, 181, 202, 203; Department of Geography, Institute of Community and Area Development, University of Georgia, *An Atlas of Multi-County Organizational Units in Georgia*, 207; Edwin L. Jackson, 7, 61, 79, 86, 106; Maps on pages 10, 66, 70 and 72 were based on original work by Marion Hemperley, Deputy Surveyor-General of Georgia.

Photo credits: Atlanta Braves, 205; Atlanta Historical Society, 99, 109, 127, 130, 134, 171, 183 top; *Atlanta Journal-Constitution,* 179, 185, 191; Atlanta Symphony, 206; Atlanta University Archives, Atlanta University Center, Woodruff Library, 149; Charles Forrest Palmer Papers, Special Collections Department, Robert W. Woodruff Library, Emory University, 172; Georgia Agrirama, 199; Georgia Department of Archives and History, 10, 74, 98, 104, 107, 116, 131, 132, 137, 140, 141, 142, 157, 160, 162, 163, 167, 169, 170, 173, 182, 184, 187; Georgia Department of Natural Resources, 119, 180; Martin Luther King, Jr., Center for Non-violent Social Change, 192, 196; Reid McCallister, 12, 31, 84, Walker Montgomery, 23, 198; Carl Rooks, Glynn County Schools, 153; Smithsonian Institution, 16; University of Georgia Library, 25, 39, 55, 81, 93, 117, 118, 120, 122, 155, 161, 176, 177, 183 bottom; Sam Walton, 201.

Illustrations: Office of the Secretary of State, Georgia—Anthony M. Hood, 11, 14, 76, and Liz Carmichael Jones 48, 53; Deborah Keener 35, 139.

The author wishes to acknowledge the contributions of persons who helped bring this project to fruition.

David Lovett, research assistant, tracked down many primary sources and conducted most oral history interviews.

Several colleagues at the University of Georgia critically reviewed manuscript chapters: F. N. Boney and Charles E. Wynes, Department of History; Thomas G. Dyer, Institute of Higher Education; and Charles Hudson, Department of Anthropology.

A number of Georgia educators reviewed and/or classroom-tested parts of the manuscript: Helen W. Richardson, coordinator of social studies, Fulton County Schools; Howard B. Sims, Jr., social science coordinator, Atlanta Public Schools; Sherry Malone, principal, Clarke County Schools; and the following Fulton County teachers: Patricia Avery, C. June Bryant, Luci Fleming, Sam Harvey, Missy Loeb, Woodie Persons, and Kim H. Pruitt.

Portions of this book are based on material that first appeared in *Changing Culture: Georgia History*, Ruby H. Crowe and Jeanette B. Moon, editors; published by the Atlanta and Fulton County Schools, 1971.

Co-worker Ed Jackson is responsible for many good ideas that became part of this book.

Responsibility for errors of fact and judgment is, of course, the author's alone.

CONTENTS

MAPS

FIGURES

UNIT I
Digging Up the Past

1. How to Do History
2. Earliest Georgia

GEORGIA EVENTS	DATE	EVENTS ELSEWHERE
Paleo-Indians hunt large game	c.10,000	Animals domesticated in Near East
Archaic Indians, hunters and gatherers	c. 8,000	Agriculture appears in Near East
	c. 4,000	Civilization develops in Near East; beginning of recorded history
	c.1,700	Judaism founded by Abraham
Woodland Indians develop agriculture	c.1,000	
	753	Founding of Rome
	BC ⎯⎯ AD	Birth of Christ
	476	Fall of Rome
Mississippian Indians, the "mound-builders," develop permanent towns	c. 800	Charlemagne's Empire brings order and Christianity to Europe
	1492	Columbus discovers New World
	1521	Protestant Reformation begins in Europe
DeSoto explores region; beginning of historic period	1540	Potatoes from Americas introduced as food into Europe
	1565	Spanish found St. Augustine, Florida
Spanish missions built on St. Simons and Jekyll islands	1595	
	1607	Virginia Colony settled by English
	1619	Black slaves brought to Virginia
English trade with Indians	1650	Corn from Americas first used as food in Europe
Indians attack South Carolina frontier	1715	
British build Fort King George on Altamaha River	1721	

1 How to Do History

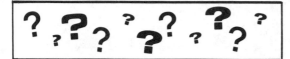

James and Ellen Young wanted to buy a home of their own. One evening, the couple found an ad in the newspaper:

House in Older Subdivision. Close to Downtown. 3 BR, 2 baths. Needs some minor fixing-up. Reduced to $47,750. Hurry on this one!

"This sounds just like what we want— an older place with plenty of room," said James.

"But is it worth the money?" asked Ellen. "And how much fixing-up will it need?"

To answer these questions, the Youngs had to have information about the *history* of the house. They talked to a real estate agent and to the owner. They asked a carpenter to check the condition of the house. They even talked to people who owned houses in the neighborhood. Then they had a lawyer check court records on the property. Finally, they felt they knew enough to make a wise decision. They decided to buy the house.

To know the present condition of their house, the Youngs had to find out about its past. They asked questions. They used different sources of information.

To understand present conditions in Georgia, the United States, and the world, you have to know something about past events. Why do we have problems of energy shortage, pollution, and violent crime? Why are the United States and the Soviet Union bitter rivals? Why are average wages higher in New York and California than in Georgia and South Carolina? None of these questions can be fully answered without knowing what happened in the past.

Finding Out What Happened

Persons whose job is to find out what happened in the past are called historians. They may study what happened to a group of people (such as Indians), a geographic location (such as Savannah), or a part of culture (such as agriculture). In any case, historians do their work by asking questions and using many sources of information.

Questions

The study of history begins with questions concerning an event, person, or group. What caused the first settlers to come to Georgia? How did slavery get started in the colony? Why were the Indians forced out of the state?

From what historians already know about such things, they form *hypotheses,* or tentative answers, to the questions. One historian may think the settlers were seeking religious freedom. Another may think they left England because they were in debt.

To *verify*, or test, the accuracy of their hypotheses, historians have to gather evidence. There are many sources of information to which historians may turn for evidence.

Sources of Information

Historians distinguish between two kinds of sources: primary sources and secondary sources.

Primary sources provide the evidence on which historical research is based. They are first-hand or original accounts of what happened. Examples of written primary sources are letters, diaries, speeches, newspaper reports, government documents, and business records. Other kinds of primary sources are oral accounts by persons who recall an event and physical remains such as buildings, tools, clothing, art work, and even gravemarkers. Old photos and maps are also primary sources. In general, primary sources date closely in time to the event under study.

 In this text, primary sources are identified by the quill pen symbol.

 Some primary sources have a mini-symbol.

Secondary sources are derived from primary sources. They are the products of historical research and are often far removed in time from the events they describe. Secondary sources such as bio-graphies, textbooks, and reference books are useful for getting background information on a topic.

 In this book, you can spot secondary sources by the book symbol.

PRIMARY AND SECONDARY SOURCES*

Examples of Primary Sources—
1. Letter: From General Sherman, U.S. Army, to General Hood, Confederate States Army, Sept. 7, 1864
2. Photograph: Fortifications on Peachtree Road, 1864
3. Diary: Of Dolly Lunt Burge, Covington, Georgia, Nov. 19, 1864
4. Proclamation: By Governor Joseph Brown, July 9, 1864
5. Map: Confederate line of defense, City of Atlanta, 1864
6. Newspaper advertisement: *Daily Intelligencer* (Atlanta), May 11, 1864

Examples of Secondary Sources—
1. History book: William Key, *The Battle of Atlanta,* 1958
2. Biography: John P. Dyer, *Fightin' Joe Wheeler,* 1941
3. Novel: Margaret Mitchell, *Gone With the Wind,* 1936
4. Story: Joel Chandler Harris, "A Baby in The Siege," in *Tales of the Home Folks in Peace and War,* 1898
5. Article: Stuart Emmrich, "The Day Atlanta Surrendered," *Atlanta Journal and Constitution,* Sept. 3, 1977
6. Textbook: Albert B. Saye, *Georgia History and Government,* 1973

*These are some sources you might use to study the fighting in and around Atlanta during the Civil War.

Using Primary Sources

One of the historian's most important tasks is criticizing, or questioning, the sources. Is the source real or a forgery? Who was the author of the source? Was he or she an actual eyewitness to the event under study? If so, what was the witness's *frame of reference?* A witness's view of an event can be influenced by his or her social group, religion, occupation, and political attitudes. These characteristics make up the witness's frame of reference. The more historians know about *why* a source came to be written, the better they can judge the value of the information it contains.

Telling What Happened

Finally, historians have the task of telling what happened. This involves pulling together pieces of evidence from primary sources. They have to weigh each piece and decide which is most reliable. The unreliable is set aside.

Now the historian is ready to make *generalizations,* or conclusions, about what happened. Actually, the historian is answering the questions asked at the start of his research. These answers may be quite different from the original hypotheses, or tentative answers. Perhaps the historian will conclude that the first settlers came to Georgia for several reasons: to make a fortune, to escape persecution, to get away from bad economic conditions.

Finally, historians describe to others what they have found. In doing this, they try to be objective. They try not to be influenced by their personal feelings. Whether or not they like what they find, historians try to be guided only by the evidence.

Of course, as other historians dig up new evidence about the same past event, they may describe things differently. In that case, our view of the past may change.

This Book

This book will help you study history, not just memorize facts, dates, and names from the past. You will be asking questions and thinking like a historian. To do these things, you will examine the same kinds of sources historians use to find out what happened.

Before you begin Chapter 2, however,

there is one matter to get out of the way—dates.

The Dating Game

You will find plenty of dates in this book—dates like 1492, 1620, 1776, 1981. Are dates important? By itself a date has little meaning; by itself a date is not really important.

However, knowing when one event occurred *in relationship to when other events occurred* is important. Why?

Let's look at some events in a murder case being investigated by a detective:

1. victim found shot in own house
2. victim overheard threatening business partner in office
3. business partner stopped for speeding in distant city
4. business partner bought handgun in local store
5. victim and business partner seen laughing together in restaurant
6. victim's wife reports house broken into

In order to solve the case, the detective has to know the time relationship of these events: In what order did the events occur? Which occurred at about the same time? Exactly when did each occur?

Knowing the *chronology* (time order) of events enables the detective to place each event in context (in its surroundings). This helps the detective to reconstruct what happened. It also provides clues as to why something happened. Knowing the context of an event is just as important to a historian as to a detective.

In solving a murder case, the detective tries to find possible motives, or causes, for the act. Likewise, the historian tries to find out what caused certain events to take place. Sometimes one event appears to cause, or lead to, another event. Historians call this relationship *cause and effect.* Often, they discover that not just one but several causes preceded an event. Most big happenings—for instance, the settling of the New World, the American Revolution, the

Civil War—stem from many previous happenings. This principle is called *multiple causation*.

Then, are dates important to know? If you need to know when one event happened *in relation to when other events happened*, dates are very important. Out of context, by themselves, dates are not important.

Time Lines

A time line is a chart which shows at a glance the chronological order (time order) of events. Each of the following units in this book includes a time line to help you keep track of the relationship of events. The time lines include Georgia events plus other important events.

By examining the time lines at the beginning of each unit you may be able to form some hypotheses about possible cause and effect relationships among events.

Dating Sources of Information

It is usually far easier to determine the date for an event in a historic period than in a prehistoric period. For one thing, calendars were in use in historic times. For another, historical documents usually contain clues to when they were written. Many, such as letters and diaries, have dates written in them.

The dates of events in a prehistoric period have to be calculated from examination of physical remains, such as pottery, tools, and human and animal bones. Persons who study such prehistoric remains are called archeologists. They often work together with historians who specialize in written records. Today, using scientific methods, archeologists can date physical remains many thousands of years old.

ACTIVITIES FOR CHAPTER 1

These activities give some tips on how to use this book.

A. Table of Contents and Time Lines

This book is divided into 15 chapters grouped in six units. The units cover long periods of time, starting with earliest Georgia and continuing up to the present. The chapters within each unit are organized around topics—such as "Georgia Indians," not around blocks of time—such as "1840-1860." Therefore, events described in one chapter may overlap in time events in another chapter.

To help you keep Georgia events in proper sequence—and relate them to events elsewhere—time lines appear at the beginning of each unit. For practice in using time lines—

1. Turn to the Table of Contents.

2. Locate the time lines for the units.

3. Find out when each of these Georgia "firsts" happened: (a) first newspaper established, (b) first cotton mill built, (c) first black citizens vote, (d) first child labor law passed, and (e) first radio station broadcasts.

B. List of Maps

A map is a source of information about the location and distribution of a subject. A listing of all maps in this book appears with the Table of Contents.

For practice in using maps as sources of information, do the following:

1. Locate the county in which you live, using the Reference Map on page 207.

2. Find the same approximate location on each of these maps:

a. Georgia Physical Regions, page 7.

b. Land Lotteries, page 66.

c. Georgia in the Civil War, page 109.

3. Answer these questions:

a. In which physical region is your county located?

b. When was your county opened to settlement?

c. Was your county in the path of the "March to the Sea" in 1864?

2 Earliest Georgia

At first the earth was flat and soft and wet. The great buzzard, father of all the buzzards we see now, flew over the earth to see if it was yet dry. When he reached the Cherokee country, he was tired, and his flapping wings touched the ground. Wherever they struck the earth there was a valley. Where they turned up again there was a mountain.

—from a Cherokee myth

To stay alive, people everywhere must solve the same basic problems. They must find food to eat, water to drink, air to breathe, and shelter from the rain or snow, heat or cold.

Sometimes, to meet these needs, human beings have to adapt to their surroundings. Sometimes they change their surroundings in ways that help them survive.

The different peoples who have inhabited Georgia have used their surroundings—their physical environment—in different ways. This chapter focuses on the Indians and how they used their physical environment. Later chapters will look closely at the Europeans and Africans who came to Georgia.

THE PHYSICAL SETTING OF GEORGIA

What did the first inhabitants find when they came into the territory we now call Georgia? The following reading describes what the first inhabitants probably found. It is written as if it were a report made by space explorers traveling in a futuristic airship. Like the American astronauts who explored the surface of the moon, these fictional explorers made aerial surveys. They also landed and looked closely at the physical environment. They took measurements and collected samples of plant and animal life, soil, water, and minerals. Here is the report.

THINK ABOUT IT

1. What are the three physical regions of the territory now known as Georgia? How do the regions differ from each other?
2. What kinds of plants and animals were available to the first inhabitants of the territory?

Preliminary Report: We have spent one full year examining the territory. It measures approximately 320 miles in length, north-south, 260 miles in breadth, east-west; and has over 100 miles of coastline.

The territory has a generally humid climate. The weather is influenced by westerly winds and the nearness of the saltwater ocean. Many rivers and streams flow from higher elevations down to this ocean.

The territory has several distinct physical regions: (1) the Coastal Plain, (2) the Piedmont, and (3) the Appalachian, which is divided into the Blue Ridge, Ridge and Valley, and Plateau sub-regions.

We have prepared a map of the territory showing rough physical features. Please refer to it as you read the following descriptions.

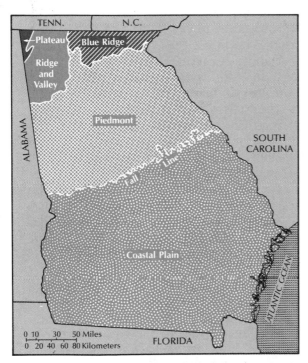

MAP 1. *The Physical Regions of Georgia. Note the "fall line" which will become an important location in Georgia's history.*

The Coastal Plain

The Coastal Plain is a mostly flat region extending inland from the ocean coastline for about 150 miles. It covers probably 60 percent of the territory.

We have determined that millions of years ago the Coastal Plain was the ocean floor. The movement of water made it smooth and even. As the planet Earth's surface changed, this area slowly rose from beneath the water.

The soils of the Coastal Plain are yellow and gray; they are sandy and not very fertile. Waterways wind slowly through the sand and soft rock; their banks are usually low and overhung with trees.

We have observed, by flying along the coastline, many sandy islands and small bays, saltwater marshes, and beaches backed by sand dunes. Near the coast the land is low-lying. Cypress trees and cane grow in the swampy areas. On higher sandy ridges grow dense forests of longleaf pine and live oaks hung with moss. In great open areas, which we call savannahs, wire grass and saw grass grow.

Further inland, the Coastal Plain rises to several hundred feet above sea level. Here the land's surface may be gently rolling, but there are no steep hills or deep valleys.

The climate of the Coastal Plain is very mild. We estimate rainfall to be 40 to 60 inches per year. The growing season should be long, perhaps 200 to 240 days.

In our surface explorations we have found the Coastal Plain to be rich in edible wild plants including blackberries, palmetto, grapes, and prickly pear. From coastal and inland waterways we have collected samples of clams, oysters, mussels, crawfish, and crabs. We observed many other animals, including turtles, alligators, and fur-bearing mammals such as otter, muskrat, raccoon, and oppossum.

The Piedmont Region

The Piedmont makes up about 30 percent of the territory. It is an upland region, gently rolling to hilly, with many valleys. In the south, where it meets the Coastal Plain, it is about 500 feet above sea level. From there it rises to almost 2,000 feet at the Blue Ridge in the northeast.

The Piedmont and the Coastal Plain meet at the "fall line"—the old shore-line of the ocean. At this line, the harder clay soils of the Piedmont meet the soft sandy soils of the Coastal Plain. Here the rivers and streams fall from the higher Piedmont through rapids and shoals onto the plain. We have determined that up to this point, the fall line, some rivers could be open to navigation by boats.

Our surface examination of the Piedmont has revealed the topsoil to be as much as two to three feet deep in some places. Underneath, the soils are generally red to dark brown in color. They are mixtures of clay and rock or clay and sand. We have collected samples of this red soil (which is unusually difficult to wash from our skin and our flight suits).

Beneath the Piedmont soils is hard rock. This rock sometimes appears as large humps on the surface. It seems as if the soil has washed away, leaving the rock exposed.

Numerous streams flow across the Piedmont, generally from north to south. They move faster than on the Coastal Plain and have rapids and waterfalls.

The climate in this region is very agreeable. It is mild like that of the Coastal Plain, but summer is cooler and winter is colder in the northern part of the Piedmont. We have calculated rainfall to be about 50 inches per year. The growing season should be 180 to 200 days.

Our aerial survey has revealed that over 90 percent of the Piedmont is covered with thick forests. Pine and such hardwoods as oak, sweetgum, tulip, and sycamore are plentiful. We have also noted hickory, pecan, persimmon, and wild plum trees.

Wildlife in the Piedmont includes deer, black bear, beaver, and raccoon. Bobwhite quail and turkey live here, too. At times great flocks of ducks, geese, and passenger pigeons fill the sky, probably on their yearly migrations. (They could be a menace to air travel.)

The Appalachian Region

The Appalachian region is part of the mountain system that begins just southwest of the territory and runs north for over a thousand miles. This region has three distinct parts that altogether cover about 10 percent of the territory.

In the northeast is the Blue Ridge. Here are rugged highlands and mountains. Steep slopes are covered by oak, hickory, chestnut, and poplar trees. Most of the Blue Ridge is more than 3,000 feet above sea level. At least two dozen peaks rise higher than 4,000 feet. For the most part the soil is rocky. Rivers flow very swiftly through deep narrow channels, sometimes dropping through chasms, rapids, and waterfalls. A few flow northward.

Immediately to the west of the Blue Ridge lies the lower Ridge and Valley subregion. Its broad open valleys, 600 to 800 feet above sea level, run in a general northeast to southwest direction. The valley bottoms contain rich, fertile soil. Parallel to the valleys and rising up to 700 feet above them are narrow ridges. In this part of the territory the streams cut deep channels through rock, then twist and turn along the broad valley floors.

In the far northwest corner of the region is a small Plateau area. It consists of high flat-topped plateaus, but it also has peaks and valleys. In this sub-region the soils are generally poor, and level land is scarce.

The climate of the whole Appalachian region varies according to location and elevation. We have figured the annual rainfall to range from 50 inches in the northwest to over 70 inches in the extreme northeast. Winter and summer temperatures are, of course, lower in the high elevations. The growing season should range from only 150 to 180 days in the mountains to 180 to 210 days in the lower valleys.

This concludes our first report. We shall provide more details upon our return. However, we wish at this time to suggest further discussion of proposals to colonize this earth territory. We believe it has great possibilities for development. □

This physical setting for what is now Georgia changed only slightly during the first 10,000 years after the arrival of humans. A few patches of woodland were cleared; here and there mounds of earth piled up. The population was very small then—never more than a few thousand people.

Later, the population would number in the millions. Changes in the Coastal Plain, the Piedmont, and the Appalachian regions would be great.

The following section traces the development of the earliest ways of life in Georgia.

THE FIRST INHABITANTS

THINK ABOUT IT

1. How did the Archaic Indians make better use of natural resources than their Paleo-Indian ancestors? What advances did the Woodland Indians make?
2. What do the mounds and other ceremonial places reveal about the Woodland and Mississippian peoples?
3. How did Indian cultures change with the arrival of Europeans?

We now have evidence that as long as 25,000 years ago Asian people migrated from Siberia to Alaska. Gradually, their descendants spread southward and eastward. By 10,000 B.C., they had arrived in what is now Georgia.

Over several thousand years, these people developed four *traditions* in the Southeast. Each tradition had its own culture, or way of life, and lasted for a long time. These four traditions are called (1) Paleo-Indian, (2) Archaic, (3) Woodland, and (4) Mississippian.

Paleo-Indian Tradition

Georgia's first inhabitants left behind large well-made stone points, called "Clovis" points. The points were used on heavy spears for jabbing, not throwing, and are evidence that Paleo-Indian hunters killed large game. At the time these people lived in Georgia, mastodons and giant bison roamed North America.

These Indians lived in small bands and led a nomadic (or wandering) life. Constantly on the move in search of food, they stayed in one place for only a brief time.

Archaic Tradition

Around 8,000 B.C., the culture of Georgia's Indians was changing. Big game had died out. The people now depended on a combination of hunting, fishing, trapping, and gathering berries, nuts, and other wild plant foods.

The Indians of this period still lived in nomadic bands, traveling much of the time in search of food. The smaller throwing-spear points they left behind are clues that they hunted smaller game. Other clues suggest that these Indians remained in certain places for longer periods of time than did earlier Indians.

For example, at sites along the coast, there are great heaps of seashells. Shellfish were an important part of the people's diet. The size of these shell mounds shows not only that the people stayed longer in one place but also that they returned to it year after year.

These Indians also burned small areas of the forest. The undergrowth that grew up in the cleared areas attracted deer and other game.

Around 2,500 B.C., the first pottery appeared among Indians living along the coast. It was made of fibers of Spanish moss, grass, or roots mixed with the clay to strengthen it for firing. This pottery shows that the Indians cooked food with water or oil and that life was becoming more settled. Pottery couldn't be easily carried long distances without being broken.

Did these Indians have religion? We don't know much about that, but it ap-

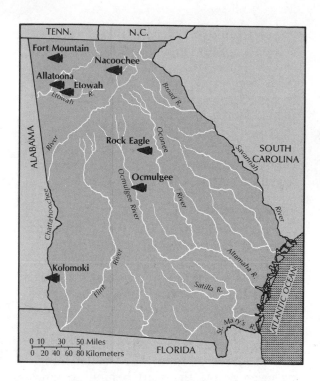

MAP 2. *Pre-Colonial Indian Sites. From these sites archaeologists have collected physical remains that provide clues to early Indian cultures.*

Rock Eagle. An example of an effigy mound built around A.D. 200 by Indians of the Woodland Tradition.

pears that proper burial of the dead had become important. These people used small pits for burials.

Woodland Tradition

By 1,000 B.C., a new cultural tradition had started. Like their Archaic ancestors, Woodland Indians were at home in the forest, but they made better use of resources. For hunting, they developed a new weapon, the bow and arrow.

Even more important, agriculture appeared. Woodland Indians began to save seeds in the fall for spring planting in cleared forest areas. This practice eventually increased the food supply. The population increased, bands joined together to form tribes, and small villages began to appear.

Archeologists have collected evidence indicating that Woodland Indians traded throughout what is now the eastern United

States. Artifacts made of copper from as far away as the Great Lakes have been found in Georgia.

This evidence also reveals that Georgia's Indians shared religious ideas with other Indians of the eastern woodlands. Earth and stone burial mounds, often containing jewelry, pottery figurines of humans and animals, and other ceremonial objects, along with corpses, have been unearthed. Woodland Indians also had special sites for ceremonial purposes. Sometimes, they built huge "effigy" mounds of rock and dirt in the shape of animals.

Mississippian Tradition

Between A.D. 700 and A.D. 900, a new Indian tradition—Mississippian—developed in the Southeast. These Indians lived along the Mississippi River and in other places that offered (1) rich bottomlands by rivers, (2) long moist growing seasons, and (3) good deer and turkey hunting.

Wild foods remained important to the Indians of the Mississippian period, but they also had come to rely on agriculture.

A Mississippian Village. This artist's drawing is based on archaeological evidence. Do the features shown indicate this was a permanent settlement?

They cultivated beans, corn, pumpkins, squash, and other plants. They stored their harvest in community storehouses. This meant they had a constant food supply and, in some years, even a surplus.

Agriculture supported a larger population. It enabled the Mississippian people to live in large permanent settlements. A Mississippian settlement was usually protected by a wooden palisade (a wall made of tall posts) and a moat (wide ditch) outside the palisade. It contained many houses of wood and clay.

Above the tribe level there developed a new social organization, called a chiefdom. At the top a priest-chief ruled, perhaps over several villages. This job was handed down through the ruling family. Below were nobles and ordinary people.

Mississippian Indians also had a highly organized religious system. They built large flat-topped mounds with temples and other buildings for ceremonies at the top. Inside and at the base of mounds were burial places—some simple pits, others elaborate log tombs. Buried along with the dead were food, tools, ornaments, and ceremonial objects of wood, copper, seashell, and stone.

Indian culture reached a high point during the Mississippian period. Evidence recovered from the many sites of the period tells us more about these people than we know about any of their ancestors. We know that Indian traders regularly traveled along waterways and forest trails between settlements such as Etowah, Ocmulgee, and Kolomokii. Artifacts unearthed from burials show the high artistic level of the people. We even know what games they played, and that they smoked tobacco and decorated themselves with jewelry, feathers, and tattooing. We know that their lives were full of ceremony and that they had special places to conduct ceremonies.

HISTORIC PERIOD

The first written descriptions of what is now Georgia were made by one of the men accompanying the Spanish explorer, Hernando DeSoto. In 1540, DeSoto came up from Florida with more than 600 men, looking for gold and other wealth. They marched to the northeast, crossing the Ocmulgee and Savannah rivers. Later, they turned to the northwest into the mountains, finally crossing into what is now Alabama.

A member of DeSoto's force kept a log book which reveals how the Indians were treated by these Spanish soldiers. Their food supplies were quickly taken over. Indian men and women were captured and made to work as slaves for the soldiers. Many died in bloody battles.

After DeSoto, other explorers came to the southeast. However, few details are known about what happened during the next hundred years. Many Indians died, probably from smallpox and other diseases brought to America by the Europeans. Weakened by the onslaught of war and disease, the great Mississippian tradition finally crumbled. From it, several tribal groups, or nations, emerged. In Georgia, the most powerful were the Cherokee and the Creek.

In the 1600s and 1700s, Spain, England, and France struggled for control of what is now the southeastern United States. The Europeans built forts in the region. The Spanish built a string of missions on the coast to convert the Indians to Christianity. English traders swarmed into the back

Etowah. A major Georgia site of the Mississippian Tradition, as it looked in 1982. At one time, the mound was topped by a building.

country, setting up trading posts where they swapped all sorts of goods for deerskins and furs.

All this contact with the Europeans changed the Indians' culture. Tools of stone, bone, and shell were discarded. European cloth, iron hoes and hatchets, and brass kettles and pots appeared in Indian villages. And the Indians learned to use the white man's guns and ammunition.

The Indians traded goods with the white man—deerskins for rifles, for example—and became more dependent on European goods. Sometimes, in return for goods, they agreed to choose sides and war on their neighbors. So the Indian nations were drawn into and used in the European nations' struggle for land and power. Some Indians understood this, but they had little choice.

Here is what Brim, a Creek chief, had to say to an Englishman who came to talk about an alliance.

I am a true friend to the English and always have behaved myself as such. And, I find that when any of our people goes to your great King that they receive presents. I have not such presents to give as we receive from you, but hope that you will accept of such as I have. Though I never was down to see your great King, yet I am as straight hearted as the best of them that has been down. For, I do not find that the talk your great King gives them lasts any longer than the present he makes them. As soon as the present is wore out, the talk is forgotten. □
[Adapted from "Tobias Fitch's Journal to the Creeks, 1725," in *Travels in the American Colonies,* edited by Newton D. Mereness (New York, 1916), 177.]

Two Cultures in Conflict

The European brought to North America a pattern of life different from that of the Indians. Of course, the Cherokee, the

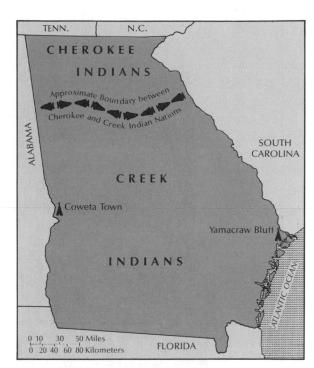

MAP 3. *The Creek and Cherokee Nations, 1733. At the time of first contacts with Europeans, the nations did not have definite boundaries. Individual tribes moved about within the areas shown.*

Creek, the Chickasaw, and others in the southeast did not all live exactly the same way. Each tribe had its own economy, government, religion, and family patterns. Generally, though, Indian values and customs differed greatly from those of the Europeans. As a result, a conflict of ideas soon developed between the Indians and the whites.

Different ideas about land ownership caused the biggest fight between the two races. For the Indian, an individual could no more actually own the land than the air or the rivers. Rather, a person could manage the land and use it. Thus, a tribe might have the right to use certain hunting grounds, and other tribes would respect that claim. But once that tribe stopped using the grounds (perhaps by moving away), it lost its special right to it. The European belief in the right of an individual to own land obviously clashed with the Indian idea about land rights.

A Young Man Becomes a Warrior. Ceremonies such as this one were an important part of the Indian cultures of the Historic Period.

Cherokee Lifestyle

What were the Indians like and how did they live? Many of the Indians who lived in the Appalachian region of Georgia, the Carolinas, Tennessee, and Alabama, were Cherokee. The Cherokees made up one of the most numerous Indian peoples of the southeast.

The Cherokee economy was based on agriculture, although hunting and trading were very important. In addition to houses, a village contained corn cribs and granaries, storehouses for hides and furs, and a "town house"—sort of a community center. Here the Indians held religious ceremonies and the councils (meetings) of leaders.

Nearby there were open areas for ceremonies and games. Out from the village were the large fields for planting.

The Indian economy had a division of labor by sex. Generally, the men hunted and traded and the women cared for the crops, ground corn, and wove clothes and baskets. However, everyone—even the chiefs—cleared the land, broke the ground, and planted the seed.

The Cherokee were governed by councils of head-men drawn from the ruling families. The whole nation, as well as each village, chose a peace chief and a war chief. During peacetime, the peace chief was the leader. As soon as war broke out, the war chief took command.

Decisions were made by the councils, not by the chiefs alone. Advice was given by the priest-physician (called the "medicine man" by whites) who was both religious leader and healer.

One of the Europeans who traded with the Indians recorded many details of Indian life. James Adair was an Englishman who lived among several Indian groups for some 40 years, beginning in 1735. Adair has provided us with many details of their life.

The following reading consists of excerpts from James Adair's accounts of Indian life. This material first appeared in print in 1775.

THINK ABOUT IT

1. What does the excerpt on "War" tell us about the Indian attitude toward warfare?
2. How does Adair's description of "Ball-play" tell us this was an important part of Indian life?
3. How was agricultural work organized? Who was expected to work?

 A Trader Among the Indians
(Excerpts adapted from James Adair, The History of the American Indians, London: 1775)

War

The Indians are not fond of waging war with each other, unless prompted by some of the traders. When left to themselves they carefully consider all the circumstances of war.

Should any young warriors violate a treaty of peace (perhaps by murdering someone from another nation), their nation usually sends some neutral Indians as friendly ambassadors to the offended side. The ambassadors ask them to accept some sort of payment for the offense and to continue their friendship. They assure the offended side that the unfriendly action was not approved but was condemned by the head-men of the whole nation.

If the proposal is accepted, the damage is made up, sometimes by the death of one of the aggressors. However, if the offended side is determined to go to war, they say, "it is finished, they are weighed, and found light." In that case, the offended side proceeds in the following manner.

The war leader announces that he is going to invade the enemy. He beats a drum three times around his winter house and flies the war signal.

A number of warriors and others, usually 20 to 40 persons, arm themselves. They go into the winter house and there drink a concoction of herbs and roots. They stay there for three days and nights, sometimes without any other refreshment. This is to get the deity to guard and help them in the coming danger.

At the fixed time they set off, whooping and halooing. The war leader goes first, striking up a solemn song. The rest follow in one line. In this manner, they proceed until quite out of the sight and hearing of their friends.

As soon as they enter the woods, all are silent so that their ears may inform them of danger. Their small black eyes are almost as sharp as those of the eagle or the lynx. With their feet, they resemble the cunning panther crawling up to its prey.

When they arrive at the enemy's hunting ground, they signal each other by mimicking the birds and beasts in the area. Sometimes a few set an ambush by fixing buffalo hoofs or bear paws on their feet and making tracks to draw out the enemy. At other times, the company will walk in three different rows, as a decoy. Everyone lifts his feet high as not to beat down the brush. In this way, each row makes the track of only one man.

At the signal of the war cry, everyone hides behind a tree or in some cavity in the ground. The leader on each side blows a small whistle. Now hot work begins—guns firing, bullets flying, hickory bows twanging, barbed arrows whizzing by, the javelin striking death, the tomahawk killing or disabling the enemy.

After the battle, the victors begin with mad rapture to cut and slash those unfortunate persons who fell. Their first aim is to take off the scalp. (Later they tie their trophy of blood in a small hoop with bark or deer sinews, to preserve it.)

They are now satisfied for the present and return home. As they reckon they have become impure by shedding human blood, they observe a fast of three days. In rites held by the war chief, they are cleansed of their sins.

Agriculture

The Indians begin to plant their outfields when the wild fruit is so ripe as to draw off the birds from picking up the grain.

Among the several nations of Indians, each town usually works together. Before planting, an old beloved man warns the inhabitants to be ready to plant on a prefixed day. At the dawn of it, he announces to them that "the new year is far advanced—that he who expects to eat, must work—and that he who will not work, must expect to pay the fine according to the old custom, or leave the town, as they will not sweat themselves for a healthy idle waster."

About an hour after sunrise, they enter the field agreed on by lot, and fall to work with great cheerfulness; sometimes one of their orators cheers them with jests and humorous old tales, and sings several of their most agreeable tunes. Also, he beats with a stick on top of an earthen pot covered with a well-stretched deerskin. Thus they proceed from field to field, till their seed is sown.

Every dwelling house also has a small field pretty close to it. In the spring, they plant a variety of large and small beans, peas, and corn. Around this they fasten stakes in the ground and tie a couple of long saplings to keep off the horses.

Yet many of the old horses will creep through these enclosures almost as readily as swine. The women scold them and give them ill names, calling them ugly mad horses and bidding them "go along." Thus they argue with them. If a horse does not observe the friendly caution, the women will strike him with a tomahawk.

Ball-Play

The Indians are much addicted to gaming, and will often stake everything they possess. Ball-playing is their most favorite game.

Ball-Play. How does this 1836 painting by George Catlin compare with Adair's description? Note that one team is painted white. Why?

The ball is made of a piece of deer-skin stuffed hard with deer hair and strongly sewed with deer's sinews. The ball sticks are about two feet long. The lower end somewhat resembles the palm of a hand and is worked with deerskin thongs. Between these thongs they catch the ball and throw it a great distance.

The ball ground is about 500 yards in length. At each end of it, they fix two long poles in the ground, three yards apart but slanting outwards. The side that throws the ball over these, counts one.

The players are equal in number on each side. At the beginning of play, they throw the ball up high in the center of the ground. During play, the ball is mostly flying different ways by force of the sticks without falling to the ground. They are not allowed to catch it with their hands.

It is surprising to see how swiftly they fly. Commonly they throw the ball perhaps a hundred yards.

It is very unusual to see them act spitefully in any sort of game. Once, indeed, I saw some break the legs and arms of their opponents by hurling them down when running at full speed. But, I afterward understood, there was a long family dispute between them. That might have caused it as much as the high bets they had at stake. □

HISTORICAL EVIDENCE FROM MYTHS

A people's myths are another source of information about their way of life. Myths are traditional stories, handed down from generation to generation, which explain a people's origin, their culture, and the natural environment.

Myths tell us something about a people's values—what they believed was important. Myths also provide clues to how the people viewed the world, how they looked at things.

The next reading contains several Indian myths written down by an anthropologist who lived with the Cherokee in the 1800s, long after they had been forced out of Georgia.

THINK ABOUT IT

1. How do the Cherokee myths explain nature?
2. What values are reflected in these myths?
3. Which myths provide clues about Cherokee values such as hard work?

Myths of the Cherokee Indians

Excerpts adapted from James Mooney, *Myths of the Cherokee, Nineteenth Annual Report* (Bureau of American Ethnology, Smithsonian Institution, 1900).

How the World Was Made

The earth is a great island floating in a sea of water, and suspended at four points by a cord hanging down from the sky vault which is of solid rock. When the world grows old and worn out, the people will die and the cords will break and let the earth sink down into the ocean, and all will be water again. The Indians are afraid of this.

When all was water, the animals were above, beyond the earth. It was very crowded and they wanted more room. They wondered what was below the water. At last, the little water-beetle offered to go and see if it could learn. It darted over the surface of the water but could find no firm place to rest. Then it dived to the bottom and came up with some soft mud, which began to grow and spread on every side until it became the island which we call the earth. It was afterward fastened to the sky with four cords, but no one remembers who did this.

At first the earth was flat and soft and wet. The great buzzard, father of all the buzzards we see now, flew over the earth to see if it was yet dry. When he reached the Cherokee country, he was tired, and his flapping wings touched the ground. Wherever they struck the earth there was a valley. Where they turned up again there was a mountain. When the animals above saw this, they were afraid that the whole world would be mountains, so they called him back. But, the Cherokee country remains full of mountains to this day.

The First Fire

In the beginning there was no fire and the world was cold. Then the thunders sent their lightning and put fire into a hollow sycamore tree that grew on an island.

The animals knew it was there but they could not get to it because of the water. They held a council to decide what to do.

Every animal that could fly or swim was anxious to go after the fire. The raven went first because he was big and strong. His feathers were scorched black; he was frightened and returned without the fire.

Then the owl tried, but the smoke nearly blinded him and hot ashes blew up, leaving white rings around his eyes. He, too, came home without the fire.

Next the little blacksnake swam to the island. He crawled to the tree and went in by a hole at the bottom. He was almost set on fire, and after twisting about he found his way out by the same hole. His body had been scorched black, and ever since he darts about and doubles back on this track as if in close quarters.

The great blacksnake swam over and climbed up the outside of the tree. He looked in, was choked by the smoke and fell inside. Before he could climb out again, he was as black as the little snake.

At last, the water spider said she would go. She spun a thread from her body and wove it into a bowl. She fastened this on her back. Then she crossed over to the island where the fire was still burning. She put one little coal into her bowl and came back with it. Ever since, we have had fire, and the water spider still carries her bowl.□

ACTIVITIES FOR CHAPTER 2

Discussion

A. The year A.D. 1540 roughly divides Georgia's Indian past into two periods: prehistoric (before written records) and historic.

1. About which features of prehistoric Indian cultures do we have more information: material culture (food, housing, technology) or non-material culture (religion, education, government)? Why?

2. From written records of the historic period, give examples of the kind of evidence we lack for the prehistoric period.

3. Sometimes it is difficult to separate fact from opinion in written records. Do Adair's accounts reveal his attitudes or opinions about the Cherokees? Give examples.

B. The year 1540 also was the first time Indians and Europeans met in the region that would become Georgia.

1. In what ways were Indian cultures changed by these contacts?

2. How was the Indian idea of land use different from the European view of land ownership?

3. How might this difference lead to conflict between Indians and whites?

Writing Project

Reread the "Preliminary Report" for the physical region in which you live. (Check the map on page 7.) Rewrite the report as if you were a space explorer flying over the region today. Tell which features of your region changed the most and which changed the least.

UNIT II
1733 - 1790: A New Life in the New World

3. The Georgia Colony
4. Life of the People
5. Revolution and Statehood

GEORGIA EVENTS	DATE	EVENTS ELSEWHERE
Georgia Colony founded	1733	
Battle of Bloody Marsh	1742	British begin building cotton factories in England
First merchant house in Savannah	1744	Ice cream introduced in America
Slaves imported legally	1750	
End of Trustee government	1752	Gregorian calendar adopted in British colonies
First royal governor in Savannah	1754	Outbreak of French and Indian War
Parishes created	1758	
Georgia Gazette established	1763	End of French and Indian War
Sons of Liberty organize	1765	Stamp Act protests in colonies; Watt develops steam engine in Britain
	1770	Boston massacre
	1773	Boston Tea Party
Patriots take control	1775	American Revolution begins
Royal government ends	1776	Declaration of Independence
First state constitution written	1777	Major battles in northern colonies
British capture Savannah	1778	France joins fight against Britain
Royal government restored; fighting continues in upcountry	1779	
	1781	British Army surrenders to Washington
Fighting ends in Georgia	1782	
	1783	Treaty of Paris ends American Revolution
University of Georgia founded	1785	Oglethorpe dies in England
Augusta becomes capital	1786	
	1787	U.S. Constitution written
Second state constitution	1789	Washington becomes president; French Revolution begins

3 The Georgia Colony

EUROPEANS COME TO AMERICA

The story of the Georgia colony begins on October 12, 1492. On that date Christopher Columbus, an Italian navigator employed by the king and queen of Spain, discovered the New World. Soon after, Spain sent more explorers to North and South America. They brought back tales of gold and silver, fertile lands, and strange cultures.

Spurred on by the promise of riches, the Spanish set out to build an empire in the New World. Explorers claimed large land areas for Spain. Then settlers came to mine gold and silver, farm the lands, and build cities. Spain soon became the richest nation in Europe.

Not to be outdone by Spain, England, France, Portugal, and Holland also sent out explorers. In the 1500s, the leading nations of western Europe began competing for empires in the New World and elsewhere. The more territory a nation controlled, the more powerful it became. This rivalry would last over 250 years.

In addition to her control of most of South and Central America and the West Indies, Spain took large areas of North America, including what is now Mexico, California, Texas, and Florida. France carved out an empire further north along the St. Lawrence River to the Great Lakes and down the Mississippi to the Gulf of Mexico. Meanwhile, England claimed lands along the Atlantic coast of North America.

English Colonization

By the early 1700s, Great Britain* had 12 colonies along the Atlantic seaboard. The colonies were set up by English trading companies and wealthy individuals. Some were self-governing; some were run directly by the king's government. Most of the settlers who came to these colonies were from England. But some came from Scotland, Ireland, Germany, Holland, and France. One group of settlers were brought by force from Africa.

Why were these colonies established? Suppose you asked that question in the 1600s. Depending on whom you asked, you might get these answers:

> King's Minister in London: "To increase our power. If we didn't colonize these regions, Spain and France would."

---

*In 1707, England and Scotland were united into one country—Great Britain. From that date, the government should be called "British," not English.

Planter in Virginia: "To get ahead. There's more opportunity here than in England where all the land's been taken. I might even get rich here."

Merchant in London: "To make a better profit. It's far cheaper to get raw materials from one's own colony than from a foreign nation. Besides, colonies are a ready market for the goods I make."

Puritan settler: "To allow us to practice our religion in peace. We had no such freedom in England."

Church of England official: "To convert the heathen Indians to true Christianity."

So, there were many reasons for colonizing, from personal and religious reasons to business and military reasons.

The Mercantile System

A government, however, favored colonies—territories inhabited by some of its people and under its control—for one very important reason. Colonies would support a system of trade known as the *mercantile system*. Through this system, a country aimed to make itself rich, mainly by selling to other countries more than it bought from them.

For a country to come out on top, it needed to be as self-sufficient as possible. That meant not having to rely on other countries for raw materials or manufactured goods. If a country had colonies that could provide those raw materials, it might be able to manufacture all the goods it needed at home. The same colonies might also grow agricultural products the country needed. Furthermore, colonies could consume the excess goods a country manufactured.

Raw materials and manufactured goods were shipped not only between the colonies and their mother country (the country which set them up), but also between the colonies themselves. Sometimes these shipments went by way of ports in the mother country. On the next page you can see how it worked for Great Britain and the colonies it set up across the Atlantic.

Exports and Imports of the 13 Colonies	
EXPORTS	**IMPORTS**
fish, whale oil, furs, lumber, rum, corn, wheat, meat, iron, rice, tobacco, hides, naval stores*	goods manufactured in Great Britain, including cloth, glass, tools, china, furniture, and metalware; tea, wine, sugar, and molasses from other colonies around the world.

*Naval stores included tar, pitch, and resin which were vital to merchant and navy sailing ships.

MAP 4. The 13 Colonies. Georgia was the youngest and southernmost of Great Britain's colonies along the Atlantic Seaboard.

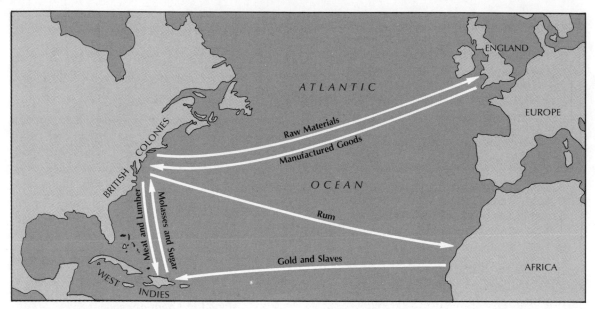

MAP 5. *Colonial Trade Routes. Examples of shipping routes between England and the colonies.*

OGLETHORPE AND THE FOUNDING OF GEORGIA

Georgia was the last of the 13 British colonies set up on the Atlantic seaboard. It was founded in 1733, over 60 years after the Carolinas had been settled. Why was Georgia settled? Would it fit into the mercantile system? Was its location important? The map above should provide some clues. But to really understand how the Georgia colony began, let's flash back to England in the early 1700s and observe the life of a remarkable Englishman, James Edward Oglethorpe.

THINK ABOUT IT

1. What were the principal reasons for colonizing Georgia?
2. What kind of people made up the first group of colonists sent over by the trustees?
3. What role did Oglethorpe play in the founding of the colony?

In the 1720s, the English were having hard times at home, especially in their cities and towns. There were not enough jobs, and many people were in debt. Those who couldn't pay their debts were often thrown in prison with criminals. Prison conditions were terrible.

Some English people were angry that honest citizens who were down on their luck were being locked up in such unfit places. So the government set up a committee to study prison conditions. Heading the committee was a young member of Parliament (the lawmaking body of the British government) named James Edward Oglethorpe. His investigation confirmed the harsh and cruel conditions of the prisons and led to the release of many debtors.

Oglethorpe was a humanitarian, a man concerned about human suffering. He wanted to help the poor and the jobless. In 1730, he and his friend John Percival and some others thought of a way to help unemployed but "worthy" persons. They asked the king for land "on the southwest of Carolina for settling poor persons of London."

On June 9, 1732, King George II granted them a charter to start a colony. Why did the king do this? The charter's opening lines provide some evidence:

Whereas we are credibly informed that many of our poor subjects are, through misfortune and want of em-

James Edward Oglethorpe. This photo of an oil painting shows Oglethorpe about 15 years before the founding of Georgia. Artist unknown.

ployment, reduced to great necessity, insomuch as by their labor they are not able to provide a maintenance for themselves and families, and if they had means to defray the charges of passage, and other expenses incident to new settlements, they would be glad to be settled in any of our new Provinces in America. . .

Where by cultivating lands at present waste and desolate, where they might not only gain a comfortable subsistence for themselves and families, but also strengthen our colonies and increase the trade, navigation, and wealth of our realms.

And whereas our Provinces in North America have been frequently ravaged by Indian enemies; more especially that of South Carolina, which in the late war by the neighboring savages, was laid waste by fire and sword, and inasmuch as this

whole southern frontier continues unsettled,

And whereas we think it highly becoming Our Crown and Royal Dignity to protect all our loving subjects, and to relieve the wants of our above mentioned poor subjects. . .

Know ye therefore, that we do, for these reasons, grant that John Lord Viscount Percival, James Oglethorpe [and other persons named] shall be established as a corporate body, *The Trustees for Establishing the Colony of Georgia in America.* □

The king, then, had three main reasons for establishing the Georgia Colony:

1. *Charity:* To provide relief from poverty. It would also draw off some of the unemployed from British cities.
2. *Economics:* To increase Britain's trade and wealth. Georgia should fit neatly into the mercantile system, providing needed agricultural products and a market for British goods.
3. *Defense:* To provide South Carolina a buffer against attack by the Spanish in Florida and their Indian allies.

Though not stated as such in the charter, *religion* was a fourth reason for settlement. Georgia became a haven for Protestants being persecuted in Catholic European countries. However, according to the charter, Georgia would not have complete freedom of religion.

There shall be liberty of conscience allowed in the worship of God to all persons inhabiting or which shall inhabit or be resident within our said province. And that all persons, except Papists [an unfriendly term for Roman Catholics], shall have a free exercise of their religion. □

Oglethorpe and his friends saw the new colony as a chance to set up a kind of model society, neatly planned and controlled for the good of all.

Under the charter, the trustees were granted all lands between "the most northern stream of a river there commonly called the Savannah, all along the sea coast, to the southward unto the most southern stream of a certain other great water of river called the Altamaha, and westward from the head of said rivers respectively in direct lines to the south seas. . . ." (Do you think King George knew that this grant cut right through the territory claimed by Spain?)

Setting Up the New Colony

The Georgia charter gave Oglethorpe and 20 other trustees the power to set up and run the new colony. First, though, they had to raise money to transport the settlers to America, and to pay for the food and tools they'd need once there. Sermons, pamphlets, speeches, and newspapers carried appeals for contributions.

Then they had to decide who would go. The trustees used the newspapers to announce the opportunity to go to Georgia. From those who volunteered, the trustees selected the ones who would go over "on charity." Each applicant was investigated. The trustees turned down those who could "earn their bread" in London, those who were lazy, and those who might be running away from their debts, or from their wives and children. They tried to choose only the "worthy poor"—good hardworking people.

The families chosen to go received more than free passage to Georgia. Once in Georgia, they were given weapons, tools for building and farming, seed, food to support them until the first harvest, and land to work. In return the colonists had to agree to clear lands, build houses and defenses, and raise crops according to direction. In short, they had to obey orders.

On November 17, 1732, Oglethorpe and 114 settlers sailed from England on the good ship *Anne*. The Atlantic crossing was a good one; only two infants died. On

January 13, 1733, the *Anne* dropped anchor off the Carolina coast.

While the settlers waited, Oglethorpe and a small party looked along the Savannah River for a place to live. On a bluff about 18 miles upriver from the ocean, Oglethorpe found the spot. The Yamacraw Indians already lived there, but that didn't stop Oglethorpe. He worked out an agreement with their chief, Tomo-chi-chi, that allowed the English to settle there.

On February 12, 1733, Oglethorpe brought his colonists to the site that would become the city of Savannah. The Georgia colony was born.

Oglethorpe laid out the town of Savannah according to a special plan. Open spaces called "squares" were one of its main features. Around each square were 40 house lots, each one 60 by 90 feet. Each square was to be a kind of neighborhood center where markets might be held. Special lots were set aside for churches and stores.

In addition to a house lot, each settler received 5 acres for a garden on the town's edge and 45 acres further out in the country for farming. Oglethorpe quickly set his people to work.

What did they think of him? A visitor from South Carolina described Oglethorpe's position among the colonists this way:

He is extremely well beloved by all his people; the general title they give him is Father. If any of them is sick, he immediately visits them, and takes a great deal of care of them. If any difference arises, he is the person that decides it. . . . He keeps a strict discipline; I never saw one of his people drunk, or heard one swear, all the time I was there. He does not allow them rum, but in lieu [instead] gives them English beer. It is surprising to see how cheerfully the men go to work, considering they have not been bred to it. There are no idlers

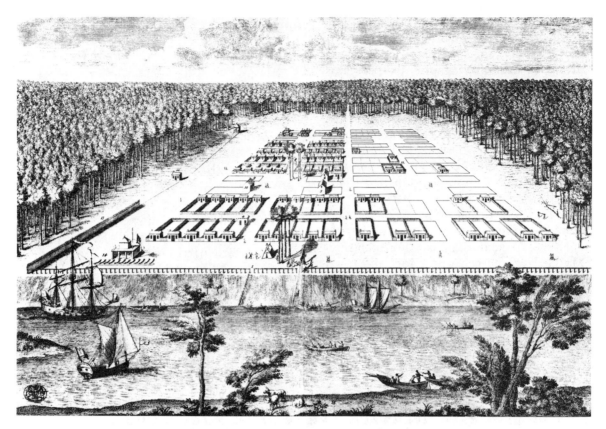

Savannah, 1734. One year after Savannah's founding, Oglethorpe's plan was taking shape. Note the house lots, the open squares, and Oglethorpe's tent near the river.

there; even the boys and girls do their parts. □

[From a letter in the *South Carolina Gazette*, Charles Town, March 22, 1733, reprinted in *Colonial Records of Georgia*, III, Allen D. Chandler, ed., 1905, p. 406.]

The next year, Oglethorpe returned to England a hero. Tomo-chi-chi and several other Indians Oglethorpe brought with him created quite a stir in London. They even met with the king and queen. This visit helped to advertise the new colony. Many people applied to go to Georgia, and Parliament granted a large sum of money for the colony's defense.

Over the next few years, the trustees sent over "on charity" hundreds of men, women, and children. Hundreds of others came at their own expense.

Growing Pains

As the colony grew, so did problems in running it. For the first few months, Oglethorpe had run it almost single-handedly. In July 1733, he had sworn in the colony's first officials: the "Town Court of Savannah and the Precincts thereof." These officials were to "preserve the Peace and Administer Justice Without fear or affection to the Terror of the Evil Doers and to the Comfort of those who do Well."

The "great experiment" wasn't working as planned. Relations with the Indians were getting worse. And Oglethorpe's decisions were not always respected. Some colonists, in fact, opposed Oglethorpe and the control he and the trustees had over them.

In addition to civil problems, there were military matters to be handled. Trouble was brewing along the Georgia-

Florida border. From the start of the British colony, the Georgia-Florida border had been disputed. More people were settling in Georgia, despite its problems, and the Spanish didn't like the growing presence of the English. In 1736, Oglethorpe and the Spanish governor at St. Augustine worked out a temporary treaty. But how long could they keep the peace?

Oglethorpe began to prepare for war. In 1735-36, he settled a group from Scotland in the new town of Darien on the Altamaha River, on Georgia's southern boundary. They were tough soldiers he hoped could guard against the Spanish in Florida. Next he laid out a fort and town, named Frederica, on St. Simons Island. Then he got Tomo-chi-chi to help him pick sites for forts as far south as the St. Johns River in Florida. As relations with the Spanish grew worse, Oglethorpe went to England to raise a regiment of soldiers.

He returned as "General and Commander in Chief of the Forces of South Carolina and Georgia."

Indian Relations

General Oglethorpe was worried about the attitude of the Indians. The colony needed the Indian trade, and if war broke out with the Spanish, they would need the Indians on the British side.

To improve relations with the Creeks and other Indians, Oglethorpe made a 500-mile round trip by horseback to Coweta Town on the Chattahoochee River. A member of his party described Oglethorpe's meeting:

At the Cowetas on 11th day of August 1739, was held a general meeting of the Estates of the Creek Nation; and the Mico's or King's, Chief Men and Deputies from all the towns of

MAP 6. The Georgia Colony, 1750. Note that only a small part of the territory claimed for Georgia was actually being settled. How does this map show that Georgia's location was of strategic (military) importance?

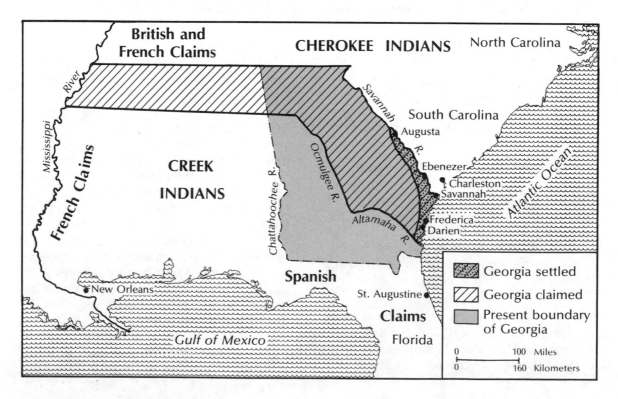

that nation were assembled there. This meeting of the Creek Indians continued till the 21st day of August 1739 and gave strong assurances of fidelity to his Majesty and proposed several regulations for maintaining the peace of the country, to which the General agreed. He and the gentlemen that accompanied him endured much hardship in their march, being obliged to pass through great woods, where for 240 miles there was neither house nor inhabitants of any kind and were forced to swim their horses over several large rivers. The Indians received his Excellency with the greatest respect and friendship, and entertained him and his men with plenty of fowls, beef, pork, venison, melons and other fruit. The General was ill with a burning fever in the Indian town, but is perfectly recovered. □

[*Colonial Records of Georgia,* XXII, pt. 2, Allen D. Candler, ed., 1913, pp. 214-15.]

In a treaty made at this meeting, the Indians agreed that only the trustees, not the Spanish, could settle lands between Savannah and the St. Johns River. But bad news awaited Oglethorpe on his return to Savannah. Britain and Spain were at war.

War with Spain

The Spanish struck first, raiding Amelia Island. General Oglethorpe decided to take the offensive. In 1740, with additional troops from South Carolina and Indian allies, he led his Georgians into Florida. However, the Spanish held out in their fort at St. Augustine, and Oglethorpe's forces withdrew to St. Simons Island.

For two years, the Spanish prepared to wipe out the Georgia colony. Finally, the Spanish force approached St. Simons Island. On July 7, 1742, enemy troops had landed on the island and were within two miles of Frederica.

Although greatly outnumbered, General Oglethorpe attacked. The Spanish were taken by surprise and fled. Later the same day, other Spanish troops on the island were ambushed by Oglethorpe's men. This victory, named the Battle of Bloody Marsh, discouraged the Spanish. They soon retreated to St. Augustine. The Georgia colony was saved.

In 1743, General Oglethorpe tried again to take St. Augustine, but he failed. A few months later, he sailed for England, never to return to Georgia.

The Colony Declines

After Oglethorpe left, the future looked bleak for the Georgia colony. Many colonists gave up and returned to England or went to other colonies. The colony wasn't producing much, so its export business was poor. The trustees' officers in Savannah worked to keep things going amidst crop failures and discontent among the colonists. For a time, it looked as if Georgia might have to be absorbed into South Carolina. Then the trustees made an important decision.

GEORGIA BECOMES A ROYAL COLONY

THINK ABOUT IT

1. How did the trustees' plan for Georgia fail? What mistakes did they make?
2. How did Georgia settlers react to the trustees' regulations for running the colony?
3. What changes took place in Georgia after it became a royal colony?

In 1751, the Trustees for Establishing the Colony of Georgia decided to give up their charter. This meant that authority to run the colony passed from the trustees to the king.

What happened? Why did the trustees become discouraged and give up their dream of building a model society?

Georgia was both a success and a failure under Oglethorpe and the trustees. By the time the trustees gave up control, over 5,500 colonists had settled there, about 2,000 of them on charity. Georgia's settlements were scattered along the coast and far inland. Persons fleeing religious persecution in Europe had found a haven in Georgia. For the British government, Georgia had served well in the war with Spain.

However, the Georgia colony failed to live up to the trustees' expectations. In 1732, they had seen Georgia as a great experiment. It was to be a model society. There the poor and oppressed might live without the bad social and economic conditions that plagued England and other countries. The trustees believed that they could make Georgia a model society by (1) their own careful plans and strict rules and (2) the hard work of carefully selected colonists. But almost from the start, they had trouble making their plans work in the real world.

For one thing, Georgia did not fit into the mercantile system as neatly as planned. Great Britain had expected the new colony to supply her with certain expensive goods, such as silk and wine. Georgia's warm climate fooled the planners into thinking it a perfect place to produce both of these. So, they required the settlers to grow mulberry trees (for raising silkworms) and grapevines. Although some good silk was produced, it never amounted to much. Wine production was a total failure. Plant diseases and insect pests put an end to both efforts. Other plans also failed.

A major problem with the trustees' plans centered around the rules that colonists were forced to obey. Three main rules caused problems in the colony:

1. Each male settler was allowed only 50 acres of land to hold for life. He could pass it on to his son, but he could not sell it, lease it, or mortgage it.
2. The settlers could not have slaves. The trustees believed slavery would make the settlers lazy and encourage the growth of classes—one very rich and the other very poor.
3. The settlers could not import rum or other strong liquor. Only "wholesome" English beer and wine were allowed.

The colonists felt these rules kept them from earning a good living. For example, lumber, cattle, and rice were being produced successfully in Georgia. But, to make a good profit from these products, a settler needed to own a lot of land. He also needed cheap labor to help with the work.

Furthermore, to make a profit on these products, the settler needed nearby markets. One nearby market for Georgia's lumber and other products in the 1700s was the West Indies. But, a most important West Indies product that could be taken in trade was molasses for making rum, which the trustees had forbidden in Georgia.

So, the colonists resented the trustees' regulations. The trustees in London were too far away to understand the colony's problems. Oglethorpe was in a tough position. If he enforced the rules, many of the colonists protested; if he relaxed the rules, the trustees objected.

The trustees gradually relaxed their restrictions on landowning. They gave in on rum and slaves. By then, however, the experiment was over. In 1751, the discouraged trustees asked the British government to take control of the colony.

The New Royal Colony

Georgia became a royal colony under the direct control of the king. The colonists were delighted with the change.

The first royal governor, appointed by the king, arrived in Savannah in 1754. But, the governor was to be only one part of the colony's new government. Like the other 12 colonies, Georgia would have its own legislature (the lawmaking body in a government). Called the General Assembly, it would be modeled after Britain's Parliament. An appointed Upper House would double as the governor's council of advisors. More important to the colonists, a lower house—the Commons House of Assembly—would be an elected body. This meant the colonists would have a voice in their own government.

White men who owned at least 50 acres

could vote for assemblymen. Those holding 500 or more acres could serve as members of the assembly.

The governor or king could veto laws made by the colonial assembly. So, the colonists did not get complete self-government, but they did get much more than they ever had under the trustees.

The Colony Prospers

With no more restrictions on land, rum, and slaves, new settlers began to rush to the Georgia Colony. They came from Europe and from other colonies. Many brought slaves with them. By 1766, Georgia had 10,000 white settlers and 8,000 blacks. In another 10 years, there were 50,000 colonists, about half of them black slaves. At the same time, new lands were opened for settlement.

Georgia's economy grew strong. More land was plowed. Towns sprang up. Rice, lumber, and livestock, plus furs and hides from the Indian trade, were shipped to Britain and the West Indies. The Georgia colony gained a new life. But what was life like for the settlers themselves? How was it changing from the earliest days of the colony? How was it different for different groups of people in the colony? Chapter 4 looks more closely at the lives of colonial Georgians.

MAP 7. Indian Cessions. In 1733, 1763, and again in 1773, Creek tribes ceded (granted) the territory settled by the Colonists.

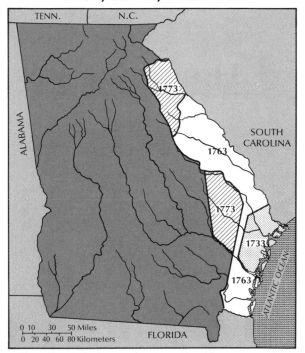

ACTIVITIES FOR CHAPTER 3

Discussion

A. Arguments for establishing colonies were often based on the mercantile system.
  1. How was this economic system supposed to work?
  2. How was the Georgia colony supposed to fit into the system?

B. James Oglethorpe has been called the Father of Georgia.
  1. What things did he do to put the trustees' plan into operation?
  2. What unforeseen problems did he have to deal with?
  3. Do you think Oglethorpe deserves the title?

C. Georgia really prospered only after it became a royal colony.
  1. Why was Georgia probably more attractive to white settlers after the trustees' rule ended?
  2. In your own view, what was the biggest weakness in the trustees' plan?

Writing Project

In the 1730s, settling in Georgia meant a dangerous voyage to unknown hardships. The trustees had to advertise to get people to go.

Assume you are a London printer with the job of making up advertisements to be posted in churches and public buildings. Design an advertisement that would attract the kind of settlers the trustees wanted for Georgia.

4 Life of the People

What was it like to live in the Georgia colony? Perhaps some Europeans setting out to cross the Atlantic asked that same question. No simple answer could have prepared them for what they found.

The Europeans who came to Georgia had to adapt to an environment quite different from what they were used to. They found no comfortable houses in which to live, no roads on which to travel, not even any cleared land on which to raise crops or livestock.

Instead they found wilderness, a hot humid climate, strange plants and animals—including fierce biting insects—and even soils they had never seen before. And they often found a hostile native population.

For many settlers, their European culture—their knowledge, their habits, their techniques, even the seeds they brought and the clothes they wore—did not serve well in the new land. Thousands died and many others gave up and left for Europe and elsewhere.

Others, however, learned to adapt, to survive, and eventually to prosper in Georgia. Sometimes they learned by trial and error, sometimes from the experiences of other settlers or from the Indians. They learned to use the resources Georgia had to offer. Gradually, the clothes they wore, the foods they ate, and the techniques they used to farm and build became quite different from those of Europe. A colonial culture was developing.

Adapting to the new environment, though, did not require the settlers to give up all their European culture. They kept their ideas about political rights and ownership of private property. They held on to European values of hard work and family ties. And they maintained religious beliefs. These elements of culture in England, Scotland, Germany, and elsewhere in Europe became part of colonial culture.

Coming from different countries, the settlers brought a variety of ideas, values, and beliefs to the colony. There was no "average" colonial Georgian. Not all the settlers adapted in the same way either. People differed from one another in the 1700s, just as they do today.

For the most part, however, Georgia settlers developed an *agrarian culture,* one centered around farming. Their communities were usually small and far apart. For most people, life was simple: survival was the aim and hard work the rule.

The four readings that follow tell about the lives of some colonial Georgians. The first consists of one primary source. It is an actual eyewitness account of daily life in the Ebenezer settlement during the first years of the colony. The second reading is a story, a fictional account based on historical research. It presents the life that white settlers probably experienced on the frontier in the 1760s and 1770s. The third reading contains two primary sources that provide some evidence of how black slaves lived. Black Georgians were forced to come as slaves to the colony. Their experience was quite different from that of most white settlers. The final reading in the chapter looks at Georgia society and culture late in the colonial period. It focuses mainly on life in Savannah.

THE EBENEZER COMMUNITY: AN EYEWITNESS VIEW

In 1734 a group of German-speaking settlers arrived in Savannah. Persecuted because of their religious beliefs in their native city, Salzburg (now in Austria), these Lutheran Protestants had made their way to England. There the trustees raised funds to send them to Georgia.

Like the British settlers, the Salzburgers received land and provisions. They became citizens of Georgia with the same rights as the British. They also had to obey the rules of the trustees.

Their settlement, about 25 miles up-river from Savannah, was named "Ebenezer." Oglethorpe laid it out and sent workers from Savannah to help the Salzburgers clear the land and put up temporary shelter.

Ebenezer quickly grew to almost 200 people, but things did not go well for the settlers. The location was swampy, the soil poor, and the river—the only transportation route to Savannah—too difficult to reach. In 1736 the Salzburgers asked Oglethorpe for a better location. A spot known as Red Bluff, where Ebenezer Creek met the Savannah River, became the New Ebenezer. At Old Ebenezer nothing remained but a cow pen.

Disease and hardship followed the Salzburgers. So many adults had died by 1737 that an orphanage had to be built for their children.

But later the Salzburgers began to prosper. They produced and sold lumber, rice, beef, and pork. Eventually, Ebenezer led all Georgia communities in producing silk and grew the first cotton in Georgia.

Ebenezer was a religious community. The minister was the leader, and each settler had to follow strict church regulations. The settlers worked according to a set plan that required them to support the church and its school and orphanage with their labor. No hard liquor, dancing, gambling, or other frivolous activities were allowed in the community. The minister watched over the behavior of the people.

Jerusalem Church at Ebenezer. The Salzburgers' church, built in 1767, is the oldest public building in Georgia still in regular use.

Those who misbehaved were punished according to church rules.

For many years, the Salzburgers' German language and close-knit society kept them somewhat apart from other Georgians. As they adopted English and became involved in the economic and political life of the colony, they became more like other Georgians. One Salzburger, a former schoolteacher named John Adam Treutlen, became the first governor of the state of Georgia.

Pastor Boltzius's Account

John Martin Boltzius was the Salzburgers' pastor, their community leader, teacher, and spokesman from the time they landed in 1734 until he died in 1765. During those years, Pastor Boltzius kept a daily diary of happenings at Ebenezer. He sent detailed reports on the community back to the Lutheran Church in Germany and wrote many letters to officials of the trustees' government. Excerpts from his writings during the first five years appear below.

These primary sources offer an eyewitness view of life in a colonial Georgia community. Remember, though, as you read these sources, that they present the Ebenezer community as seen through the eyes of only one witness, Pastor Boltzius.

THINK ABOUT IT

1. From Boltzius's account, what were some of the Salzburgers' values?
2. What kinds of problems did the Salzburgers have to deal with? How did they deal with them?

1734
March 12 (Savannah)

Nearly all the inhabitants of Savannah had assembled where our ship was to land. They fired several cannon and shouted for joy.

The Salzburgers, who were feasted with fresh meat while still aboard ship, received some good English beer afterwards on land.

March 13

A Jew, who had also received some land here, took the Salzburgers in and treated them to breakfast with a good rice soup. God has awakened some people here so that they are very friendly toward us and show great kindness.

March 14

This afternoon someone led us to the Indians who live in this neighborhood. We found them in circumstances that made our hearts bleed. We thanked God for the Holy Gospel. We had seen among the Indians what a great pity it is not to have it.

March 15

Mr. Oglethorpe is a man of exceptionally fine qualities. Since it means a great deal to him to bring true knowledge of God to the poor Indians, he urged us today to learn their language which has only about one thousand primitive words.

Our Salzburgers have been cautioned very much not to drink a certain sweet-tasting brandy, called rum, because this drink has already brought death to many.

[*Detailed Reports,* Vol. I, 1734, University of Georgia, 1968.]

1735
May 28 (Ebenezer)

Mr. Causton (government storekeeper in Savannah) has sent several bushels of rice for planting. He desires that the Salzburgers should clear some swampy and wet places and try this seed.

The people intend to be obedient and start with this tomorrow.

November 22

The rice which had been planted by the Salzburgers in communal labor as an experiment did not do very well because there was no rain for too long a period. But we see that planting it does not require much more labor than is required for other fruits of the land. It is said that the hardest labor is required in threshing the rice to separate it from its hulls. Only Negro slaves are used to perform this labor in Carolina.

[*Detailed Reports,* Vol. II, 1734-35, University of Georgia, 1969.]

1736

February 17

I wish that Mr. Oglethorpe were here to see our garden, which has again been nearly half under water since the recent rainy weather. Then he would be able to comprehend what was recently told him.

We still hope that the Salzburgers will enjoy the rights and liberties of Englishmen as free colonists. It appears to me and to others that the Salzburgers are a thorn in the eyes of the Englishmen, who would like to assign them land that no one else wants. Just as Mr. Oglethorpe has made it very clear that he can not give our people this or that land on account of the Englishmen, and is thereby still causing us difficulty.

[*Georgia Historical Quarterly,* Vol. 53, 1969.]

February 27

At the end of the sermon, I had to apply the discipline of the church, in the presence of the congregation, against Ruprecht Zittrauer who had offended the congregation last Wednesday by getting drunk once again.

April 17 (New Ebenezer)

Most of the people are already living here now. Only a few women and children will stay at Old Ebenezer to watch out for the seeds planted there and wait on the sick. Everyone seems pleased with living here, and the air seems healthier than there.

[*Detailed Reports,* Vol. III, 1736, University of Georgia, 1972.]

1737

July 21

Toward evening we received a slaughtered ox from Old Ebenezer, where the Honorable Trustees have recently begun to have cattle kept. Due to difficulty in bringing it here, the carcass had almost spoiled.

July 25

An Englishman from a Carolina plantation has sold some butter here. When we asked him for the sale of some corn, he told us of the terrible scarcity of foodstuffs further up the river.

July 27

The heat is so great that we can hold school only in the morning with the few children who are still well.

July 28

A man told me that his corn was so badly blighted by the worms that he had little hope of a good harvest, if God were not to prevent further damage. He was quite composed, however, and trusted in the Lord.

The boat returned to Savannah today to buy a few more kegs of flour, and we intend to contribute money from the poor box to those who cannot afford it.

July 30

Paul Lemmenhofer was very fatigued for a long time and could find no rest day or night. Although his condition seemed improved this morning, he died suddenly and against all expectations.

Of the congregation who have been with us from the beginning, 31 adults have died here and in Old Ebenezer and 24 children; among the living are 89 adults, and 43 children.

August 9

Our poor people are about to lose most of their fowl and other small livestock. They cannot give them much feed at home and therefore let both chickens and hogs run free so they may find food in the swamps and bushes. There they are preyed upon by bears, crocodiles and a certain type of large wild cat.

August 14

While most in our community suffer from weakness caused by the fever, this does not prevent them from listening to the Lord's word. They attend the sermon; and, when the fever strikes them, they simply leave, which is otherwise rare in our meetings.

[*Detailed Reports,* Vol. IV, 1737, University of Georgia, 1976.]

1738
March 16

Some Indians have come to our place again with their wives and children and are bringing pieces of meat for rice. One of them brought an entire deer for the orphanage. We like to do as much as we can for them, but then we have them around our necks all the more, as long as they are at our place. □

[*Detailed Reports,* Vol. V, 1738, University of Georgia, 1980.]

The Settler Family: A Story

The following reading provides a glimpse into the life of the Settlers, a fictional colonial family. Although the story is made up, it is based on knowledge we have about life in Georgia over 200 years ago.

THINK ABOUT IT
1. What was expected of a woman in colonial society?
2. How were the Settler children an economic asset to the family?
3. What did it mean for the Settler family to be self-sufficient?

"I believe that's all, Samuel," sighed Elizabeth after shoving the bundle of clothes into the wagon.

"Then we'll be off as soon as I get this fixed," her husband grunted as he struggled with the wheel that had come loose.

Elizabeth noted that everything they owned was packed into the wagon. They had the board table and two chairs Sam had made, the patchwork quilt she had sewn, and a feather mattress. Some smaller items were on the wagon too—a few tools for planting and building, some iron pots, and Sam's musket. These goods were the barest necessities to begin life in their new home.

Elizabeth turned as she heard her father and mother coming from the house. She was born in that house 17 years before and had never been more than 10 miles from it. She thought about spending four days in the wagon bouncing over rough trails into the upcountry. Before their marriage, Sam had bought some land there, cleared an acre of woods, and built them a place to live. It was one room, made of logs, with a dirt floor.

"Here's your seed corn," her father called out, holding up a small sack.

"And a jug of good cider for your journey," added her mother.

Elizabeth's father hugged her. "Daughter, we wish you weren't going so far. Can't I talk young Mr. Settler into changing his mind?"

Sam looked up from his work and frowned. Like most colonial husbands, Samuel Settler would run his family affairs with a firm hand. He would make the decisions and give the directions. Elizabeth was expected to obey her husband. When they were married even the few things she owned became her husband's to use as he saw fit. Later, their children would be taught to respect and obey both their parents and to expect a prompt beating from their father if they didn't.

Elizabeth's father saw the determination in Sam's face. He remembered his son-in-law saying, "There's more and better land above Augusta than any you'd find in this parish and I mean to have some of it." He clasped Sam's hand. "Good-bye and Godspeed," he said.

As the wagon creaked off into the distance, Elizabeth's mother waved one last time and picked up her hoe. The sun was already high in the sky and she had much to do.

During their first year together, Sam and Elizabeth worked almost every day from sunrise to sunset. At dawn, Sam went into the woods to hunt and check his traps. Elizabeth split wood, built a fire, and prepared their food. Later in the day, they tilled their corn fields or cleared brush. In bad weather, Sam stayed inside and worked on the tools. Elizabeth repaired clothes or made new ones.

The Settlers were practically a self-sufficient economic unit. Almost everything they needed to live, they produced on their few acres or brought back from the forest. After they had stored and dried the corn, Elizabeth ground it into meal. The deer, rabbits, squirrels, and raccoons that Sam hunted and trapped provided hides and furs for clothing. The trees Sam cut supplied fuel for cooking and heat.

The Settlers needed a few things they didn't produce themselves, such as salt for preserving meat and wool for spinning yarn. To get such items, they bartered with their neighbors or the peddlers who came up from Augusta.

When she wasn't working in the fields with Sam, Elizabeth tended a garden of peas, potatoes, and other vegetables near the cabin. Every day she battled the birds and other animals that tried to eat the seed and young plants.

One day, as Sam chopped down trees in the woods, he heard a shot, then

The Settlers in the Upcountry. A one-room cabin was home for the Settlers who worked from sunrise to sunset. With only hand tools it took years to clear a few acres for farming. How has the artist shown the strength of the Settlers?

another. He raced back to the cabin. His wife was nowhere in sight. He called and called. Finally she appeared, musket in hand.

"While I was down at the creek washing the clothes, our neighbor's cattle got into the garden. I've driven them off, but look," she cried, pointing at the trampled garden. "There's blessed little left for us to eat. Sam, if only I had a fence around it. . . ." Elizabeth sat down on a stump and sighed, "And a well near the cabin so that. . . ."

Sam protested, "You know I must clear more of the woods for planting before any fence or well can be. . . ." His voice softened as he looked down at his wife. "But you shall have them, dear Bess, perhaps before our first child is born."

As any married woman in colonial Georgia, Elizabeth was expected to raise a large family. Long hours of heavy work and primitive living conditions made childbearing and childrearing difficult. Many colonial women died young. The Settlers, however, were blessed with good fortune. They raised eight healthy children.

In only a short time the Settler children, too, contributed to the economic unit. At age six, they were able to pile brush to burn, chase birds from the cornfields, and gather eggs. At seven, they helped with the planting and harvesting. As the boys grew older, Sam taught them to hunt and trap, to plow, to cut logs into lumber, to make tools, and to build fences. Elizabeth taught the girls to grind corn into meal and to preserve meat, fruits, and vegetables. She trained them to spin, weave, sew, and prepare animal skins. Year by year, the children took on more work. The farm grew; the Settler family prospered.

In the twelfth year of their marriage, Sam had to leave Elizabeth and the children for the first time. His parents had died, and Sam had to go to Savannah to settle his father's estate.

When he returned, Sam told Elizabeth, "I'll have a good bit of money coming to me when I've sold my father's merchant house.* And it will come at a good time, for our neighbor's land along the Little River is for sale."

"More land! Why?" asked Elizabeth. "Haven't we enough to work now? Would it not be better to keep a merchant business that's prospering so? You could find a good partner to. . . ."

"No! I want no partners. Nor to be bound to any merchant house in Savannah. I mean to buy the land. Land is the main source of income in Georgia. Owning land is the foundation of a man's wealth, and his independence. The land will be here to give to my sons long after any merchant business has failed."

"Then it's settled. But what of your sister, Sarah?" asked Elizabeth.

"Unless she is to marry soon, there's no place for her to live but here," Sam replied.

"Aye, it's true there's no place in Georgia for an unmarried woman," Elizabeth agreed. "But where will she sleep? We've no room."

"We now have four rooms," Sam replied firmly. "I can add another. Sarah has known hard work in Savannah. She will be a help to you raising our youngest. We shall welcome her into our family."

A few years after Aunt Sarah came to live with them, the Settlers' way of life began to change. Sam and the boys cleared the land along the Little River and planted many more acres of corn and even a few of wheat.

Elizabeth stood back admiring the corn drying in the cribs. "It's more than I ever thought we'd harvest, Samuel."

"Aye, certainly it's a fine crop. More than is to be traded with our few neighbors. I'll be selling the meal in Augusta this year. That much meal, plus the hides and furs you've readied, should bring enough to buy the beginnings of a good flock. I've heard that a dealer from Virginia is in Augusta with fine stock to sell. I'll be going to see him."

*shipping and trading firm

The sheep were a good investment. The Settlers sold wool and meat, as well as grain, to the merchants in Augusta. Sam bought cattle and cleared more land for pasture. Soon the farm had several sheds for livestock, barns for grain and hay, corn-cribs, and a smokehouse.

Sam had money to buy tools, plows, and other equipment that was better than he himself could make. As the family's income grew, Elizabeth began using English cloth for her family's clothing instead of coarse homespun. In time, she even had a dress made in Augusta, and Sam had boots from Boston. They drank tea from India sweetened with sugar from the West Indies out of cups made in England. The Settlers were no longer self-sufficient.

Eventually, the Settler children grew up, married, and had families. Sam, Elizabeth, and Aunt Sarah were never very far away from them, however. Most had settled down within a few miles of the old farm. One son, however, decided to strike out with his young wife for the frontier to the northwest.

Everything they owned was packed into a wagon. They had a board table, two chairs, a patchwork quilt, and a . . . . □

BLACK PEOPLE IN GEORGIA

Black people from Africa also settled the Georgia colony. Unlike the settlers from Europe, however, blacks did not come by choice. They were brought as slaves to work for white settlers.

Slavery lasted in Georgia until 1865. Slave labor was an important part of Georgia's economy.

THINK ABOUT IT

1. Why did European colonists turn to slave labor? What was the argument for slavery in Georgia?
2. How was being a slave different from being an indentured servant? How was it similar?
3. From Equiano's account, what can you tell about the values of Africans? How reliable is Equiano's account?

4. From the Slave Code of 1770, what can you tell about the relationships of blacks and whites in colonial society? What can you tell about the values or beliefs of the authors of the Code?

Background on Slavery

Slavery existed in Europe, Africa, and other parts of the world for thousands of years. Many societies used slavery to control certain people and put them to work. These people included captives taken in war and criminals.

In general, slaves were men, women, and children forced to work without pay for someone who had control over them. Yet slavery was not the same thing in all societies. In some places, slaves were freed after several years and became regular members of the society. In other societies, however, slavery was forever.

The use of African slaves in the New World began in the 1500s. Portuguese and Spanish sugar plantation owners in the West Indies and South America needed cheap labor to make a profit. At first, the owners tried enslaving native Indians. In just a few years they lost thousands of Indian slaves—wiped out by diseases spread from Europe and by cruel working conditions. Other Indians ran off where their masters couldn't hunt them down. Plantation owners then turned to Africans, who were more resistant to old world diseases and who wouldn't be able to escape, as the Indians had, to nearby friendly tribes.

As more plantations were built in the New World, more slaves were needed. For their supply of slaves, the Europeans were helped by warfare among African tribes. One tribe would capture members of a rival tribe and sell them as slaves.

Soon the British, Dutch, and French joined the slave trade. They built trading places, called "slave stations," along the west coast of Africa. From there, they shipped slaves to colonies in the West Indies and mainland America.

The Europeans used money to encourage tribal warfare and the taking of captives for slavery. Some of the tribes of west Africa knew what was happening and refused to supply any more slaves. Still, the slave traders could always find new sources of supply. Between the years 1500 and 1800, as many as 20 million black Africans were enslaved and brought to the New World.

Slavery in British America

Great Britain's colonies also had a labor shortage. They had far more work—farming, lumbering, building and so forth—than they had workers to do it. This was a big problem in southern colonies.

The southern colonies seemed particularly suited to plantation-style agriculture. A plantation is a large-scale operation that requires many workers doing the same simple tasks at the same time. To be profitable, the plantation's work had to be done cheaply.

To meet the need for cheap labor, some landowners used indentured servants—white settlers who were too poor to pay their own way to America. An indenture was a contract. A person agreed to work without pay for a set number of years—usually from four to seven—for anyone who would pay his or her passage to the colonies. At the end of the contracted time, the indentured servant became a free person with all the rights of other colonists.

But indentured servants didn't work out so well. Their masters complained that they refused to do certain kinds of hard work. Moreover, they often ran away before their indenture was worked off.

On the other hand, African slaves, some colonists said, were better suited to plantation work than were white servants. They could work harder in the hot summer sun, needed fewer clothes, could be fed a poorer diet, and didn't have to be replaced every few years. Obviously, the landowners pointed out, blacks couldn't run away as easily because "they would always be recognized."

The first Africans arrived in the Virginia colony in 1619. Whether they were slaves or indentured servants is not clear. However, by the time Georgia was founded, black slavery had become common in the British colonies.

Although black slaves could be freed, they seldom were.* Permanent enslavement was based on the Europeans' ideas about private property. They believed they had a "natural right" to use or dispose of their property—land, houses, livestock—as they alone saw fit. Owners of slaves extended this idea to include slaves. They argued, "I paid good money for the slave, so he is my property. Therefore, if I choose, I can set him free or I can keep him a slave until he dies." The slaveowner also maintained that the children of his slaves were born his slaves.

Not all the British colonists agreed with this argument. Many believed that all people, not just white European people, had natural rights—to life and liberty. For many years, though, the opponents of slavery were in the minority.

A Slave's Account

What was it like to be brought to America as a slave? As slaves were seldom allowed to learn to read and write, there are very few firsthand accounts by slaves. One that does exist, however, is by Olaudah Equiano.

Olaudah Equiano was born in 1745 in the Kingdom of Benin in west Africa. When he was 11 years old, he was captured, sold to slave traders, and taken by ship to the West Indies. From there he was taken to Virginia and Pennsylvania.

Equiano was renamed Gustavus Vassa by his master. Unlike most slaves, Equiano learned to read and write and was eventually given his freedom. Later, he moved to England where he was active in anti-slavery efforts.

---

*There were small numbers of freed blacks in all the colonies. (About 30 or 40 lived in colonial Savannah.)

The following account is taken from Equiano's autobiography, published in 1791.

The first thing I saw when I got to the coast was the sea and a slave ship waiting for its cargo. These filled me with much astonishment and terror.

When I was carried on board, I looked around and saw a large furnace boiling and many black people chained together. I no longer doubted my fate.

I was soon put down under the decks. There with the terrible stench and crying, I became so sick and low that I was not able to eat. I wished for death to relieve me. Soon two white men offered me food. When I refused to eat, one of them held me by the hands. My feet were tied and I was severely whipped. . . .

In a little time, I found some people from my own nation among those who were chained. I asked them what was to be done with us. They told me that we were to be taken to the white people's country to work for them . . . .

The closeness of the hold, the heat of the climate, so crowded was it that each person scarcely had room to turn. . . .it almost suffocated us. This brought on sickness and many died. I became so low I was put on deck.

One day two of my countrymen who were chained together jumped into the sea. They preferred death to a life of such misery. Then another followed their example. I believe that many more would have done the same if they had not been prevented by the ship's crew. Two of the wretches were drowned, but they got the other and flogged him unmercifully for attempting to prefer death to slavery.

Finally, we came in sight of land . . . Many merchants and planters came on board. They put us into separate groups and examined us with great attention. We thought we would be eaten by these ugly men. . . .

Soon we were taken to the land where we were led immediately to the merchant's yard. There we were penned up together like sheep without regard to sex or age.

In a few days, we were sold. On a signal, the buyers rush into the yard where the slaves are kept. They choose those they like best. The noise and clamor which accompany this, and the eagerness in the faces of the buyers, serve to increase the fear of the terrified slaves. In this manner, relatives and friends are separated, most of them never to see each other again. . . . ☐

[Adapted from *The Interesting Narrative of The Life of Olaudah Equiano, or Gustavus Vassa, the African, Written by Himself*, Vol. 1, First American Ed. (New York: W. Durrell, 1791).]

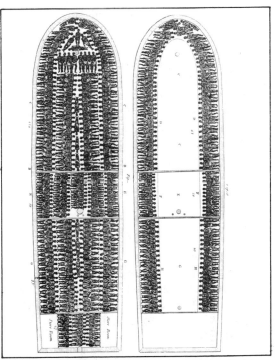

Diagram of a Slave Ship. Called a "slaver," this sailing ship was specially designed to squeeze aboard as many persons as possible. The confinement, heat, and lack of sanitation killed thousands of Africans before they reached America.

Slavery in Georgia

The trustees had intended that there be no slavery in Georgia, and Oglethorpe vigorously opposed any attempts to bring in slaves.

However, in December 1738, a group of Savannah colonists petitioned the trustees to allow slaves into the colony. They argued that they could never raise enough products for export without help. How could they compete with the Carolinians who had slave labor? Besides, the Georgia climate was too hot for white farm workers. Rice, they said, could be raised only by black workers.

Other Georgians objected to slavery. In January 1739, Scottish settlers at Darien asked the trustees to keep their ban on slavery. They argued that having slaves would take away the white settler's will to work hard. Moreover, said the Scots, "it's shocking to human nature, that any race of mankind . . . should be sentenced to perpetual slavery; . . . freedom to them must be as dear as to us." The Salzburgers, too, spoke out against slavery. They laughed at the idea that white workers couldn't raise rice. They themselves had already done so.

The trustees rejected the Savannah petition, but slaves were brought in anyway. Some planters "rented" slaves from their Carolina owners or sneaked them in to work in their fields. The slavery faction grew. Finally, in 1749, the trustees gave in.

Once slavery was permitted, many more blacks were brought from South Carolina, other colonies, and the West Indies. In 1752 alone, more than 1,000 slaves were brought to Georgia. Eventually many opponents of slavery accepted it. Even some of the Salzburgers at Ebenezer had slaves. By 1773, the colony had about 15,000 slaves,* almost as many people as the 18,000 whites.

---

*Almost all slaves were blacks, but working alongside them in the fields were a handful of Indian slaves.

Slave Codes

The growing number of slaves in the colony required laws to govern their behavior and regulate their treatment. A few sections of the Slave Code of 1770, passed by the colonial General Assembly, show something of the legal position of Georgia's slave population.

Therefore be it enacted,

- That all negroes, Indians, Mulattoes, or mestizoes, who now are, or hereafter shall be in this province, (free Indians in amity with this government, and negroes, mulattoes, or mestizoes, who now are, or hereafter shall become free, excepted) and all their offspring are hereby declared to be and remain for ever hereafter absolute slaves, and shall follow the condition of the mother, and shall be deemed in law to be personal property in the hands of their respective owners.

- That no person whatsoever shall permit any slave under his care or management, and who lives in any town, to go out of the limits of the town, or any slave who lives in the country to go out of the plantation to which such slave belongs, without a ticket signed by the master or other person in charge of such slave. Every slave who shall be found without a ticket, or without a white person in his or her company, shall be punished with whipping on the bare back not exceeding twenty lashes.

- That if any slave shall presume to strike any white person, such slave, upon trial and conviction before the justice or justices, shall, for the first offense, suffer such punishment as the justice or justices shall think fit, not extending to life or limb, and for the second offense shall suffer death.

- That if any person shall on the Lord's day, commonly called Sunday, employ any slave in any work or labor (works of absolute necessity excepted), every person so offending shall forfeit the sum of ten shillings for every slave he, she, or they shall so cause to work or labor.

● That all and every person and persons whatsoever, who shall hereafter teach, or cause any slave or slaves to be taught to write or read writing, or shall employ any slave in any manner of writing whatsoever, every such person and persons shall for every such offense forfeit the sum of twenty pounds sterling. □

[Adapted from Slave Code: 1770, Act of May 10, 1770, in *Watkins Digest*, 163- 77.]

The slave became an important part of Georgia's economy. With cheap labor available, plantation agriculture grew rapidly.

The next reading describes how colonial life in Savannah changed, in part because of slave labor.

SOCIETY AND CULTURE IN SAVANNAH

As some of the colonists began to prosper, social classes based on wealth and status began to form. These colonists had time for other activities besides work.

THINK ABOUT IT

1. Why did social distinctions grow as the colony grew?
2. What kinds of social activities were there in colonial Savannah?
3. Were religion and education the same for all colonists?

The model society the trustees planned for Georgia allowed for few social differences. The trustees expected all settlers to be hardworking "common folk." Each family would hold the same amount of land and have about the same kind of life. According to plan, life in Savannah during its first years was indeed fairly simple.

Life in Savannah 40 years later, however, was quite different. Oglethorpe's settlement had grown up. It had over 250 houses and was the capital of a colony of 33,000 people, about half of them black slaves. Many of the slaves worked on great rice plantations stretching out from Savannah. Some Georgia planters had become very wealthy. Sir James Wright, the royal governor, owned eleven plantations with about 26,000 acres and 525 slaves.

By 1773, Savannah had become a busy seaport of the British Empire. In that year,

Changing Colonial Lifestyle. According to the cartoonist, one aspect of life changed greatly during the colonial years. Does such a change indicate increased wealth in the colony?

it had about 30 merchant houses. Merchants exported, in 225 shiploads from Savannah, over 11,000 tons of rice, deerskins, lumber, naval stores, salt beef and pork, corn, and other Georgia products. Most of Savannah's trade was to and from Great Britain, but some shipments went directly to and from the West Indies, Africa, and northern colonies.

As the colony prospered, the society of Savannah changed. Back in 1733, each colonist had to work with his or her own hands just to survive. By 1773, many had the help of hired laborers, indentured servants, or slaves.

In 1733, the settlers had to do many things for themselves, such as raising food, building shelter, and making tools and clothing. In 1773, residents of Savannah could turn to many kinds of specialists to provide the things they needed. Savannah had artisans and mechanics, such as shoemakers, tailors, cabinetmakers, coopers, blacksmiths, gunsmiths, masons, saddlers, wheelwrights, and sailmakers. The city also had scribes and printers, as well as millers, bakers, and butchers. As the capital of the colony, Savannah also used the services of trained professionals: lawyers, doctors, clergymen, and schoolteachers.

So, by 1773, the population of Savannah was made up of distinct groups. The structure of Savannah's society may be likened to a ladder. Depending on their ability and ambition, persons might move up (or down) the ladder.* Blacks, however, were locked into their position as slaves.

The small group of wealthy rice planters and shipping merchants at the top of the ladder provided most of the colony's leaders. Other men who owned property had a smaller voice in the colony's affairs. They included the professionals; owners of small farms, shops, and other businesses;

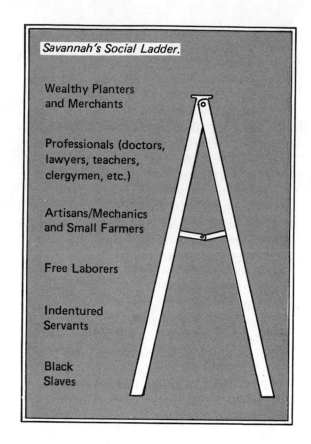

Savannah's Social Ladder.

Wealthy Planters and Merchants

Professionals (doctors, lawyers, teachers, clergymen, etc.)

Artisans/Mechanics and Small Farmers

Free Laborers

Indentured Servants

Black Slaves

and some artisans and mechanics. Laborers, indentured servants, and slaves had no such voice.

Savannah Culture

For the lower ranks, life in Savannah varied little from one day to the next. It was mostly work.

Those higher up the ladder, though, had time for social activities. Public celebrations and military ceremonies, as well as weddings and funerals, were big events. The biggest event was the annual celebration of the king's birthday. Men and women attended dances, picnics, and other social events.

Some of the men of the city belonged to social clubs and fraternities. For others, Savannah had several taverns where drinking and gambling were popular.

Those who could read acquired books from the city's several booksellers and

---

*This statement applies only to white men. There was little opportunity for a woman to be independent. Her position in society was tied to her husband's.

libraries. In 1763, they could also buy Savannah's first newspaper, the *Georgia Gazette*.

Many colonial Georgians, however, could not read or write. Neither the trustees nor the royal government established a school system for the colony.

In Georgia, as in other American colonies, children were taught mainly by their parents. A boy learned a trade or how to farm from his father. A girl learned from her mother the skills she would need to be a good wife and mother. Sometimes, boys who were orphans or from poor families would be "bound out" to a skilled mechanic or artisan to learn a trade. Similarly, girls might be bound out to a family to learn how to run a household.

From time to time, schools were set up in Savannah, but only one, Bethesda Orphan House, lasted very long. Schoolmasters were often clergymen, and religion was taught along with reading, writing, and arithmetic. The larger plantations often had schools for the planters' children. Most children in colonial Georgia, however, never went to school.

Religion in Colonial Savannah

The trustees who founded Georgia were concerned about the religious life of the settlers. In 1733, the good ship *Anne* carried, along with the first group of colonists, hundreds of Bibles, prayer books, and other religious works. The trustees also provided for clergymen to go to the colony.

In Great Britain, the Anglican Church (Church of England), raised money for the new colony. Most of the settlers who came with Oglethorpe were Anglicans. However, all religious groups except Roman Catholics were welcome to settle.* The first Jewish families arrived in Savannah in 1733. Later came Lutherans, Presbyterians, Congregationalists, and Quakers.

---

*Only after the Revolutionary War were Catholics allowed to settle in Georgia. They built their first church in Wilkes County in 1796.

The new colony also attracted three Anglican clergymen who would become famous as founders of Methodism. John and Charles Wesley came in 1736 to minister to the colonists and to try to convert Indians to Christianity. They were followed by George Whitefield who established Bethesda Orphan House. Whitefield preached a "great awakening" of religion in the American colonies and for 30 years was one of the best known colonial clergymen.

When Georgia became a royal colony, its government continued to take an interest in religion. The royal governor was required to see that the Sabbath was properly observed. In 1758, the colonial General Assembly passed an act which established the Church of England as the official church and divided Georgia into eight parishes. The parishes were to administer church affairs, including the upkeep of buildings and cemeteries, and local government affairs. All Georgians were taxed to support the official church, but they remained free to worship as they chose.

Four years later, the Assembly passed another law regarding religion. This one prohibited certain social activities on Sundays.

And be it further enacted . . . that no public sports, or pastimes, as bearbaiting, bullbaiting, football playing, horse racing, shooting, hunting or fishing, interludes or common plays, or other games, exercises, sports or pastimes whatsoever, shall be used on the Lords day by any person or persons whatsoever.

All and every person or persons offending . . . shall forfeit for every such offense the sum of five shillings sterling. □
[Act of the General Assembly, March 4, 1762. *Colonial Records*, XVIII, 510.]

At the same time, the Assembly prohibited most travel on Sundays. How well these laws were enforced is not known.

By the end of the colonial period, Savannah had several churches of different religious groups. Anglicans were the largest group. Elsewhere in the colony, the place of religion in colonial life varied greatly. In Ebenezer the church was the center of community life. In the upcountry, except for Augusta which had an Anglican church, religion barely existed. That would change with the arrival of Baptist and Methodist missionaries about the time of the Revolutionary War.

As the colonial period drew to a close, Georgians enjoyed greater prosperity than ever before. Much of that prosperity came with royal government in the 1750s. Among the people of Savannah, Sir James Wright was well-respected and trusted. Yet, when the time came, in 1776, Georgia would join the other 12 colonies in a revolution. Why? That's the subject for the next chapter.

ACTIVITIES FOR CHAPTER 4

Discussion

A. Georgia's settlers developed an agrarian culture. Almost every settler farmed for a living. Their whole lives, including their family relationships and values, were influenced by working the land.

   1. In what ways does the Settler story illustrate an agrarian way of life?

   2. Was the Salzburger culture agrarian?

   3. How would a story about a Salzburger family differ from the story about the Settler family?

B. In 1739 the Scots at Darien predicted slave labor would have a bad effect on the colony. After 1750, Georgia's agricultural economy came to depend more and more on slave labor.

   1. Did the presence of black slaves influence the colony's prosperity? How?

   2. Did their presence affect the culture of Georgia in other ways?

   3. Do you think the Scots were accurate in their prediction?

Writing Project

How was life for a teenager in colonial Georgia different from what it is today? Write an essay on this question. To get started: (a) figure how much time you spend each week on work, school, church, recreation, and travel; (b) figure how much time you might have spent on these five activities in colonial times. Tell why you think there would be differences between life in colonial Georgia and present-day Georgia.

5 Revolution and Statehood

From 1754 to 1763, Great Britain and France fought a war over territory in North America. American colonists, many of whom fought alongside British troops, called it the French and Indian War because many Indians fought on the side of France. On the frontier, the fighting was savage, with scalpings and cruelties.

Great Britain won and gained Canada and all of France's territory east of the Mississippi River, except New Orleans. The British also took Florida from Spain, France's ally in the war. These actions removed the foreign threat to the Georgia colony. But, the outcome of the French and Indian War led to new problems for Britain and its 13 colonies.

In 1763, Great Britain found itself with a huge empire, not only in North America but also in other parts of the world. British leaders determined that they needed a new policy, a new overall plan, for governing this empire. They devised a new imperial policy. It was aimed at (1) tightening Britain's control over its colonies and (2) having the colonists share more of the cost of government, including military costs.

In forming this new policy, however, Britain's leaders did not give a voice to the American colonists. Many colonists saw things differently and had interests different from Britain's leaders. In a little over 10 years, these differences would lead to the American Revolution.

The following reading outlines the conflicts between Great Britain and the colonies that led to war.

THINK ABOUT IT

1. How had the colonists put the idea of representative government into practice?
2. According to the colonists, how did Parliament violate this idea?
3. For what purpose did Parliament pass a series of tax acts? Why did it pass the "intolerable acts"? How did some colonists react to these laws?

THE CLASH OF BRITISH AND AMERICAN IDEAS

The American colonists' views on government and economics were influenced by several ideas they brought with them from the old world.

The first of these ideas is called government by *consent of the governed*. It means that government should rule only so long as the people consent (or agree) to be governed. If the government doesn't protect the people against enemies or doesn't respect their rights, the people may take away their consent to be governed. They may even rebel.

Related to the consent idea is the idea of *representative government.* It means that the people have the right to elect persons to represent them in making decisions that affect their lives. These elected representatives must be able to gather in assemblies (or legislatures) to make laws and set taxes.

The third idea was the idea of *limited government.* It means that the power of government is limited by natural law. Natural law is higher than any government. This law says the people have natural rights which the government cannot take away because they come from God. The most basic natural rights are life, liberty, and property.

In addition, American colonists had developed their own ideas about self-government. They had held town meetings to decide on local problems such as building roads. They had set up legislatures to make laws such as those requiring men to serve in the militia and to pay taxes to support the militia. From these experiences, they had come to believe that only their own elected representatives could pass laws and set taxes in the colonies.

The colonists also developed their own economic ideas. They felt that they should be free to make anything they wished and sell it to whomever they wished. Such a notion of free enterprise clashed with Britain's mercantile system. It also conflicted with laws Parliament had passed to control colonial manufacturing and trade. Some colonists ignored British laws and carried on illegal trade (smuggling) with French, Dutch, and Spanish merchants.

By 1763, then, the American colonists were used to doing things their own way. British leaders were probably not fully aware of what had happened. After all, they were separated from America by an ocean, with communication only by sailing ship. So, when they stepped in with new laws to govern Britain's empire, they ran smack into the angry opposition of the Americans.

Taxes

Taxes were a major source of conflict between the colonies and Britain. Starting in 1764, Parliament passed a series of tax laws designed to raise money from the colonies to help pay the costs of running the empire.

Some of these laws, such as the Sugar Act (1764) and the Townshend Acts (1767), placed customs duties (taxes on imports) on products coming into the colonies. These products included sugar, coffee, tea, wine, paper, lead, glass, and paint. The Stamp Act (1765) required a government tax stamp on all printed paper used in the colonies. Such tax laws made these items more costly for the colonists.

The colonists protested these laws to Parliament. They organized such groups as the Sons of Liberty (or Liberty Boys) to rouse the people to oppose the government's actions. They boycotted (refused to buy) goods that were taxed, and they continued to smuggle non-British goods into the colonies. Sometimes, officials trying to collect taxes met with threats and even attacks.

Parliament finally backed down and repealed most of these taxes. But by then an anti-British attitude had formed in the minds of many colonists.

Rights

Britain's new laws conflicted with the political beliefs of the American colonists in several ways. First of all, the tax laws violated their right to be taxed only by their own elected assemblies. One new law required colonial legislatures to raise money to support British troops in the colonies. When some colonists resisted, their assemblies were suspended.

Second, some of the laws permitted government officers to search homes without a specific search warrant. (And, accused smugglers could be hauled before military courts with no rights to trial by jury.) To the colonist who believed that "a man's home is his castle" and that every person had a right to a trial by jury, these laws were outrageous.

As public protests and violence against government officials grew, Britain sent more troops to the colonies. This only added to the trouble.

The Final Straw

In 1773 Parliament passed a law, the Tea Act, giving one British company a monopoly on importing tea into the colonies. Tea-drinking was very popular among the colonists, but many refused to buy this company's tea—even though it was priced cheaply. They felt it was being forced on them by the government. Meanwhile, some colonial merchants, who had been illegally importing Dutch tea, saw their businesses threatened. On the night of December 16, the Boston Sons of Liberty dumped several shiploads of tea into the harbor. In other ports, tea was also dumped overboard or burned.

To punish Massachusetts and control the colonies, Parliament passed several harsh measures. These included (1) closing the port of Boston until the tea was paid for, (2) not allowing the people of Massachusetts to elect their own officials or hold town meetings, and (3) requiring the people in all the colonies to feed and house soldiers.

These "intolerable acts," as they were called by the colonists, only increased the opposition to Britain. The patriots in each colony joined in protest. A Continental Congress, with delegates from all colonies except Georgia, met in Philadelphia and agreed to boycott all British goods. In incidents around the colonies, government officials were beaten up, British goods were burned, and persons openly loyal to Britain were tarred and feathered.* Britain sent more troops to the colonies to control the situation.

---

*Smeared with tar and covered with feathers as a punishment.

Finally, on April 19, 1775, Massachusetts "minutemen" and British troops battled at Lexington and Concord.

News of the battles spread quickly throughout the colonies. Colonial assemblies voted to raise militia to defend themselves against the British. The war had begun.

Georgia Chooses Sides

Georgia was much younger than the other colonies and didn't have a long history of self-government. Many Georgians had arrived from England only recently and still felt strongly attached to their homeland. The colony owed much of its prosperity to its efficient royal governor. So, when the colonies began gradually to move toward revolution, Georgia lagged behind.

However, as Britain's policies became more distasteful to them, Georgians, too, began to take sides. As in the other colonies, the anti-British Georgians were known as "Whigs," later "patriots." Supporters of Britain were called "Tories" or "loyalists."

Discussion of Views in 1775: A Story

The following story is a discussion between two Georgians and their British visitor early in 1775. Although the account is fictional, it presents the different ways people viewed the events leading up to the Revolutionary War.

Characters:
> Charles Winston, a British merchant visiting in Savannah on business
> Henry Bradshaw, a wealthy Savannah merchant
> John Bradshaw, his son and also a merchant

Setting: The Bradshaw home overlooking Savannah's harbor. The Bradshaws and their guest have just finished dinner.

THINK ABOUT IT

1. What action by the colonists affected Winston's pocketbook?
2. Which of the British government's actions conflicted with young Bradshaw's beliefs?
3. Why might the Bradshaws see things differently from their visitor? Why might they see things differently from each other?

"Well, tell us Charles, how goes your business in London?" asked Henry Bradshaw.

"Not very well, Henry. The boycott is ruining me. I have several warehouses full of clothing and hardware. If I don't sell some of it soon, I'll go broke. Why can't people in the other colonies be reasonable like you Georgians and buy our goods?"

"Excuse me, sir," John Bradshaw interrupted. "I think all of us in the colonies have been too reasonable for too long. For years, the government has ruined *our* businesses by imposing unfair taxes on imports we badly needed. Also, it has strangled our trade with strict regulations.

"Your government ignored our protests. Then it passed those 'intolerable acts' to punish our friends in Boston. That made us decide to boycott all trade with Britain. Soon Georgia will join that boycott, I'm proud to say."

Charles Winston huffed, "Was it reasonable of your friends in Boston to dump tea worth a thousand pounds into the harbor?"

Henry Bradshaw spoke up, "Destroying property is criminal. Differences should be settled lawfully. The Bostonians anger too easily. I assure you, Charles, the people of Savannah are more reasonable."

Drawing Room of the Bradshaw Townhouse. Only Savannah's wealthier merchants and planters would have a home like this one.

"Not for long!" John interrupted. "The people of Savannah will *not* accept unfair taxation."

"Please excuse my son," said Henry Bradshaw. "He's been associating too much, I fear, with the Liberty Boys, who . . . ."

"Ah, you have them in Savannah, too," sighed Mr. Winston. "They've certainly made trouble in Massachusetts with their leader, that hothead Sam Adams."

"You can thank your Stamp Act for Georgia's Liberty Boys. They were organized to prevent the sale of those hated stamps. And, they did all right," John smiled.

Winston's face reddened. "We in Britain pay far heavier taxes than you in the colonies. And one reason is that it cost His Majesty's government so much money to save your scalps from the Indians," thundered Charles Winston. "Such tax measures were a fair way to have you Americans pay part of the cost. Anyway, the tax was carefully considered by Parliament before it was voted on."

"Voted on? By whom?" John demanded. "By what right does Parliament impose taxes in the colonies? We Georgians have no vote, as you have, in electing members to Parliament. We stand firm with our brothers in the other colonies: *no taxation without representation*!" John declared.

Charles Winston cleared his throat, "Well, if it's a simple matter of taxes that's bothering you colonials, there's really no reason to fight over. . . ."

"It's not that simple," John replied firmly. "It's a matter of the rights we are entitled to as free-born Englishmen. The government has allowed its agents to enter at will and search private homes. It has denied the protection of trial by jury to persons accused of crimes. These measures are certainly unjust."

Henry Bradshaw, who had been listening patiently, spoke up. "I'm afraid, Charles, that His Majesty's government has made some foolish mistakes that have driven even decent people into a hostile attitude. For example, the government forced our assembly to vote funds to quarter and supply its troops," said the elder Bradshaw. "Many Georgians resented that action."

"But you need our British regulars to defend you from Indian attacks," replied Winston.

"Ha! Those troops are stationed here only to force us to behave as the government wishes. In England you wouldn't put up with soldiers in your towns!" John argued. "The government is mistaken if it thinks that military force will resolve our differences."

"And how do you think they must be resolved, young man?"

John looked the Englishman squarely in the eye. "You in Britain must treat us as equals. We must have the same economic and political freedoms as you. Americans are no longer your children; we are adults. If Britain does not treat us as adult members of the family, we shall leave her and make our own way in the world.

"That is all I have to say." John left the room quickly.

Stunned, Charles Winston turned to his old friend. "Henry, which way will Georgia go?"

"If you had asked me that question a year ago, I'd have confidently answered 'with the king.' But, now I fear the king's power is slipping away. Georgia will be joining the other colonies at the Continental Congress in Philadelphia."

"But, why?" wondered the Englishman. "So many Georgians are still loyal to the king."

Henry Bradshaw got up, walked to the window, and gazed out at the harbor. "Last week I talked to a ship's captain from Boston. I asked him why they were so hot for rebellion up there. He answered, 'We have always governed ourselves and we always mean to.'

"That attitude has spread like an infection from Massachusetts to Georgia. If Britain means that we shouldn't govern ourselves, it will be war. And, Georgia will be in it." □

AFTER LEXINGTON AND CONCORD

On May 10, 1775, news of battles at Lexington and Concord, Massachusetts reached Savannah. The American Revolution had begun. The following reading describes the events during that struggle.

THINK ABOUT IT

1. Who took control of Georgia's government in 1775-1776?
2. Who was given the power to make laws under the Constitution of 1777? How were lawmakers chosen?
3. What problem did the new state government face?

Independence for Georgia

Savannah patriots greeted the news of Lexington and Concord by openly defying royal authority. They raided the government gunpowder storehouse and disrupted the governor's celebration of the king's birthday. Amid much confusion, royal government began to fall apart. Gradually a new revolutionary government run by the Whigs took its place.

In July, a "Provincial Congress" of delegates from Georgia's parishes met in Savannah. The delegates voted to join the colonies' complete boycott of trade with Great Britain. The Whigs also set up a "Council of Safety" to enforce the boycott and to work with other colonies.

Later in 1775, the Whigs took over the militia, ousting Tory officers. They set taxes to finance Georgia's defense against British attack. They also took control of the courts and other government activities—such as handling Indian relations. Governor Wright was powerless to do anything about these actions.

In January 1776, the Council of Safety arrested Wright and other officials loyal to the king. Two months later Governor Wright escaped to a British warship in the harbor. Royal government ended.

The Declaration of Independence

Meanwhile, the Second Continental Congress, including delegates from Georgia, was meeting in Philadelphia. The delegates had to decide what to do. Should they give in to Great Britain or resist? They took two actions: (1) they sent King George III a message stating their loyalty to him, but asking him to stop his government's hostile actions against the colonies; and (2) they organized an army and named George Washington of Virginia to command it.

Through the rest of 1775 and into 1776 more fighting broke out between the colonists and British troops. Yet, the Americans did not agree on what they were fighting for. Some felt they were fighting for their rights *as Englishmen*; they had no desire to separate from their mother country. Others, however, accepted more and more the idea that full independence was their goal.

On July 4, 1776, the Second Continental Congress adopted the Declaration of Independence. It was mainly the work of a Virginian, Thomas Jefferson. All the delegates signed it, including Button Gwinnett, Lyman Hall, and George Walton from Georgia.

What did the Declaration of Independence contain? It included the following ideas:

1. All men are created equal.
2. Everyone is born with certain rights—life, liberty, and the pursuit of happiness.
3. Government gets its power from the people.
4. The people can do away with a government that is unsatisfactory.

Reaction in Georgia

On August 8, 1776, the Declaration of Independence was publicly read in Savannah. Patriots shot off cannons and staged a mock funeral and burial for King George III. Other Georgians, however, did not celebrate. Some 1,500 Tories left the colony. Others stayed to protect their property, but kept quiet about their loyalist feelings.

The Continental Congress asked each of the former colonies to set up state governments if they hadn't already done so. Georgia already had formed a Provincial Congress, with a set of "Rules and Regulations" for governing the state. Archibald Bulloch became the first "President and Commander-in-Chief of the Province of Georgia."

Georgia's First Constitution

But the "Rules and Regulations" were only the barest outline for government. The patriots decided that Georgia needed a more permanent form of government. Under Bulloch's leadership, they gathered to write a constitution.

A constitution is a plan for the operation of government. It spells out the government's powers—what it can do and what it cannot do. It tells how the laws will be made, how the laws will be carried out, and how disputes will be settled according to the laws. Also, a constitution states what officers the government will have, how they are to be chosen, and how they are to carry out their duties.

In February 1777, the new state constitution was finished. The Constitution of 1777 set up a unicameral (or one-house) legislature with the power to "make such laws and regulations as may be conducive to the good order and well-being of the State." The legislature, named the House of Assembly, had the power to elect the governor and other state officers. The governor had very little power and was limited to a one-year term.

The Constitution set up eight counties,* to replace the colonial parishes. Each county had to have its own officials, courthouse, schools, and militia unit. To settle disputes, each county had a court, called the superior court. The Constitu-

---

*Burke, Camden, Chatham, Effingham, Glynn, Liberty, Richmond, and Wilkes.

tion stated how cases were to be tried.

Much of Georgia's first constitution focused on representation and voting. Here are some excerpts:

● The legislature of the State shall be composed of the representatives of the people . . . the representatives shall be elected yearly . . . .

● The representatives shall be chosen out of the residents in each county, who shall have resided at least twelve months in this State . . . and they shall be of the Protestant religion, and of the age of twenty-one years and shall (possess) two hundred and fifty acres of land, or some property to the amount of two hundred and fifty pounds.

● All male white inhabitants, of the age of twenty-one, and possessed in his own right of ten pounds value, and liable to pay tax in this State, or being of any mechanic trade, and shall have been resident six months in this State, shall have a right to vote in all elections for representatives, or any other officers . . . .

● No person shall be entitled to more than one vote . . . nor shall any person who holds any title of nobility be entitled to a vote . . . .

The Constitution also provided for freedom of religion and other rights:

● All persons whatever shall have the free exercise of their religion; provided it be not repugnant to the peace and safety of the State.

● Freedom of the press and trial by jury (are) to remain inviolate forever.

Problems of the New State Government

In May 1777, the new Constitution went into effect. John Adam Treutlen became the first governor of the state.

The new government faced great difficulties. First, thousands of Georgians were still loyal to the king. They wanted to see the new government fail.

Second, squabbling among the Whigs weakened the government. Two rival parties struggled for control of the government.

Bitter feelings between members of a radical upcountry party and a conservative city party led to the death of one of Georgia's signers of the Declaration of Independence. In the 1700s, a man protected his honor with sword or pistol. When Lachlan McIntosh, a conservative, publicly called Button Gwinnett, a radical, "a scoundrel and lying rascal," Gwinnett challenged him to a duel. On May 16, 1777, the rivals exchanged pistol shots outside Savannah. Both were wounded and Gwinnett died three days later. The rivalry between the factions continued for many years.

Of course, the biggest difficulty facing the new government was war. In the war with Great Britain, the colonial forces started out as the underdog. The story of Georgia's place in that struggle appears in the following reading.

GEORGIA IN THE REVOLUTION

THINK ABOUT IT

1. In what sense was the American Revolution (especially in Georgia) a civil war?
2. What part of Georgia could the British not regain?
3. What happened to Georgia's state government (the Whig government) after Governor Wright restored royal government in Savannah?

The American Revolution began in the northern colonies, and most of the fighting continued there until 1778. But even during the first years of the war, there was no real peace in Georgia. Only about one-third of the Georgians were Whigs. Another third were Tories, and the rest remained neutral, waiting to see what happened. From 1776 to 1778, with the Whigs in control, some of the Tories were driven out of Georgia, their property taken over by the state. In addition to this fighting between Georgians, fights erupted between Georgia patriots and Florida loyalists.

The British Return

In 1778 the British decided to turn their efforts toward regaining control of the Carolinas and Georgia. They counted on the large number of loyalists in the South to help them.

In December, a British army from New York reached Savannah. A force of 600 patriots faced 2,000 British soldiers. The battle was over quickly. The leaders of Georgia's Whig government barely escaped, and over half the American defenders were either killed or captured.

British troops captured Sunbury, Augusta, and Ebenezer. By the end of January 1779, every important town in Georgia was in the hands of the British.

Meanwhile, Sir James Wright, the last royal governor, returned to Savannah to reestablish royal authority. Many loyalists

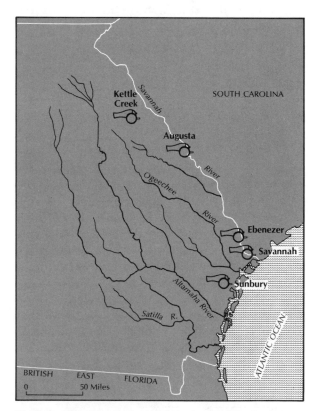

MAP 8. The Revolutionary War in Georgia. In Georgia there were fewer major battles than in the northern colonies.

came out of hiding to openly support the crown. The British called on the people to come over to their side. Some wealthy coastal planters did take the oath of allegiance to the king, but the upcountry farmers held out for independence.

In the upcountry, the state government's leaders tried to carry on the fight, meeting wherever they could. The British and the Tories, however, kept them on the run.

Kettle Creek

Early in 1779, at Kettle Creek in Wilkes County, a force of Georgia patriots, aided by South Carolinians, attacked a Tory force. The Tories scattered, their British commander dead.

Although the Battle of Kettle Creek didn't involve large armies, it was important to the patriot cause. The patriots gained badly needed arms, ammunition,

and horses. The battle reinspired many Georgians who had become lukewarm to the patriot cause. And never again were the Tories able to gather a large force in the upcountry.

The Battle of Kettle Creek was fought between Americans—patriots and loyalists. In fact, the Revolutionary War in Georgia was in some ways like a civil war. Frequently, neighbor fought neighbor, and sometimes whole communities were split down the middle.

Siege of Savannah

During the fall of 1779, the patriots—aided by France, which had joined the American side in 1778—tried desperately to retake Savannah. An American army and a French fleet laid siege to the city for three weeks. After a fierce bombardment, the Americans tried to take the city by storm. In a daring cavalry charge, Count Pulaski,

Fighting in the Upcountry. The type of fighting once carried on in Georgia is often called "guerilla warfare." Small units of patriots and loyalists carried on almost continual skirmishes, ambushes, and raids.

a Polish nobleman who had come to America to help the patriots, was killed. The attack failed.

In the end, the British were able to hold Savannah and lost only 150 men. The Americans and their allies had 1,000 men killed or wounded and gained nothing.

The End of the War

During 1780, the British controlled most of Georgia, the only one of the 13 former colonies in which the king's government was restored. However, the Whigs and the Tories continued their bitter fighting in the upcountry. Families were driven from their lands, their homes burned, their livestock killed, and their crops destroyed.

In 1781, the Whigs recaptured Augusta. Meanwhile a large British army surrendered to General Washington at Yorktown, Virginia. In the spring of 1782, the Tories and the British troops gave up Georgia. As the American troops marched joyfully into Savannah, over 2,000 Tories and their slaves left the state. All of Georgia was once again under control of its own government.

The Revolutionary War ended formally with the signing of the Treaty of Paris in 1783. Georgia, along with the other former colonies, was now a free and independent state. However, all her troubles were not over. Britain had given Florida back to Spain, causing peril along the southern border. Unfriendly Indians, some of whom had taken the British side in the war, posed a threat along Georgia's frontier. Georgia would face some of the same problems that she had before the war. This time, however, she would handle them as a state, not a colony.

Georgia Patriots

". . . We mutually Pledge to Each Other Our Lives, Our Fortunes and Our Sacred Honor." So ends the Declaration of Independence. Who were those upcountry fighters who refused to swear allegiance to the British Crown, and suffered at the hands of the Tories and the British?

Unfortunately, little is known about most of Georgia's patriots. During the war, few records were kept. Not much reliable information exists about the activities of the Whig government either.

The heroic deeds of the patriots, however, spread by word of mouth. Years later, people still talked about them. During the 1800s, people wrote down different versions of these stories, now a part of Georgia's tradition.

These stories are a blend of fact and fiction; thus they are secondary, not primary sources. But, for a look into the lives of the upcountry patriots, they are all we have.

The stories as presented here are adapted from versions published in 1854.

THINK ABOUT IT

1. What useful information do these stories contain? What parts are likely to be fictional?
2. What clues do these stories provide about the values and beliefs of the patriots? About the values the storytellers had?

 Aunt Nancy Hart

The Rev. Mr. Snead of Baldwin County, a connection of the Hart family, says he remembers Aunt Nancy, as she was usually called, and stories about her. He describes her as being about six feet high, very muscular, and erect in her gait. Among the stories about her is the following:

On an excursion from the British camp at Augusta, a party of Tories penetrated into the interior. They savagely murdered Colonel John Dooly in bed in his own house. They then proceeded up the country to commit further outrages. On their way, five of them crossed the Broad River to pay a visit to their old acquaintance, Nancy Hart.

On reaching her cabin, they entered it unceremoniously, receiving from her no welcome but a scowl. They ordered her to give them something to eat. She replied,

Nancy Hart Captures Some Tories. This photo was made from an artist's impression published in the early 1800s.

"I never feed King's men if I can help it. The villains have put it out of my power to feed even my own family and friends. They have stolen and killed all my poultry and pigs, except that one old gobbler you see in the yard."

"Well, and that you shall cook for us," said one, who appeared to be the head of the party. Raising his musket, he shot down the turkey and handed it to Mrs. Hart. She stormed and swore awhile—for Nancy occasionally swore. But, at last she agreed to cook it, assisted by her daughter, Sukey, who was some 10 or 12 years old. Nancy now seemed in a good humor, exchanging jests with the Tories. They invited her to partake of the liquor they had brought with them.

Before cleaning and cooking the turkey, Mrs. Hart sent Sukey to the spring, a short distance from the house, for water. At the spring was kept a conch shell. It was used as a crude trumpet by the family to give information, by means of various notes, to Mr. Hart, or his neighbors, who might be at work in a field. Mrs. Hart had directed Sukey to blow the conch in such a way as to inform her husband that Tories were in the cabin.

Later, after they had become merry over their jug, the Tories sat down to feast upon the slaughtered gobbler. They had cautiously stacked their arms where they were in view and within reach. Mrs. Hart attended to her guests at the table and occasionally passed between them and their muskets. She had slipped out one of the pieces of pine chinking between the logs of the cabin. Then she put out of the house, through that space, two of the five guns.

She was detected in putting out the third. The men sprang to their feet. Quick as a thought, Mrs. Hart brought the gun she held to her shoulder and declared she would kill the first man who approached her. All were terror-struck. At length one of them made a motion to advance upon her. True to her threat, she fired. He fell dead upon the floor! Instantly seizing another musket, she brought it to the position of readiness to fire again.

Sukey, who had returned from the spring, took up the remaining gun and announced, "Daddy and them will soon be here." This information increased the alarm of the Tories. They proposed a general rush.

No time was to be lost by the bold woman; she fired again, and brought down another Tory. Sukey had the other musket in readiness. Her mother took it, and positioning herself in the doorway, called upon the party to surrender.

Her husband and his neighbors came up to the door. They were about to shoot down the Tories. Mrs. Hart stopped them, saying they had surrendered to *her*. She swore that "shooting was too good for them." The dead man was dragged out of the house. The wounded Tory and the others were bound, taken out, and hanged.

The tree upon which they were hanged was pointed out, in 1838, by a person who lived in those bloody times. This person also showed the spot once occupied by Mrs. Hart's cabin, with the remark, "Poor Nancy—she was a honey of a patriot, but the devil of a wife." [Since this sketch was written, a new county has been formed, named Hart, and we understand it is proposed to call the seat of justice *Nancyville*.] □

[Adapted from George White, *Historical Collections of Georgia* (New York: Pudney & Russell, Publishers, 1854).]

 Austin Dabney

The following account of Austin Dabney, a remarkable free man of colour, was given by Governor Gilmer—

In the beginning of the Revolutionary conflict, a man by the name of Aycock moved to Wilkes County. He brought with him a mulatto boy, named Austin, who passed as Aycock's slave.

As the conflict in that area became bitter, Aycock was called on to join the fight. He wasn't much of a fighter, though, and offered the mulatto boy as a substitute. The patriots objected, saying that a slave could not be a soldier. Thereupon, Aycock admitted that the mulatto boy was born free. Austin was then accepted into service, and the captain to whose company he was attached added Dabney to his name.

Dabney proved himself a good solider in many a skirmish with the British and Tories. He fought under Colonel John Dooly and was with Colonel Elijah Clarke in the battle at Kettle Creek. At Kettle Creek, he was severely wounded by a rifle-ball passing through his thigh. He was taken into the house of a Mr. Harris, where he was kindly cared for until he recovered. The wound made him a cripple for life. Dabney was unable to do further military duty and afterwards labored for Harris and his family.

After the war, when prosperous times came again, Austin Dabney acquired property. Later, he moved to Madison County, carrying with him his benefactor and family. Here he became noted for his fondness for horseracing and he betted to the extent of his means. His means were aided by a pension, which he received from the United States on account of his injury.

In the distribution of the public lands by lottery among the people of Georgia, the legislature gave Dabney some land in the county of Walton. At the election for members of the legislature the year after, the County of Madison was divided. They voted according to whether the candidates were for Dabney or against him. People were incensed that a mulatto should receive a gift of land. Some felt such gifts belonged to the white freemen of Georgia.

Dabney soon after moved to the land given him by the state, and carried with him the Harris family. He continued to labor for them and contributed whatever he made to their support, except what he needed for his own clothing and food. He sent the eldest son of Harris to Franklin College, and afterwards supported him while he studied law. When Harris was undergoing his examination, Austin waited outside. When his young friend was sworn in, he burst into a flood of tears. Upon his death, Austin Dabney left the Harris family all his property. □

[Adapted from George White, *Historical Collections of Georgia* (New York: Pudney & Russell, Publisher, 1854).]

GOVERNMENT RESPONDS TO NEEDS OF A NEW NATION

After the Revolutionary War, the states faced the challenge of forging a strong nation. In May 1787, delegates from every state except Rhode Island met in Philadelphia, Pennsylvania to tackle a big problem—how to improve their national government.

Across the country, the economy was shaky. In some places, business was almost at a standstill. State governments discouraged trade by taxing the products of other states. Some of them issued nearly worthless paper money that many merchants refused to accept.

In Massachusetts, disgruntled citizens rebelled and were put down by the state militia. Other state governments squabbled over boundaries and the control of navigation and shipping on interstate rivers.

Operating under a constitution called the Articles of Confederation, the U.S. government could do very little about this situation. The Articles had left most powers to the individual states. For example, the central government had no power to impose taxes. When it asked the states for money, they usually refused to give it. The national government had no money for an army or navy, or even for roads or post offices. It had no power to regulate trade among the states and no courts to settle disputes between citizens of different states.

The delegates to the Philadelphia Convention debated, often bitterly, for four months and finally produced the Constitution of the United States. It provided for a new government that would guarantee the principles Americans had fought for in the Revolutionary War. The new government would have power to make and enforce laws to protect the people from foreign enemies and to bring order to the land.

Under the Constitution, the state and national governments would function side by side, each with certain powers spelled out, in what is called a *federal* system.

To prevent the national government from growing too powerful, the delegates at Philadelphia divided its powers among three separate branches. They created a *legislative* branch to make the laws, an *executive* branch to carry out the laws, and a *judicial* branch to settle disputes according to the laws. They built into the United States Constitution a plan of "checks and balances" to prevent any of the branches from overpowering the others.

Georgians supported the idea of a strong national government. On January 2, 1788, Georgia became the fourth state to ratify (or approve) the Constitution of the United States. A year later the new national government took power, with George Washington as the first president of the United States.

State Government

That same year, 1789, Georgia adopted a new state constitution, one more in line with the new national constitution. Like the national Congress, the Georgia legislature would be bicameral (or two-house), with a Senate and a House of Representatives.

The state government was designed to have three branches, like the national government. It had a legislature (the General Assembly) to make laws, an executive branch headed by a governor to enforce the laws, and a judicial branch consisting of courts to settle disputes among the citizens. But the branches were not balanced. Almost all the power rested with the legislature. It controlled raising and spending money and even chose the governor, the judges, and other state officials.

The highest courts in the state were

the *superior courts*. Superior court judges traveled a regular "circuit" by horseback or stagecoach, handling the most serious cases in several counties. Each county had an inferior court for less serious cases, and each community had a justice of the peace court to handle minor matters.

Local Government

The state constitution allowed for local governments to be set up. In each county, the justices of the inferior court not only tried cases but also had to maintain county property, such as the courthouse, jail, local roads, and bridges. Counties were (and still are) local extensions of state government. They are not independent governments; they have no power except what the General Assembly assigns to them.

Cities and towns were a somewhat different case. Their powers were (and are) given to them in *charters*—sort of mini-constitutions—approved by the General Assembly. Not all charters are alike, but they each set up a city as a kind of corporation. A city's charter gives a city the power to make local laws, called *ordinances*, which have effect within the city limits. The charter spells out what services a city can provide, how it can raise money, and what officers it will have.

Under the new state constitution, government in Georgia was very small. In 1790, state government spent only about $25,000 each year, and the state had only 11 county governments.

By 1840, state government was spending about $300,000 a year, and the state had 93 county governments.

What caused these changes? Events surrounding this growth will unfold in the next chapter.

ACTIVITIES FOR CHAPTER 5

Discussion

A. What were the causes of the American Revolution?

Historian No. 1: "The main cause? The colonists wanted to get rid of the mercantile system."

Historian No. 2: "No, it was the denial of rights the Americans were due as Englishmen."

Historian No. 3: "The British government was at fault. It was misinformed and antagonized the Americans."

1. If you lived in Savannah in 1775, with which of the historians would you have most likely agreed? Why?

2. Do you think war could have been avoided? How?

B. The Revolution brought great changes to Georgia. Gone were the loyalists, British taxes, the mercantile system, and the official church and its parishes. Georgia had self-rule, with its own constitution that guaranteed rights.

1. Which of these changes do you think were the most important?

2. What problems did Georgia and the other colonies face after the Revolution that spurred them to form a new government under the Constitution?

Writing Project

One of the slogans the Whigs (or patriots) used to whip up support for their cause was "no taxation without representation." What other slogans might the patriots have used in Savannah or the upcountry? What slogans might the Tories (or loyalists) have used to win the people to their side?

Write two slogans for each side. Be able to tell at whom the slogans are aimed and why you think they would be effective.

UNIT III
1790 - 1840: The Pioneer Spirit

6. Growth and Prosperity
7. The Indian Problem "Solved"

GEORGIA EVENTS	DATE	EVENTS ELSEWHERE
	1790	First cotton mill in U.S. built
Whitney invents cotton gin	1793	
Yazoo Fraud; state capital moved to Louisville	1795	Metric system adopted in France
Importing slaves prohibited	1798	Jenner develops vaccination
	1800	Washington, D.C., becomes U.S. capital
First land lottery held	1803	Louisiana Purchase
Milledgeville becomes capital	1807	Fulton develops steamboat
	1812	War between U.S. and Britain begins
Creeks give up Southwest Georgia	1814	Battle of Horseshoe Bend, Alabama
Steamboat *Savannah* crosses Atlantic	1819	U.S. buys Florida from Spain
	1820	Missouri Compromise over slavery
Plans drawn for the city of Macon	1823	U.S. issues Monroe Doctrine
Chief McIntosh killed	1825	Erie Canal links East and West
Last Creek lands ceded	1827	First railroad chartered
Gold discovered at Dahlonega; first cotton mill built at Athens	1829	Jackson becomes president; photography invented by Louis Daguerre
Lottery of Cherokee lands	1832	Democratic Party organized
Georgia Railroad chartered	1833	Great Britain abolishes slavery; American Anti-Slavery Society organized
Treaty of New Echota	1835	Seminole War in Florida
Terminus (later Atlanta) founded	1837	John Deere invents steel plow
Cherokees removed from state	1838	"Underground Railway" set up

6 Growth and Prosperity

It is 1790. A family's dinner is interrupted by a knock on the door. "Come in," says the father. A U.S. marshal enters. "Who is the head of this household?" he asks, looking at the father. "How many free white males are there under 16? How many 16 or over? How many free white females? How many slaves? Any other free persons living here?" He tallies the answers on a sheet of paper and writes down only the name of the father. As he is going out the door he adds, "If you want to change anything, the information about you and the rest of the town will be posted in the tavern."

. . . The event was the first U.S. census. The marshal was an official census taker, one of 17 marshals and their 200 assistants who went door-to-door to count the number of people in the brand-new American nation. The Constitution, ratified only the year before, required a census to be taken within three years of the first meeting of the Congress and every tenth year after that. . . .

. . . The most important reason for taking a census then (and now) was to ensure that citizens were fully represented in the federal government of the new nation—not a surprising goal considering that one of the grievances leading to the Revolution was "taxation without representation."

[From *How America Studies Itself: The U.S. Census, A Teaching Module* (Washington, D.C.: Population Reference Bureau, Inc., 1980).]

In the 50 years between 1790 and 1840, the population of Georgia quadrupled. The first United States govern-ment census, in 1790, counted about 4 million people living in the 13 states. The census in 1840 showed more than 17 million people.

A vibrant new nation was emerging. Americans pushed westward from the original states, settling the land between the Appalachians and the Mississippi River. The United States almost doubled its land area when it purchased the Louisiana territory from France in 1803. Later it bought Florida from Spain.

As the thousands of settlers poured into the fertile lands to the west, the Indians retreated, hopelessly outnumbered.

During this period technology advanced rapidly, changing the way Americans did things. Steamboats and railroads brought faster and cheaper transportation. New machines, such as those developed by Samuel Slater to make textiles, helped create the factory system of manufacturing. Other inventions, such as Eli Whitney's cotton gin and Cyrus McCormick's mechanical reaper, changed agriculture.

These developments affected both the size and the location of Georgia's population. In this chapter, you will see how the population, its activities, and the land itself changed. Then you will see how the government tried to deal with these changes.

POPULATION CHANGES IN GEORGIA

During the colonial period, Georgia's white inhabitants came from Europe. They settled mainly along the Atlantic coast and navigable waterways, especially the Savannah River up to Augusta.

In 1776, Savannah was the population center of a colony with 40,000 to 50,000 people, almost half of them black slaves. Savannah was the largest settlement, and it was also the political, economic, and cultural center of the coastal region.

But population changes were underway that would alter the character of Georgia's politics, its economy, and its way of life. After the Revolutionary War, change came rapidly. What were those changes? Clues for answering that question lie in quantitative data.

Quantitative Data

Quantitative data is factual information about the quantity, amount, or number of something. For the historian, such data can be important evidence. Knowing, for example, *how much* of a certain crop was produced at a particular time and place and *how many* people lived at that time and place may help explain why things happened in the past as they did. Quantitative data from such primary sources as government documents, business records, and newspaper reports can be especially useful.

Quantitative data can be written out like other kinds of information—"The factory turned out 1,257 pianos in 1890 and 1,377 in 1891." Or it can be presented in tables, graphs, and maps. These are each a kind of shorthand used to present much quantitative data in little space.

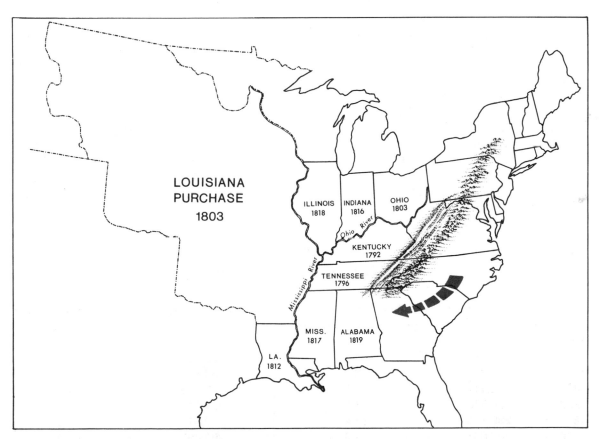

MAP 9. Population Movement in the Early 1800s. How might an event, the Louisiana Purchase, and a natural feature, the Appalachians, influence migration? What future conflict might be foreseen by looking carefully at this map?

The following reading includes tables, graphs, and maps presenting data on Georgia's population, 1790 to 1840. They help answer *when* and *where* as well as *how much* and *how many*.

1. During which decade (a 10-year period, such as 1810-1820) did the number of people in Georgia increase the most? During which decade did the population increase at the fastest rate (percentage increase)?
2. During which decade did the number of people in the United States as a whole increase the most? At the fastest rate?
3. The average number of people per square mile (total population number divided by total square miles number) indicates how densely people are settled in an area. In which decades was Georgia more densely settled than the United States as a whole? How could the U.S. population density decrease while the population was increasing? (Hint: What happened in 1803?)
4. Overall from 1790 to 1840, which population increased at the greater rate, that of Georgia or that of the United States?

TABLE 1

Population: Georgia and the U.S., 1790-1840*

	Georgia			United States		
	Total Population	Increase (%)	Per Sq. Mi. of Land	Total Population	Increase (%)	Per Sq. Mi. of Land
Year						
1790	82,548		.6	3,929,214		4.5
1800	162,686	97.1	1.5	5,308,483	35.1	6.1
1810	252,433	55.2	4.3	7,239,881	36.4	4.3
1820	340,989	35.1	5.8	9,638,453	33.1	5.5
1830	516,823	51.6	8.8	12,866,020	33.5	7.4
1840	691,392	33.8	11.8	17,069,453	32.7	9.8

*Source: U.S. Census.

TABLE 2

Georgia Population, By Race, 1790-1840*

	White Population	Percentage of Total	Black Population	Percentage of Total
Year				
1790	52,886	64.1	29,662	35.9
1800	102,261	62.9	60,425	37.1
1810	145,414	57.6	107,019	42.4
1820	189,570	55.6	151,419	44.4
1830	296,806	57.4	220,017	42.6
1840	407,695	59.0	283,697	41.0

*Source: U.S. Census.

The form in which quantitative data is presented can influence how the reader interprets (or "sees") that data. For example, Table 2 has all the data used in Figure 1. But the graph in Figure 1 makes it easier to compare the growth of the black population with that of the white population.

THINK ABOUT IT

1. During which decade did white population make the biggest increase in numbers? When did it increase at the fastest rate?
2. During which decade did black population make the biggest increase in numbers? When did it increase at the fastest rate?
3. During which decade did the number of black people most nearly equal the number of white people?
4. Which form of presentation, table or graph, is more useful in comparing these two sets of population data?

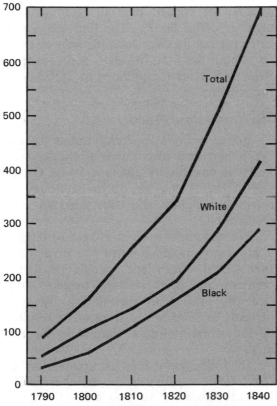

FIGURE 1. Growth of Black and White Populations of Georgia, 1790-1840 (in thousands)

How was the census data you've been working with collected? Who collected it? Each United States census, from 1790 to 1980, required persons hired by the government to go out and count every individual living in the United States.

Just how difficult was that task? The following note from an 1820 census taker (who earned just $1.00 for every hundred names he collected) was attached to his report.

 Taking the Census in Hall County

The difficulties were very considerable that attended taking the census; in the first place, the inhabitants are very dispersed, in the second place the country being but lately settled, there are but few roads, in the third place (it was) difficult to get nourishment for either myself or horse, and often when got, had to pay very high, in the fourth place had often to travel a considerable distance through fields to get to dwelling cabins, often, and generally, drench'd in dew, particularly in August and September; and often had to walk many miles where it was so steep that I could not ride, or even set on my horse.

In the whole I respectfully submit my case to the Federal, or district judge, hoping that he will recommend such additional wages to the dollar per 100, as in his judgment he may think proper.

25th of November 1820

Jos. McCutchen, Assistant to the Marshall of the District of Georgia

[From "Fourth Census, 1820, Population, Georgia," I, 77-78. Reprinted in *Georgia Historical Quarterly,* Vol. 35 (March 1951), pp. 76-77, contributed by H.B. and Kathleen C. Fant.]

Maps are especially useful for showing the *distribution* of data about almost anything—people, resources, products, and even culture traits.

The set of six maps on page 65 shows the distribution of Georgia's population, black and white, at each decennial (10-year) census, 1790-1840. The blank area is Indian territory where no census was taken.

THINK ABOUT IT

1. Which physical region of Georgia experienced the greatest population growth between 1790 and 1840? What are some physical characteristics of the region?
2. Which regions experienced less growth? What are their characteristics?
3. The first settlers entered Georgia at Savannah, then settled along the coast and navigable waterways. Does the information presented in the maps suggest this pattern continued after 1790? Explain.

GEORGIA'S LAND AREA

In its early years, Georgia grew in land area as well as in population. At one time, most of the territory claimed by the state was Indian land, not open to white settlement. Gradually the Indians gave up more and more of that land.

In 1733 the colony occupied only the small area turned over to Oglethorpe by Tomo-chi-chi. By treaty in 1763, the northern limit for white settlement was the Little River. However, after 10 years of dealing with shrewd white traders, the Indians were heavily in debt. To settle their debts, the Creeks and Cherokees in 1773 gave up more than two million acres of land. This land, in the upcountry region north and west of Augusta, opened up to buyers. Surveyors marked off tracts of land and colonial government agents distributed them.

After the Revolutionary War, the Indians ceded (turned over) more land by treaties in 1783 and 1790. These lands and other territory claimed by Georgia—about 100 million acres of land extending all the way to the Mississippi River—became the focus of great controversy.

The question was, How should these lands be distributed? Selling them would bring in money needed by state government for roads, schools, and other public services. Giving them away would encourage more people to come to Georgia to turn the forests into farms, thus stimulating economic growth.

THINK ABOUT IT

1. What systems were used to distribute land in Georgia? How did they work?
2. What was the Yazoo land fraud? Why was it important?

DISTRIBUTING PUBLIC LAND

Originally, the state of Georgia distributed land under the "head-right" system. The head of a family was granted 200 acres of land for himself plus 50 acres for each member of his family. The limit was 1,000 acres per family. War veterans were entitled to "bounties"—additional acres—ranging from 200 acres for privates to 2,200 acres for generals.

The Yazoo Land Fraud

Some Georgia leaders wanted to turn the public land into farms as quickly and fairly as possible by giving it away. Others saw the lands as a way to make money for themselves. They did this through land *speculation.*

When someone buys a tract of land at a low price, holds it until the price rises, then sells it—that's land speculation. It is a common and perfectly legal business practice. But the land speculation by state officials in 1795 was dishonest. It resulted in the worst political scandal in Georgia history.

In 1795, some land companies bribed (paid off) a majority of the members of the General Assembly to pass a law for them. The law allowed the companies to buy at least 35 million acres of the state's western

MAP 10. *Distribution of Georgia's Population, 1790-1840.*

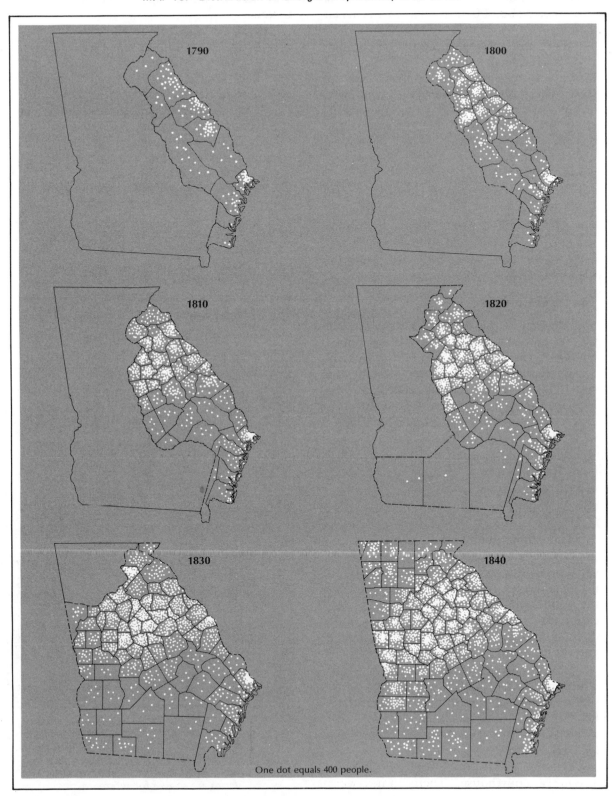

One dot equals 400 people.

lands extending to the Yazoo River. The price was $500,000—less than two cents an acre.

When the public learned of this scheme, it was outraged. Some of the dishonest legislators, fearing for their lives, fled the state. The next year, a newly elected legislature repealed (abolished) the law authorizing the Yazoo land sale. However, the buyers of the land weren't willing to give up their bargain. The Yazoo controversy landed in the courts.

Finally, Georgia ceded (turned over) its lands west of the Chattahoochee River to the United States government. In return, the United States government paid the state $1,250,000 and promised to remove the Indians from Georgia.

The Land Lotteries

Another result of the Yazoo scandal was a new system of distributing public lands in Georgia, established by the General Assembly in 1803. Under this system, the state first surveyed lands ceded by the Indians. Then it divided the land into lots that varied in size, according to the quality of the land.

By using this method of distributing land, state government helped the economy of Georgia grow.

How the Lottery Worked

The state divided the land into small parcels to encourage a large number of settlers. In the pine barrens of South Georgia, the lots were 490 acres each. In the Piedmont, they were 202½ acres each. The Cherokee lands in North Georgia were divided into 160-acre lots, with lots in the gold fields as small as 40 acres.

Next, the state held a lottery. Every white male Georgia citizen over 21 years old was allowed one draw (or chance). If he had a wife and child, he got two chances. Widows and families of orphans also got chances.

Persons who wanted land registered at a county courthouse. Their names were

sent to the state capital and written on tickets.

Each lot was numbered. The numbers of all lots to be drawn were written on a set of tickets that were then placed in a wheel. In another wheel were tickets bearing the names of persons wanting land.

A state official simultaneously drew the names and numbers from the wheels. In this manner the settlers got their land. Except for a recording fee of $4 per 100 acres, the land was absolutely free.

People who got land could farm it or sell it as they wished. In 30 years, the state held six lotteries. Under the lottery system of land distribution, the state distributed about 30 million acres of land west of the Oconee River among more than 100,000 people.

The Frontier Spirit

While most Georgia pioneers settled permanently on the lands they received,

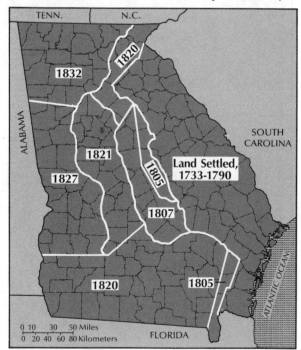

MAP 11. Land Distribution by Lottery. Usually the state held lotteries after the Indians had left the lands, but the 1832 lottery was held before the Cherokees gave up their lands. The 1982 county boundaries are shown for reference.

some moved almost constantly, along with **the** frontier. This restless spirit is illustrated in the life of Gideon Lincecum, born in middle Georgia in 1793. Gideon's father moved his family about Georgia and the Carolinas seeking better opportunity and more elbow room. Inheriting this same spirit, Gideon moved west with the frontier to Mississippi and Texas. Along the way, he learned enough to be a surveyor, school teacher, Indian trader, physician, and planter. The following excerpt from his autobiography tells about events beginning in 1804.

THINK ABOUT IT

1. What were some personal qualities of Gideon Lincecum? of his father?
2. From Gideon's account, what can you tell about how work was done on the Georgia frontier?

 Autobiography of Gideon Lincecum

My father sold his cotton for a good price and made a visit to his sister in Clark[e] County, Ga. He was gone two or three weeks, and when he returned, he told my mother that he had purchased a tract of land with a good house on it, one mile from Athens, Ga. We were soon on the road again, returning to Georgia. In the course of a week we were in our new home. Father extended every power at his new place. He planted and raised a large crop of cotton; and as soon as it began to open, every one that could pick five pounds a day was forced into the cotton field . . . . We succeeded in gathering the cotton by Christmas, and father took it to the gin and got the receipts for 4,643 pounds, for which he received five cents a pound.

He again became restless, and selling his place, put his wagon in good repair, and set out on a third attempt to get to Tennessee. Father hired a straggling old fellow to drive for us this trip, and we rolled on bravely until we came to the Saluda river. There was there a store and blacksmith shop, and we stopped until the smith nailed a pair of shoes on the outriding horse. Father and his teamster became somewhat intoxicated and got two bottles of whiskey to carry with them. The river was wide and swift, but shallow. We forded it and landed safely in South Carolina again. After going about five miles further, my father and the driver became more deeply intoxicated. The driver fell off the wagon and frightened the horses. They ran away and tore up the wagon, hurting all who were in it. My grandmother was very seriously wounded. [The family never made it to Tennessee and next year was back in Georgia.]

The lands beyond the Oconee river had been obtained by the United States from the Muskogee Indians. No one had moved into this new purchase. Father intended to settle there as soon as the Indians had completed the twelve months' hunting which had been by a stipulation in the treaty with the United States reserved to them.

Father entered my sister, brother, and me as day scholars in a little old log cabin, a mile and a half from our home, at the rate of $7 each per year. I was 14 years old, and it was the first school house I had ever seen. I began in the alphabet. There were some very small boys, seven years old, who could read . . . .

When the Indians finished their year of hunting and retired from the new purchase my father took me with him to explore the country. He preferred the country on the Little River, selected a place and we returned home to make ready for the removal as soon as possible . . . .

My father had been moving about so much that he was not entitled to a chance in the lottery,—and the place he wanted on the Little River was drawn by a man who would not part with it. Father then gave all the money he had for a place on a beautiful clear running creek.

The next year after we came there the county seat was laid off and named Eatonton. I was one of the chain carriers to survey the streets and lots. □

[From extracts reprinted in Ulrich B. Phillips, *Plantation and Frontier Documents: 1649-1863*, Vol. II (Cleveland, Ohio: The Arthur H. Clark Company, 1909).]

GROWTH OF BUSINESS AND GOVERNMENT

After the Revolutionary War, Georgia was a poor state. Many Tories had fled, taking their wealth with them. Much property had been destroyed, business was almost at a standstill, and debts were piled up. Yet, within a few decades Georgia would become known as the "Empire State of the South" because of its prosperity. How did this come about?

Several factors combined to encourage prosperity in Georgia. The invention of the cotton gin (see Chapter 8) was a major factor. The cotton gin made it faster and cheaper to get cotton ready for making cloth. Georgia had the right soil and climate for growing cotton. It had the plantation system with slave labor—a profitable arrangement for landowners. People flocked to Georgia to get in on the prosperity. As the population grew, so did the economy.

Another important factor was the advancement in the United States of an economic policy called "laissez-faire," a French term meaning "leave things alone." Laissez-faire meant that government would keep its hands off the economy. It was very different from the old mercantile system in which government tried to control what the people could make and sell. This free economic system certainly suited Americans who had recently fought so hard for their freedom. They adopted it wholeheartedly. In Georgia, as elsewhere in the nation, business was free to seek profit with few restrictions.

But even though the economy was supposed to function as freely as possible, government had to become involved in regulat-

ing business. Sometimes government acted to protect citizens and sometimes to encourage growth of business. So, as the economy and the population grew, government grew also. In the following pages, you will see how government interacted with business, and how it later took on other roles as well.

Regulating Agriculture

Both state and local governments took actions that could help create an environment in which business could prosper. Because agriculture was the main business in Georgia, laws related to it were most common. Here are excerpts from two early laws.

THINK ABOUT IT

1. What seems to be the purpose of the following laws?
2. Who might have favored these laws? Who might have opposed them?
3. Which of these laws would encourage or protect business? Which would interfere with business or make trade more costly?

 A State Law Passed by the General Assembly

An Act to compel the owners or occupiers of Cotton Machines within this State, to enclose the same, and in particular situations to remove the seed therefrom.—Approved December 10, 1803.

Section 1—. . . it shall be the duty of all owners or occupiers of cotton machines (gins) for picking (the seeds) of cotton, in all towns or villages, or immediately in the vicinity of any town or village within this State, to enclose the seed in such manner as will effectually prevent all stock, especially hogs, from eating them.

Section 2—All owners or occupiers of such machines shall secure and keep the seed dry, or remove them at least once every week from said machine, to such distance from such city, town, village, or vicinity thereof, so as to prevent all the unwholesome effects resulting from the stench and vapors arising from the seed, in their putrid state, if suffered to remain in heaps. . . .

Section 3—. . . for every week, any owner or occupier of such machine who shall neglect to comply with the several duties required of them by this act, shall forfeit and pay a sum not exceeding three dollars. □

[*Digest of the Laws of the State of Georgia* (Athens: Oliver H. Prince, 1837).]

 A Local Ordinance Passed by the City of Augusta

An Ordinance to Regulate the Public Market in the City of Augusta.

Section 3. . . . it shall be the duty of all regular butchers attending the Market, during market hours together with their servants that may cut meat for sale, to be clothed in a clean and decent apron or frock, under the penalty of being fined the sum of one dollar.

Section 7. . . . all meats and other articles sold by weight or measure shall be weighed by scales or measured by measures regulated and stamped as required by the Police Ordinance; . . . if any person shall be guilty of . . . selling by scales unfairly balanced, or by false measurements . . . on conviction thereof, shall pay a fine not exceeding fifty dollars.

Section 10. . . . no person shall be allowed to vend in the market . . . any unsound, impure, or unwholesome article of provision or other produce whatsoever, under penalty of paying a fine not exceeding fifty dollars; and, if in the opinion of the Clerk of the Market, any article comes under this description, he shall condemn same; and . . . it shall be the duty of said clerk to have

the same thrown into the river, at the expense of the owner.

Passed in Council, 14th Nov., 1818 □

[*Augusta Chronicle,* November 25, 1818, p. 2.]

Fixed prices required to be "set up in the public entertaining room" of taverns in Clarke County, 1804. (Tavern license was $8.56 per year.)

For a Well Furnished Dinner with good Spirits	$0.50
For a Well Furnished Dinner without Spirits	.37½
For a Common Family Dinner	.25
For a Breakfast with Coffee	.25
For Supper with Tea	.25
For Stabling a horse 24 hours	.50
For Feeding a horse with Grane and Fodder	.12½
For Lodging per night in good Bed	.12½
For Fourth Proof Jamaica Spirits, pr. h. pt.	.25
West Indies Rum, pr. h. pt.	.18¼
Cognac Brandy	.25½
Peach Brandy	.12½
Holland Gin	.25½
Whiskey	.12½

Tolls fixed (according to state law) for privately built and maintained bridge across middle fork of the Oconee River on road between Athens and Watkinsville, 1807. (Inferior Court gave leave to Peter Randolph and Thomas Hill to erect bridge and apply tolls.)

foot passenger	$0.06¼
man & horse	.06¼
2-wheel carriage	.25
4-wheel carriage	.50
a horse	.02
a cow, hog, or sheep	.01

Source: Clarke County Minutes of Inferior Court, 1802-1810.

Chartering Corporations

In the early 1800s, the typical Georgia business was run by a single owner-operator. Such small businesses were (and continue today to be) an important part of the economy. But the state needed large-scale enterprises—such as banks that could lend money to farmers and small businesses—to help the economy grow. Few persons in the whole United States had enough money to run large businesses by themselves. So, issuing corporate charters became one of the most important economic activities of state government.

A corporation is a form of business organization in which many people (called investors) combine their money. Corporations can undertake large projects, such as building railroads, that an individual owner-operator cannot afford to finance.

A corporation's charter spells out the corporation's powers and the rules it has to follow in doing business. Sometimes, the charter gives the corporation special privileges, such as the exclusive right to do business in a certain area.

Corporations were needed to undertake large business projects in Georgia. So the General Assembly became heavily involved in chartering banks, manufacturing companies, insurance companies, and other kinds of businesses, especially transportation companies.

Expanding Transportation

To have a strong economy, Georgia needed a more efficient way to distribute goods and move people. Whose responsibility was it to provide transportation—government or business? As you will see, transportation is an example of how government and business worked hand-in-hand.

Waterways

Waterways are a natural transportation resource. The Savannah River was the first "highway" inland for the Georgia colonists; Augusta, at the fall line, became

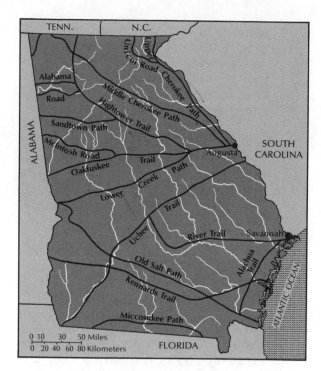

MAP 12. *Waterways and Indian Paths. For about 100 years, Georgians generally followed transportation routes first used by the Indians. Why did trading paths generally run east and west?*

Georgia's first inland trade center. From there, trade paths ran west into the Indian lands.

After 1800, other important trade centers were established along the fall line: Milledgeville on the Oconee, Macon on the Ocmulgee, and later, Columbus on the Chattahoochee. At first, flat-bottom pole boats carried river traffic. Rectangular barges—called "Oconee boxes"—carried bales of cotton downriver to ports on the Atlantic Ocean and Gulf of Mexico. With the coming of the steamboat around 1820, river travel, upstream and downstream, became faster and more efficient.

Although private companies generally operated vessels on the rivers, state government passed regulations and spent tax money to protect river transportation. It had to keep the channels free of fallen trees and sandbars, and prevent people from placing fish traps or other hazards to navigation in the rivers.

Roads

The few navigable waterways in Georgia generally ran north and south. To get products to riverside docks and move east and west in Georgia, overland transportation was needed.

Back in 1755, the colonial government had passed Georgia's first road law. It required males between ages 16 and 60 to work on local roads at least 12 days a year. The new state government continued this method of building and maintaining roads—all of them dirt in those days. Some of the early roads merely followed old Indian trails, twisting and turning through the forests. Even the best road—from Savannah to Augusta—was so bad that it took a stagecoach two to four days to make the trip.

As the interior of Georgia began to fill up with people and farms, the need for more connecting roads grew. Farmers needed roads to transport their products to the markets. To build such roads, state government tried chartering turnpike corporations.

A turnpike corporation was a private business that built and maintained roads. Travelers using the roads paid toll charges, from which the corporation took its profit. At certain points, "pikes"—long poles serving as gates across the road—blocked wagons and stagecoaches from continuing until the drivers paid the toll. Similar corporations were chartered to build bridges and establish ferries across rivers. They also earned their income by charging tolls and fees to travelers.

Railroads

Even with improved rivers and roads, transportation remained a big obstacle to Georgia's economic growth. Cotton-marketing towns such as Athens and Forsyth were far from navigable rivers. Shipping cotton by wagon over rough dirt roads was so slow and expensive that it ate into cotton-growing profits.

In the 1820s, planners proposed schemes to build a vast network of canals connecting Georgia's rivers. But before much could be done, a better form of transportation appeared—the railroad.

In the 1830s, investors were eager to build rail lines from Augusta and Savannah into the rich cotton lands of the Piedmont. However, before railroads could crisscross the state, many questions had to be settled. Through what towns would the lines run? What could a railroad do about landowners who wouldn't permit tracks across their property? Could a railroad legally refuse to carry someone's produce? What rates could a railroad charge its customers?

So even though Georgia's railroads were private businesses (except the state-owned Western and Atlantic (W&A) Railroad running to Tennessee), state government became involved in meeting these problems and regulating the railroads.

Atlanta and the Railroads. In 1836, the General Assembly passed a law for building a state-owned railroad from the Chattahoochee River in DeKalb County, through the Cherokee country, to Tennessee. This line would connect railroads already underway from Savannah and Augusta with western states.

The next year, surveyors determined the 138-mile route of the W & A Railroad. They located its southern end a few miles southeast of the Chattahoochee. There they drove a stake in the ground and marked it "Terminus" (meaning *end*). This was the beginning of the city of Atlanta.

Terminus began to grow as the W & A headquarters building went up and construction began on the railroad. On Christmas Eve 1842, a locomotive made the first run, from Terminus to Marietta.

In 1845, another line, the Georgia Railroad, arrived from Augusta. Terminus was renamed "Marthasville" in honor of the daughter of ex-governor Wilson Lumpkin, a strong backer of the W & A.

A year later, the Macon and Western Railroad linked Marthasville with the Central of Georgia Railroad from Savannah.

By 1847, town population reached

400. It was no longer a frontier village, and the name "Marthasville" didn't seem appropriate for a big-time railroad center. The chief engineer of the Georgia Railroad suggested the name "Atlanta." The inhabitants agreed and the General Assembly made it official. (Ex-governor Lumpkin was not pleased.)

In 1853 a fourth line, the Atlanta and West Point, was completed, linking Georgia's rail system to Alabama's. By 1860, Atlanta was a major railroad center of the Deep South. The main link between the Atlantic seaboard and the Middle West, it was nicknamed the "Gate City."

State Laws Affecting Transportation

Companies providing transportation needed to be both protected and regulated, so they could provide their service in a profitable and acceptable way. State government passed several acts for this purpose, including the following:

An Act to regulate the pilotage of vessels to and from the several ports of this State (Approved December 6, 1799).

This act set up a method for licensing ships' pilots and rules for their fair treatment.

An Act to regulate toll-bridges, ferries, and turnpike-roads (Approved December 22, 1808).

This act required owners of toll-bridges, ferries, and turnpike-roads to post their toll rates (as set by law) in a conspicuous place.

An Act to incorporate the Georgia Rail Road Company (Approved December 21, 1833).

This act directed the Georgia Rail Road Company to build railroads from Augusta to three interior points in the state—Athens, Eatonton, and Madison. It granted certain privileges to the company,

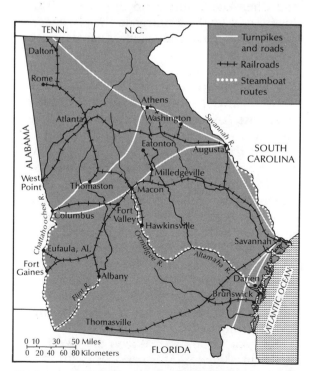

MAP 13. Rail, River, and Road Development, 1830-1860. Only the main routes are shown on this map.

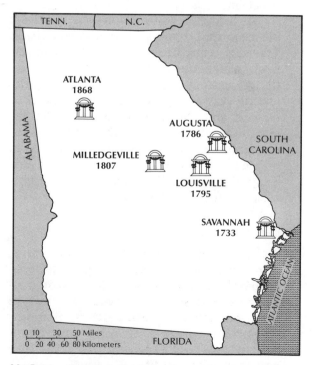

MAP 14. Georgia's Capitals. Does the movement of Georgia's capital from city to city seem related to population growth?

such as powers to purchase the necessary land. It allowed railroads to cross public roads, but required that such construction not "obstruct or injure" such roads. It also gave the company exclusive rights to transport people and goods over the railroads, but set limits on how much they could charge per mile.

Government and Town Planning

After Georgia became a state, many new towns sprang up unplanned at crossroads, ferry landings, or other places where farmers gathered to trade. Other towns followed special developments in the state. For example, when the General Assembly in 1801 selected a site in northeast Georgia for the University of Georgia, it set the stage for the founding of Athens.

Still other urban places were purposely planned by state government. When the state surveyed former Indian territory for distribution to white settlers, it reserved specific land for towns. Specially appointed commissioners then laid out streets, set aside lots for public buildings, and sold town lots to settlers.

Between 1803 and 1828, as the Creek Indians gave up their lands and moved west, state government planned three major cities to be centers of trade for the new areas of settlement.* Milledgeville, Macon, and Columbus were located at the fall line, or "head of navigation," on the Oconee, Ocmulgee, and Chattahoochee Rivers, respectively. From these points, agricultural products could be easily shipped downriver to ports on the coast. Also, goods could be brought upriver to these locations for distribution throughout the interior of the state.

The legislature's plans were not the same for all three cities. However, the plans show that the state's leaders wished them to be attractive, healthy places to live as well as successful commercial centers.

---

*Milledgeville was planned to be the state capital, which it was from 1807 to 1868.

Macon: A Planned City

Following the Creek cession of 1823, the General Assembly reserved 21,000 acres of land along both sides of the Ocmulgee River for the city of Macon. Its plan, based on a grid, shows in general what most city plans were like.

Macon's plan called for 60 city blocks, each covering four acres. A block was divided into one-half acre town lots for building houses or businesses. Along the river were partial lots.

In a large public square stood the courthouse and other public buildings. Shade trees lined the square and the broad streets, all neatly laid out at right angles.

Macon's plan also included garden lots on the edge of town and a *common*. The common was public land reserved for future growth of the city. On it the people could cut timber, farm, or graze livestock. In later years, as the population grew, the city marked off more streets and lots in the common.

To prevent land speculation in the city (someone buying up all the best lots for resale at higher prices), the legislature carefully controlled sales. It determined which lots would be sold first and limited the number of lots a person could buy.

As planned, Macon became a center of trade for middle Georgia. Cotton was the basis of its prosperity. Wharves and warehouses went up along the riverfront. In addition to shipping and trading companies, manufacturing companies, retail stores, banks, and hotels thrived in Macon.

But Macon had more than business. By the 1850s, Macon had a medical school, the state academy for the blind, and Georgia's first college for women. The city also had Presbyterian, Methodist, Episcopalian, Baptist, and Roman Catholic churches. Plays, concerts, and other entertainment were available.

State government's planning of Macon and dozens of other cities and towns helped bring orderly growth to rough frontier areas. This kind of orderly growth contributed to Georgia's economic prosperity in the early 1800s.

Government and Social Welfare

While the state in the early years focused mainly on encouraging and regulating business, it began to move into other areas. Concern about schools, prisons, and care of the needy resulted in state actions.

Education

In 1785, the General Assembly chartered the nation's first state university. Classes began in 1801, and soon the university at Athens was graduating men* who would lead the state in business and poli-

---

*Women were not admitted to the University of Georgia until 1918.

tics. As the need for more doctors became obvious, the state established the Medical College of Georgia in 1828 at Augusta.

In contrast, the state did not do much about pre-college education. Although the first state constitution called for schools in each county, the General Assembly never provided enough money to set up a true public school system for the whole state. Only a few counties had public schools. Wealthier Georgians sent their children to private or religious schools. Some even hired tutors to teach their children at home. Because schooling was not available to all citizens, many adults could neither read nor write.

Penal System

In 1816, the state enacted a new code

Town Plan of Macon, 1823. How was Macon's plan similar to Oglethorpe's plan for Savannah? How was it different? (See page 25.) Why were the "common" and the public square included in this plan?

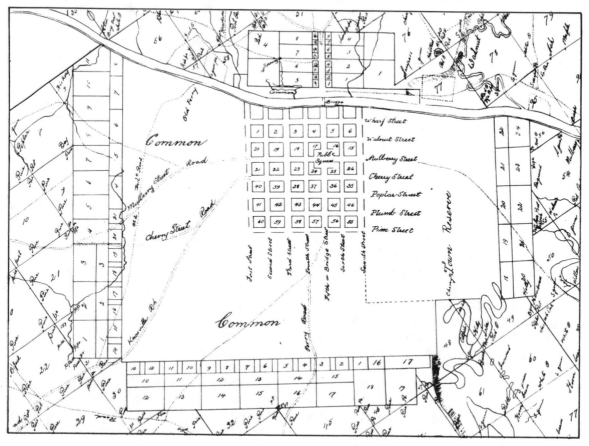

of laws abolishing cruel punishments. No longer would white men be whipped or have their hands and heads locked in the pillory for crimes such as theft. In 1817, the state opened a penitentiary (so-called because prisoners locked up there would have time to repent for their crimes). The next year the state began to furnish prisoners in county jails with clothing, blankets, heat, and medical attention. Later, in 1823, imprisonment for debt was limited.

Care of the Needy

The state also began taking care of its needy. An asylum for the insane was opened in 1842 at Milledgeville. (Formerly mentally ill and retarded persons were thrown in jail with criminals.) Five years later, a school for deaf persons was opened at Cave Springs. In 1852, the state took over responsibility for helping blind persons at the Georgia Academy for the Blind at Macon.

ACTIVITIES FOR CHAPTER 6

Discussion

A. Between 1790 and 1840, state government gave much attention to distributing public lands.

  1. How did the availability of land contribute to population growth?

  2. How did the state's lottery system meet the problem of speculation? Was the lottery fair?

B. In addition to distributing lands, state government played other roles in Georgia's growth.

  1. What are some things government did to promote economic prosperity?

  2. What are some things government did to make the state a good place to live?

Writing Project

Imagine you are a historian who must give a brief talk on "Georgia Population Growth, 1790-1840" without using maps, tables, or graphs. To do this you must "translate" information from one form to another. (This is something that historians frequently do.)

Select the most important data in the chapter and make generalizations from it. Some generalizations might be made about (1) overall growth; (2) comparisons between Georgia and the U.S., or between black population and white population growth; and (3) population distribution across the state. Limit your speech to one page.

7 The Indian Problem "Solved"

Leave us–fly–save yourselves from annihilation–all the laws ever made cannot protect you here–your fate is inevitable if you stay among us. . .go to a land provided for you beyond the Mississippi–

The *Athenian,* August 8, 1829, Athens, Georgia

When the first white settlers arrived in the area now known as Georgia, two main Indian nations already lived there–the Creek and the Cherokee.

Some Indian leaders helped the Europeans adjust to their new environment. Gradually, however, as more whites and their black slaves moved into Georgia, trouble grew between the Indians and the settlers. Disputes over land or trade deals frequently led to bloodshed. The British and later the American governments stationed troops along the frontier to protect settlers from Indian raids. But often, it was the Indian villages that were plundered and burned–by white frontiersmen and traders.

During the Revolutionary War, many Indians fought on the side of the British.

Beginning in 1783, white Georgians demanded that the U.S. government relocate Indian tribes to territory in the west. Terms for removal had to be worked out among the state government, the United States, and the Indians.

Here is the story, beginning with the Creeks.

THE CREEKS

During the Revolutionary War, some Creeks sided with the British, carrying on frontier raids against Whig settlements.

A Cherokee Indian Man about 1800. What evidence of white culture do you see in this picture?

After the war, white Georgians demanded that the Creeks give up their land between the Ogeechee and the Oconee rivers.

The Creeks were divided over what to do. While the Creeks of the Lower Towns agreed to turn over territory to the whites, the Creeks of the Upper Towns, led by their chief, Alexander McGillivray, refused to agree to any treaty.

Fighting between McGillivray's followers and white settlers on the border of the Creek Nation almost became a full-scale war. Finally, in 1790, President Washington invited McGillivray to come to New York City (then the national capital). There the Creek leader was persuaded (and, perhaps, took money) to agree to a treaty ceding the Oconee lands to the state of Georgia.

After the Yazoo Land Fraud of 1795-96 (discussed in Chapter 6), Georgia turned over its western lands to the United States government. In return, Georgia received $1,250,000 and the national government's promise to *remove all Indians from the state* as soon as reasonably and peacefully possible. (At the same time, the United States government was, in its treaties with the Indians, more or less promising to protect their lands from white takeover!)

In 1802 and 1804, the United States government persuaded the Creeks to move west of the Oconee to the Ocmulgee. In 1805 this "purchase"—as it was called by the whites—was distributed in Georgia's first land lottery. And, in 1807, the state capital was moved to Milledgeville, on the Oconee River.

The War of 1812

In 1812 the United States went to war with Great Britain. Some Creek tribes, seeing a chance to get back their lands, sided with the British and attacked border settlements.

In March 1814, an army under Gen. Andrew Jackson defeated the Creeks at Horseshoe Bend in Alabama. It was a disastrous battle for the Creeks. Forced to give up all their land in south Georgia, the Creeks had little choice but to accept the culture of the whites. They began to depend less on hunting and trading and more on raising crops and livestock. Slowly, the "white man's" religion and education became a part of Creek life.

Creek Government

The Creek Nation was a loose association of several tribal groups. The Creek towns were the main units of government. To consider matters that affected the whole nation, the town chiefs came together in a national council.

Until 1817 laws governing the Creek Nation were committed to memory, not paper. The lack of uniform laws caused problems, not only among the Creeks, but also in their dealings with whites. Therefore, in order for them to have a more regular form of government, the Creeks were urged by U.S. Indian Agent, Benjamin Hawkins, to write down their laws.

Below are excerpts from the final version of Creek Laws, set down in 1824.

THINK ABOUT IT

1. Which laws reveal something of the lifestyle and problems of the Creeks?
2. Which laws were probably made necessary by contact with the culture of whites?
3. Which laws are similar to laws in the United States today?

 Laws of the Creek Nation

Law 1. Murder shall be punished with death, the person who commits the act shall be the only one punished and only upon good proofs.

Law 5. If a man takes a weapon in hand and goes to kill another person and the person he goes to kill happens to kill first, and the fact be so proven, the person shall be forgiven as he killed the man to save his own life.

Law 8. Stealing shall be punished as follows: for the first offense the thief shall be whipped, for the second offense shall be cropped [ears cut], for the third offense he shall be put to death.

Law 10. If any person give false evidence by which another suffers punishment, he shall receive the same punishment, which he inflicted upon the one against whom he stated the falsehood.

Law 19. Should a white man take an Indian woman as a wife and have children by her and he goes out of the Nation, he shall leave all his property with his children for their support.

Law 22. If any man should think proper to set his Negroe free, he shall be considered a free man by the Nation.

Law 23. Prisoners taken in War shall not be considered or traded as slave, and it shall be the duty of the law makers to make them as free as ourselves.

Law 38. If two persons should steal and one should tell on the other, one should be whipped and the teller stand cleared.

Law 44. The Citizens of the Nation shall pay taxes for every year, or twelve months, twenty five cents per head, ten dollars per stand or store, and ferriage [ferry fee].

Law 53. If a person should get drunk and want to fight, he shall be roped until he gets sober. □

[Adapted from reprints in Antonio J. Waring, *Laws of the Creek Nation* (Athens, Georgia: University of Georgia Press, 1960), pp. 17-27.]

Pressure on the Creeks Continues

The Creeks had given up most of their land in Georgia and were adopting more and more of the white culture. Still they were in the path of white migration westward. White Georgians protested. "The Creeks still occupy much of the best land in central Georgia," they complained. "From the Ocmulgee to the Chattahoochee they roam, hunting deer where we should be building and growing and manufacturing."

The United States government, pressured by Georgia's leaders, obtained the Creek lands west to the Flint River. This wasn't enough. Georgians reminded the national government of its promise to remove all the Indians from the state. The government in Washington tried to bargain with the Indians. Most Creeks, however, had decided not to yield any more land.

Chief McIntosh

The Lower Creek Towns were led by William McIntosh, one of the five great chiefs of the nation. McIntosh, son of an Indian mother and a Scottish father, was first cousin to Georgia's governor, George M. Troup. The Creek chief was a well-known warrior who had fought under General Jackson against other Creeks at Horseshoe Bend in 1814.

Governor Troup and representatives of the United States government believed they could work through Chief McIntosh to get the Creeks to sell their remaining lands in Georgia. McIntosh evidently received thousands of dollars for accepting the deal. However, he was unable to persuade the rest of the Creek leadership to agree to it.

Next, McIntosh, whom the Cherokees had made an honorary chief of *their* nation, tried to get the Cherokees to sell their lands. He offered some of the white man's money to Cherokee leader John Ross, who turned him down. The Cherokees warned the Creeks to watch their chief closely.

The warning came none too soon. On February 12, 1825, Chief McIntosh and a few followers signed a treaty ceding all Creek lands to the United States government. They did this without the support of the Creek nation. McIntosh's days were numbered. Years before, the Creek National Council had passed a law condemning to death any chief who sold tribal lands without the council's approval.

Before dawn on May 1, 1825, Creek warriors surrounded the house of Chief McIntosh and set it on fire. When the chief ran from the burning building, he was shot down and stabbed to death. Several of his followers were also killed.

Governor Troup demanded that the U.S. government honor the treaty signed by McIntosh and remove the Creeks at once. He also directed that the Creek lands be surveyed to prepare for distribution to white Georgians by lottery.

However, the president of the United States, John Quincy Adams, thought the treaty might not be legal. He threatened to arrest any surveyor found on the Creek lands.

But President Adams backed down when Governor Troup threatened war with the United States. He wanted to avoid any military showdown with Georgia. So, by new treaties, the United States forced the Creeks to sell their remaining lands in Georgia. By the end of 1827, the Creeks were gone, to Alabama and eventually to Oklahoma.

Next came the Cherokees.

THE CHEROKEES

THINK ABOUT IT

1. What evidence is there in Sherwood's description of the Cherokees to indicate that they were prospering?
2. In their "memorial" (a statement of facts presented to a government), what did the Cherokees claim they had done? What were they asking of Congress?

With the Creeks removed, the state government turned its attention to driving

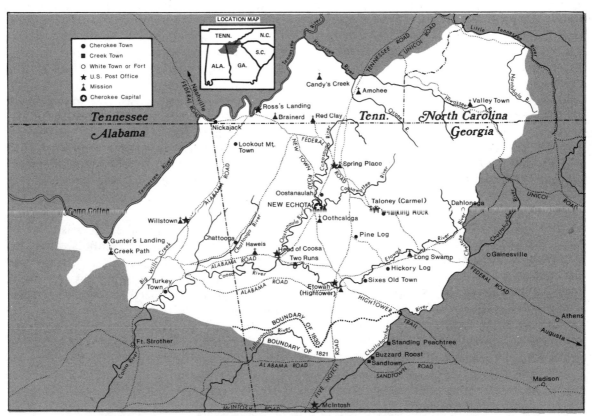

MAP 15. The Cherokee Nation, 1820-1838. Note that the Cherokee Nation overlapped Georgia's boundaries with Alabama, Tennessee, and North Carolina.

the Cherokees out of Georgia. The Cherokees survived 10 years after the Creeks were gone. Living in the mountains, they were out of the main path of white migration to the west.

In the eyes of many white Americans, the Cherokees were "civilized" Indians. Whites considered the Cherokees to be advanced far beyond other Indian groups because the Cherokees had adopted so much of the white culture.

Here is a white Georgian's description of the Georgia Cherokees, published in 1827.

 ## Progress in the Cherokee Nation

Within the last 20 years the Cherokees have rapidly advanced towards civilization. They now live in comfortable houses, chiefly in villages, and cultivate large farms. They raise large herds of cattle which they sell for beef to the inhabitants of the neighboring states. Many mechanical arts have been introduced among them. They have carpenters and blacksmiths, and many of the women spin and weave, and make butter and cheese.

The population, instead of decreasing as is the case generally with tribes surrounded by whites, increases very rapidly. There are now 13,563 natives in the nation; 147 white men and 73 white women, who have intermarried with them. They own 1,277 slaves. Total is 15,060 souls. The increase in the last six years is 3,563.

Their government is republican and the power is given to a Committee and Council, similar to our Senate and House of Representatives. The members are elected once in two years. Their judges act with authority and prevent the use of alcohol during sessions of their courts.

The Mission at Spring Place was established in 1801. Since that time nearly a dozen missions have been brought into operation in various parts of the nation. The Missionaries are assisted in their work by the U.S. Government. Some of the Missionaries have translated the New Testament into the Cherokee language. A Press is about to be established, also a Library and a Museum. A native by the name of Guess [Sequoyah] has invented an Alphabet consisting of 86 characters, by which many of the older Indians have learned to write and they thus correspond with each other. The number of children in the several Missionary Schools is nearing 500, all learning the English language. □

[Adapted from Adiel Sherwood, *A Gazetteer of Georgia* (Charleston, S.C.: W. Riley, 1827), pp. 41-43.]

Actually the Cherokees had developed their own agriculture-based civilization independently of white culture. When the whites first appeared, these Indians lived in about 80 towns, some with as many as 200 houses, stretching from northeast Alabama to Georgia, Tennessee, and on to the Carolinas and Virginia.

The most important units of government were the towns. The central government wasn't strong, although it had a national head chief.

The Cherokees also developed their own system of writing. In the early 1800s, white Americans learned that an Indian named Sequoyah was doing something that missionaries and other whites had been unable to do. He was writing and teaching others to write the Cherokee language.

The system taught by Sequoyah was a syllabary, not an alphabet. It was a set of written characters, or symbols, used to represent spoken syllables. Using the Cherokee syllabary was a way to show that Indians didn't need the white's written English.

In 1827 the Cherokees wrote a constitution for their nation. Patterned after the United States Constitution, it provided for legislative, executive, and judicial branches of government. The vote was given to Cherokee men only.

The first issue of the Cherokee's bilingual (two language) newspaper, the

D a		R e	T i	Ꮻ o	Ꮻ u	¡ v
Ꭶ ga Ꭷ ka		Ꭸ ge	Ᏹ gi	A go	J gu	E gv
Ꭺ ha		Ꭾ he	Ꭿ hi	Ᏺ ho	Ꮁ hu	Ꮂ hv
Ꮃ la		Ꮄ le	Ꮅ li	Ꮆ lo	Ꮇ lu	Ꮈ lv
Ꮉ ma		Ꮊ me	H mi	Ꮎ mo	Ꮘ mu	
Ꮟ na Ꮠ hna Ꮡ nah	Ꮄ ne	ʜ ni	Z no	Ꮕ nu	Ꮗ nv
Ꮚ qua		Ꮛ que	Ꮝ qui	Ꮜ quo	Ꮞ quu	Ꮟ quv
Ꮠ s Ꮡ sa		Ꮢ se	Ꮣ si	Ꮤ so	Ꮥ su	Ꮦ sv
Ꮧ da Ꮤ ta		Ꮥ de Ꮦ te	Ꮧ di Ꮨ ti	V to	s du	Ꮩ dv
Ꮪ dla Ꮫ tla		L tle	C tli	Ꮬ tlo	Ꮭ tlu	P tlv
Ꮰ tsa		Ꮳ tse	Ꮵ tsi	K tso	Ꮶ tsu	Ꮷ tsv
Ꮹ wa		Ꮺ we	Ꮻ wi	Ꮼ wo	Ꮽ wu	6 wv
Ꮿ ya		Ᏸ ye	Ᏹ yi	Ᏺ yo	Ᏻ yu	B yv

The Cherokee Syllabary. Why was having their own written language important to the Cherokees in the 1820s?

Cherokee Phoenix, carried the new constitution.

Although the Cherokee government had the approval of the United States government, Georgia refused to recognize it. State leaders argued that the U.S. Constitution prohibited the creation of such a state-within-a-state without the approval of the existing state's government.

In 1828 the Georgia General Assembly decided to put an end to the Indian nation. It passed an act extending the laws of the state and the authority of its courts over the Cherokee territory. Cherokee laws were declared "null and void" as of June 1, 1830. The act also provided that no Indian, or descendant of an Indian, could be a witness against a white man. An Indian could not bring a lawsuit against a white man.

Now the Cherokees protested. After all, they said, hadn't they signed treaties with the United States government? Hadn't the U.S. government agreed that they could set up their own government and laws?

In 1829 representatives of the Cherokee nation journeyed to Washington and presented their case to the U.S. Congress. An excerpt from their *Memorial* (statement) follows:

Memorial of John Ross and Others, Representatives of the Cherokee Nation of Indians, 20th Congress, 2nd Session, March 3, 1829.

. . . We . . . respectfully and solemnly protest, in behalf of the Cherokee nation, against the extension of the laws of Georgia over any part of our Territory, and appeal to the United States' Government for justice and protection.

The great Washington advised a plan and afforded aid for the general improvement of our nation, in agriculture, science, and government. President Jefferson followed the noble example, and concluded an address to our delegation, in language as follows: "I sincerely wish you may succeed in your laudable endeavors to save the remnant of your nation by adopting industrious occupations and a *Government of regular law. In this you may always rely on the counsel and assistance of the United States."* This kind and generous policy to improve our condition, has been blessed with the happiest results: our improvement has been without parallel in the history of all Indian nations. Agriculture is everywhere pursued, and the interests of our citizens are permanent in the soil. We have enjoyed the blessings of Christian instruction; and the advantages of education and merit are justly appreciated, a Government of regular law has been adopted, and the nation, under a continuance of the fostering care of the United States, will stand forth as a living testimony that all Indian nations are not doomed to the fate which has swept many from the face of the earth.

Under the parental protection of the United States, we have arrived at the present degree of improvement, and they are now to decide whether we shall continue as a people, or be abandoned to destruction.

In behalf, and under the authority of the Cherokee nation, this protest and memorial is respectfully submitted.

John Ross
R. Taylor
Edward Gunter
William S. Coody
Washington City, February 27, 1829. □

The President Speaks; the Indians Reply

In March 1829, while Congress considered the Cherokees' *Memorial,* Andrew Jackson took office as president of the United States. One of his first official acts

Indian Talk
From the President of the United States
[Adapted from *Rural Cabinet,* May 30, 1829, Warrenton, Georgia.]

Friends and Brothers—By permission of the Great Spirit above, and the voice of the people, I have been made President of the United States, and now speak to you as your Father and friend, and request you to listen. Your warriors have known me long. You know I love my white and red children, and always speak with a straight, and not with a forked tongue; that I have always told you the truth. I now speak to you, as my children, in the language of truth—Listen. . . .

Where you now are, you and my white children are too near to each other to live in harmony and peace. Your game is destroyed, and many of your people will not work and till the earth. Beyond the great River Mississippi, where a part of your nation has gone, your Father has provided a country large enough for all of you, and he advises you to remove to it. There your white brothers will not trouble you; they will have no claim to the land, and you can live upon it, you and all your children, as long as the grass grows or the water runs, in peace and plenty. It will be yours forever. For the improvements in the country where you now live, and for all the stock which you cannot take with you, your Father will pay you a fair price. . . .

Where you now live your white brothers have always claimed the land. The land beyond the Mississippi belongs to the President and to none else; and he will give it to you forever. . . .

Friends and Brothers, listen. This is a straight and good talk. It is for your nation's good, and your Father requests you to hear his counsel.

Signed, ANDREW JACKSON   March 23, 1829

was to ask Congress to pass an Indian removal bill, giving him more power in Indian matters.

Jackson also addressed the Indians directly. His message, aimed specifically at the Creeks still in Alabama, let Georgia Cherokees know exactly where the new president stood.

The reply by Chief Speckled Snake reveals an Indian reaction to President Jackson's message.

THINK ABOUT IT

1. How did President Jackson feel about Indians and whites living as neighbors?
2. What did Jackson promise the Indians if they moved west?
3. The editor of the Warrenton, Georgia, *Rural Cabinet* wrote "hurrah for Jackson" regarding the president's "Indian Talk." Why might the editor have taken this position?
4. What was the position of Chief Speckled Snake regarding Jackson's talk?

Gold Discovered

Another development in 1829 weakened the Cherokees' position in Georgia. In July, gold was discovered at Dahlonega (meaning "the place of yellow metal") in the middle of the Cherokee country. Thousands of gold seekers, many of them wild and lawless men, rushed into the Indian lands. Whites and Indians fought savagely.

To control the situation, the state government in 1830 required all whites entering the Cherokee country to have a permit and to take an oath of allegiance to Georgia. It also forbade Cherokees to dig for gold!

At the time, Protestant missionaries

Chief Speckled Snake Replies

(Speech made in council summoned to have a talk from President Jackson read to them.) [*Niles' Weekly Register,* Vol. XXVI, June 20, 1829, p. 274.]

Brothers! We have heard the talk of our great father; it is very kind. He says he loves his red children. *Brothers!* When the white man first came to these shores, the Muscogees gave him land, and kindled him a fire to make him comfortable; and when the pale faces of the south (the Spanish in Florida) made war on him, their young men drew the tomahawk, and protected his head from the scalping knife.

But when the white man had warmed himself before the Indian's fire, and filled himself with the Indian's hominy, he became very large; he stopped not for the mountain tops, and his feet covered the plains and the valleys. His hands grasped the eastern and the western sea.

Then he became our great father. He loved his red children; but said, "You must move a little farther, lest I should by accident tread on you." With one foot he pushed the red man over the Oconee, and with the other he trampled down the graves of his fathers.

But our great father still loved his red children, and he soon made them another talk. He said much; but it all meant nothing, but "move a little farther; you are too near me." I have heard a great many talks from our great father, and they all began and ended the same.

Brothers! When he made us a talk on a former occasion, he said, "Get a little farther; go beyond the Oconee and the Oakmulgee; there is a pleasant country." He also said, "It shall be yours forever."

Now he says, "The land you live on is not yours; go beyond the Mississippi; there is game; there you may remain while the grass grows or the water runs."

Brothers! Will not our great father come there also? He loves his red children, and his tongue is not forked.

were teaching and preaching among the Cherokees. Some white Georgians resented these missionaries and their schools, especially since the missionaries supported the Cherokees' resistance to removal.

Several of the white missionaries who refused to get permits or take Georgia's oath were arrested. In 1831, they were tried, convicted, and sentenced to four years hard labor in the Georgia penitentiary at Milledgeville. When Georgia Governor George Gilmer offered to pardon them, they refused. "After all, if we committed no crime, how could we be pardoned for it?" the missionaries asked.

The missionaries' situation gained national attention. Their case was carried to the United States Supreme Court. In 1832, Chief Justice John Marshall announced the Supreme Court's decision: Georgia laws did not apply in the Cherokee Nation. The missionaries should be freed.

The Cherokees celebrated. They believed the decision meant that their laws and their nation would be saved. It was not to be.

Georgia's newly elected governor, Wilson Lumpkin, paid no attention to the Supreme Court. President Jackson, no friend of the Cherokees, sided with the state of Georgia. Said the president, "John Marshall has made his decision; now let him enforce it."

The Cherokees and Their Lands Divided

The Cherokee cause now became hopeless. Their lands had already been surveyed by the state into lots of 160 acres each, 40 acres each in the gold fields around Dahlonega. In 1832 the state held a lottery to distribute the Cherokee lands to whites. Ten counties were mapped out and Governor Lumpkin urged white settlers who had drawn land in the lottery to occupy it. Cherokee families were forced from their homes by the new owners.

Most of the Cherokees continued to resist. Early in 1834, in a statement to President Jackson, they even offered to give up their own government and *part*

The Printing Shop at New Echota. This 1982 photo shows one of several restored buildings at the former Cherokee capital.

of their territory. They wanted only to stay in Georgia as citizens of the United States. Jackson replied, "The only relief for the Cherokees is by removal to the West."

Like the Creeks earlier, the Cherokees were divided. Most followed Chief John Ross in resisting any move west. Another group followed the leadership of Major Ridge, his son John, and Elias Boudinot, the first editor of the *Cherokee Phoenix*. These Cherokee leaders sincerely believed it was better for their people to move west.

In 1835, at New Echota, the Cherokee capital, the Ridge faction signed a treaty with the United States. By this treaty, these Cherokees* agreed to give up their lands and move west in return for $5 million. The majority of the nation, led by John Ross, opposed this treaty.

Some Cherokees left for Arkansas across the Mississippi. Those who rejected

---

*In 1839, after the move west, Major Ridge, John Ridge, and Elias Boudinot were killed. Like the Creeks, the Cherokees had a law against signing away tribal lands without the full consent of the people.

the New Echota treaty stayed in Georgia. Within a few years, they were driven from their farms by white settlers. They continued to present their case in Washington, with no success.

White Attitude toward the Indians

Except for the missionaries who worked among the Cherokees, few white Americans supported them in their struggle to keep their lands. Why?

Many Americans accepted President Jackson's argument that Indian removal was for their own protection. Also, many believed that it was the white people's destiny—their natural right—to possess all of North America.

Wilson Lumpkin, a leader in state politics for many years, strongly held to this belief. As governor and as a United States senator from Georgia, Lumpkin devoted much of his time in public office to removing the Indians from Georgia. Below is an excerpt from a speech he delivered before the United States Senate.

THINK ABOUT IT

1. What does Senator Lumpkin think of Indians as human beings? Does he regard them as the equals of white people?
2. Does Lumpkin's description of the Indian as "uncivilized" and "wild" fit the Georgia Cherokees of the 1830s?

 Sen. Wilson Lumpkin of Georgia Addresses the United States Senate, April 30, 1838

(Note: The United States Senate was considering a bill to provide for Indians moving to lands west of the Mississippi River.)

In thinking of the past, we may, with hearts overflowing with gratitude to a kind and beneficent Providence, congratulate ourselves at the unparalled advancement and prosperity of our beloved country, since the first settlement of our European fathers on this continent. . . . .And, still our course is onward and onward—to the summit of our destiny.

And, sir, we have wrested this delightful and magnificent land from the hands of its native lords; and whether it was brought about by force, or fraud, the obligation which now falls on us to rescue and save from oblivion the remnants of the native race is not changed. We should make an honest, sincere effort. . . .

I do not condemn, or regret, the success of our race on this continent. No, sir. I have none of that . . . sickly sympathy for these interesting people that induces me to regret that they have been supplanted by a superior race. . . . I cannot desire that this flourishing land of light and liberty— "The home of the free, and the land of the brave"—with all its various and beautiful improvements, should go back to the control of uncivilized man, and again become a wild wilderness and dense forest, for the wild man to roam and hunt in, from place to place. . . .

. . . .Unless we speedily change our policy, the day is not far distant when there will not be a solitary Indian left to tell the sad story of his ancestors. But should success speedily crown the plan (to move the Indians to the west) for which I have so long labored in the face of powerful opposition, my hopes will then be revived for the salvation of a remnant of this peculiar race of people—a people for whose real and permanent welfare I feel all the concern of which I am capable for feeling for any portion of the human family. □

[Adapted from Wilson Lumpkin, *The Removal of the Cherokee Indians from Georgia* (New York: 1907), pp. 192-95.]

Trail of Tears

Later in 1838, U.S. Army troops, under Gen. Winfield Scott, rounded up the last 15,000 Cherokees in Georgia.

Almost all the Indians resisted. The troops scoured the hills and valleys of North Georgia, breaking into cabins, seizing men, women, and children wherever they found them.

Although General Scott ordered his men to treat the Cherokees humanely, many did not. One Georgia soldier wrote many years later, "I fought through the Civil War, and have seen men shot to pieces and slaughtered by thousands, but the Cherokee removal was the cruelest work I ever knew."

The last group of Cherokees left on November 4, 1838. A young Cherokee leader reported to Chief John Ross the following:

We are now about to take our final leave and farewell to our native land, the country that the Great Spirit gave our fathers. It is with sorrow that we are forced by the authority of the white man to quit the scenes of our childhood. We bid farewell to the country which gave us birth, and to all that we hold dear.

The Cherokees were forced to march to the west on foot in the dead of winter. Exposed to bitter cold and disease, thousands of men, women and children died, including Quatie Ross, wife of the chief. The Cherokees' suffering was so great that the route they took is known as "The Trail of Tears."

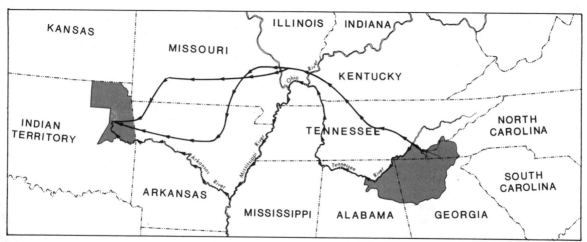

MAP 16. The Trail of Tears. Where did the Cherokees go when they were removed from Georgia?

ACTIVITIES FOR CHAPTER 7

Discussion

A. Federal Indian agent Benjamin Hawkins, who worked among the Creeks from 1796 to 1816, urged the Indians to adopt white culture in order to avoid conflicts with the whites.

1. What arguments might Hawkins have used to persuade the Indians to change their way of life?

2. How did the Creeks and Cherokees become more like their white neighbors?

B. Yet conflicts between the Indians and the whites continued. Why?

1. What was the main source of conflict?

2. What was the attitude of many whites toward the Indians?

C. The removal of the Cherokees involved three governments: the state of Georgia, the United States, and the Cherokee Nation.

1. At first, how did the U.S. and Georgia governments differ in their attitude toward the Cherokee government?

2. How did the U.S. government's position change after Jackson became president?

UNIT IV
1840-1870: Turning Point

8. Antebellum Society
9. The Civil War
10. Reconstruction Begins

GEORGIA EVENTS	DATE	EVENTS ELSEWHERE
State hospital at Milledgeville established	1842	Massachusetts limits child labor
Crawford Long uses anesthesia in surgery	1844	Samuel Morse invents telegraph
	1846	U.S. declares war on Mexico
City of Atlanta incorporated; Augusta canal opened	1847	Frederick Douglass publishes abolitionist newspaper
	1848	Gold discovered in California; Mexico cedes lands to United States
Cotton production reaches half million bales	1850	Compromise of 1850 over slavery; California admitted as free state
	1852	Uncle Tom's Cabin published
	1854	Republican Party founded
Joseph E. Brown begins eight years as governor	1857	Dred Scott decision
	1859	John Brown's raid at Harper's Ferry
	1860	Abraham Lincoln elected president
Georgia secedes, joins Confederacy	1861	Civil War begins
Battle of Chickamauga	1863	Emancipation Proclamation; Battle of Gettysburg
Sherman's invasion; Atlanta burned	1864	Grant commands Union armies
Union forces take control of the state	1865	Civil War ends; Lincoln assassinated; 13th Amendment abolishes slavery
Atlanta University founded; blacks get the vote	1867	Reconstruction begins; U.S. buys Alaska from Russia
Atlanta made capital; Constitution of 1868 adopted	1868	14th Amendment adopted
Georgia readmitted to the Union	1870	15th Amendment adopted
Democrats regain government	1872	Reconstruction ends

8 Antebellum Society

What do you propose, gentlemen of the [North]? . . . Is it that your section may grow in power and prosperity upon treasures unjustly taken from the South? . . . You desire to weaken the political power of the southern states; and why? Because you want, by an unjust system of legislation, to promote the industry of the New England states, at the expense of the people of the South and their industry. [Jefferson Davis, U.S. senator, Mississippi, 1850.]

. . .two systems have existed in different states, but side by side within the American Union. . . these antagonistic systems are continually coming into closer contact, and collision results.

Shall I tell you what this collision means? . . . It is an irrepressible conflict between opposing and enduring forces, and it means that the United States must and will, sooner or later, become either entirely a slave-holding nation, or entirely a free-labor nation. . . . [William H. Seward, U.S. senator, New York, 1858.]

"Antebellum," a word that means *before the war*, has a special meaning in the United States, especially in the South. It refers to a way of life that had developed in much of the South by the 1850s. Meanwhile, in the North a different way of life, or culture, was developing.

By 1861, the differences between southern and northern sections of the country led to a war. That war would bring an end to antebellum Georgia, its culture and its prosperity.

What were the sectional differences that split the United States? What were some features of antebellum life in Georgia? This chapter focuses on these questions.

Economic Differences. In the early 1800s, both the northern and southern sections of the United States had mixed economies, that is, some agriculture and some industry. However, the North turned increasingly industrial, especially after such inventions as the steam engine and the factory system. The northern climate provided only a short growing season for agriculture. On the other hand, the North's great forests, swift rivers and waterfalls, and natural harbors were well-suited to manufacturing and foreign trade. The middle states stayed largely agricultural.

Meanwhile, the South's special advantages—such as its long growing season—encouraged its inhabitants to stick to farming. With the invention of the cotton gin, the South became even more tied to agriculture—especially to the growing of cotton!

Dependence and Independence. In the North, the growing industrial economy led to the growth of cities. Persons who moved from farms to work in city factories could no longer be largely self-sufficient. They had to depend more on one another for such needs as food, shelter, and clothing. In the developing cities of the North, people came to expect more from government, such as police and fire protection.

In the South, however, people generally continued to live a somewhat isolated life. They had to be independent and provide for themselves.

As their economies and lifestyles became less similar, the people of the North and the South developed conflicting views. The following section examines some of those views.

THINK ABOUT IT

1. How did the United States government's tariffs affect the North and the South differently?
2. How did northerners and southerners differ in attitude toward the federal union? Was economics related to these differences?
3. In what ways was the West a source of controversy between the North and South?

CONFLICTING SECTIONAL VIEWS

Because their economies were different, the North and the South were not affected by events—such as business slumps or booms, government decisions, or even wars—in the same way. In the 1820s and 1830s, political leaders in northern and southern states often looked at national issues in terms of how those issues affected their own *section* of the United States rather than the *nation* as a whole. They made political decisions more as northerners or southerners than as Americans. This sectional approach shows up in government decisions involving several issues: tariffs, states' rights, the settling of the West, and of course slavery.

Tariffs

A tariff (also called a *duty*) is a tax on goods imported from foreign countries. Tariffs are a source of government revenue. They can also be used to protect a nation's business against cheaper goods produced in foreign countries.

For example, a tariff on foreign steam engines can make the price on them higher than the price on engines manufactured domestically (at home in the buyer's own nation). If the two were equal in quality, buyers would likely choose a domestic one because it cost less. This would, of course, provide domestic manufacturers with more profits.

To protect their industries against British competition, northern business leaders favored high protective tariffs. Southerners, however, did not.

Southerners had very few industries to protect. They depended heavily on imported goods from Great Britain and other nations, as well as on goods from New England. They wanted to pay as little for these goods as possible. But the same high tariffs that protected northern manufacturers forced southerners to pay higher prices for manufactured goods they needed.

States' Rights

The disputes over tariffs fueled a burning issue—states' rights—raised at the time the United States Constitution was adopted by the 13 original states. Within the federal system of government, what rights and powers belonged to the state?

Southerners generally favored "states' rights." They said that each state had the right to determine if a law passed by Congress—such as a high tariff that hurt that state—should be obeyed. Furthermore, some southern leaders argued, if a state decided a law was unconstitutional, that state could declare the law "null and void" (without force) within that state. This idea, called "nullification," was strongly rejected by most northern leaders.

Many northerners argued that the

states had no power to declare a U.S. law null and void. Only the United States Supreme Court could declare a law unconstitutional.

Most southerners felt that the national government was taking actions hostile to the South. This angered them. They went further and claimed that each state had a right to secede (withdraw) from the Union.

Many northerners argued that the states had no right to secede.

The West

Another source of conflict between North and South was the United States territory in the West. How would these lands be developed? Who should settle there? How would states be formed there and admitted to the Union?

The western territories, with their rich prairie soils, good climate, and great rivers were just right for growing and transporting agricultural products. People from both the North and the South were eager to make use of the region.

Generally, southerners favored distributing western lands as cheaply as possible so that they could quickly develop them into large agricultural holdings like those in the South. Northerners tended to prefer that the U.S. government sell the public lands at a good price in order to bring in revenue. (Some northern factory owners also feared losing workers if the West were made too attractive to settlers.)

Northerners favored the idea of developing the West—including roads and canals—at the expense of the government. Southern leaders opposed such activities by the national government and didn't want to be taxed in any way to support them.

As the West grew, its inhabitants developed their own sectional views. Some of the settlers in the West were from the North and some from the South. Views of the settlers there were mixed. Their main differences were over the biggest question splitting North and South—*slavery.*

THE SLAVERY ISSUE

The slavery issue was woven into all these other issues that separated North from South. Whether Americans argued about states' rights, the powers of the national government, or the development of the West, slavery was part of the issue. And, of course, the differences—both social and economic—between the two sections were tied to the use (or nonuse) of slavery.

The subject of violent debate, slavery involved basic principles of human freedom and democratic ideals upon which the United States was founded. This section looks at the slavery issue in detail.

THINK ABOUT IT

1. Which states were the first to emancipate (free) slaves? Why were these states the first?
2. What problem relating to the national government did the Missouri Compromise settle?
3. Why was this compromise only temporary?
4. What was "popular sovereignty?" Did it solve the problem of free or slave states?

Slavery once existed throughout the United States, but some states gradually abolished it.

Emancipation by the States

1780—Pennsylvania and Massachusetts
1784—Connecticut and Rhode Island
1792—New Hampshire
1799—New York
1804—New Jersey

These were states with industry and small-scale farming, not plantation agriculture, as their economic base. Pro-slavery factions were not powerful in these states, and the arguments against slavery prevailed.

In addition, in 1787, Congress had prohibited slavery in the Northwest Territory. As the United States grew, some new states entered as slave states, others as free states. By 1819 the number of free and slave states was balanced—eleven each.

The Missouri Compromise

In 1819 the Missouri Territory applied

for admission to the Union as a slave state. Northern members of Congress opposed this: It would upset the balance of free and slave states and give the slave states control of the U.S. Senate. (Because they had more population, the free states controlled the House of Representatives.)

Some northerners suggested Congress abolish slavery in Missouri before admitting it. Southerners objected that Congress had no power under the Constitution to abolish slavery.

The question was temporarily settled by a compromise. Missouri would be admitted as a slave state at the same time that Maine would enter the Union as a free state—thus keeping the balance. Also, the Louisiana Territory north of latitude 36° 30' would be closed to slavery.

Compromise of 1850 and "Popular Sovereignty"

In the 1840s, as the United States gained territory as far as the Pacific Ocean, northerners and southerners fiercely debated expanding slavery into these lands. After Texas had won its independence from Mexico, many southerners moved there with their slaves. In 1845, Texas was admitted as a slave state. In a few years, gold was discovered in California. Forty-niners seeking their fortune streamed into the territory, which then applied for admission to the Union.

The Compromise of 1850 provided that California enter as a free state. Meanwhile, the plan of "popular sovereignty" would operate in other territories. This meant that the inhabitants of a territory would decide whether or not to have slavery in their state.

Popular sovereignty proved to be no solution to the dispute. Kansas was not left alone to reach a decision about slavery without pressure from outside the territory. Thousands of slaveowners from the South and abolitionists (persons opposed to all slavery) from the North rushed to

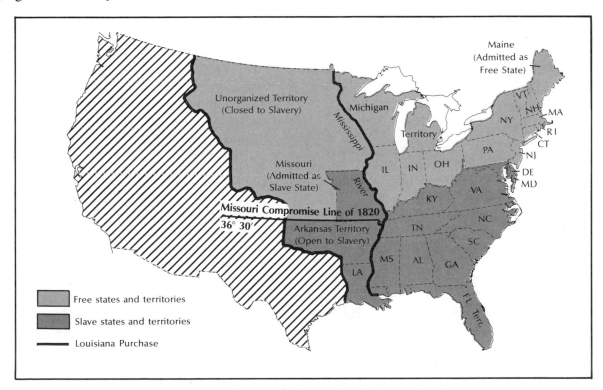

MAP 17.   The Compromise of 1820. What part of the Louisiana Territory (the far west was not yet part of the U.S.) was to be open to slavery? What part was to be closed to it?

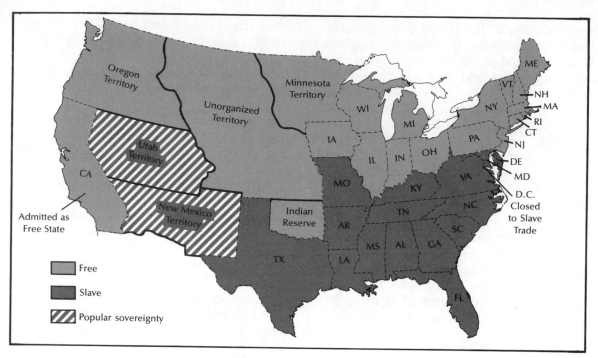

MAP 18. *The Compromise of 1850. Georgia's representatives in Congress—Howell Cobb, Alexander Stephens, and Robert Toombs—helped work out this compromise. How did it compare to the one of 1820?*

gain control of the territory. So savage were their raids on each other's settlements that the area was called "Bleeding Kansas." The slavery question now divided the nation more than ever.

SLAVERY AND COTTON IN GEORGIA

Georgia, one of the slave-holding states, was deeply involved in the conflict between North and South. Plantation agriculture and the slave system had brought economic prosperity to antebellum Georgia.

From the poorest state in the Union in the 1790s, Georgia had, by the 1850s, become "the Empire State of the South." So proud were Georgians of what they had accomplished that the Macon *Georgia Telegraph* carried this glowing account:

Georgia has over twelve hundred miles of Rail Road . . . . These Roads, with but a single exception, are mainly the results of the enterprise,

the energy and the capital of our own people. . . .

We have Cotton and Wool and Paper Factories, Rolling Mills, Foundaries, and Machine Shops—Merchant Mills—Marble Yards—Gold and Copper and Coal Mines—all in a flourishing condition. . . .

Our Banks are solvent—our Merchants in the best of credit and the people generally out of debt, with full crops of cotton, corn, etc. . . .

If then, at this time, she occupies so proud a position, what will she be when, . . .instead of a fourth, as she now has, of her rich lands in cultivation, the full half of the rich valleys of the North shall bear a golden harvest, and the plains of the South and West shall be white with the kingly staple. When that day shall come, Georgia will not only be the Empire State of the South, but the Empire State of the World. □
[*Georgia Telegraph*, October 19, 1858.]

What was this "kingly staple" the newspaper spoke of? What was its place in Georgia's economy? This section looks at the rise of "King Cotton" and the role slavery played in that rise.

THINK ABOUT IT

1. How did "King Cotton" encourage the growth of slavery in Georgia?
2. How did attitudes toward slavery change in Georgia after 1830?
3. Why did white Georgians bitterly resent the abolitionists?
4. How widespread was slave-owning among white Georgians?

The large-scale plantation system of cotton growing was made possible by three things. First, Georgia had the right combination of soil and climate and lots of cheaply available land to grow cotton. Second, Eli Whitney invented the cotton engine. As fast as cotton could be grown and picked, the cotton gin would gulp it down and spit out the seeds. The third thing was the ready supply of cheap labor to plant, hoe, and pick the cotton. Slavery was the cheapest way—claimed its supporters—to get a lot of people doing the same hand labor at the same time. These three factors made cotton plantations profitable in Georgia.

Cotton rapidly became "king" in Georgia. In 1790, only 1,000 bales (about 400 pounds to the bale) were produced. By 1840 cotton production rose to over 400,000 bales, and by 1860 to over 700,000 bales.

An Augusta newspaper reported the impressions of a traveler from South Carolina.

. . .I crossed over in the Horse-boat [ferry], with several empty cotton wagons, and found a number on the other side, loaded with cotton, going to town. From this I continued on,

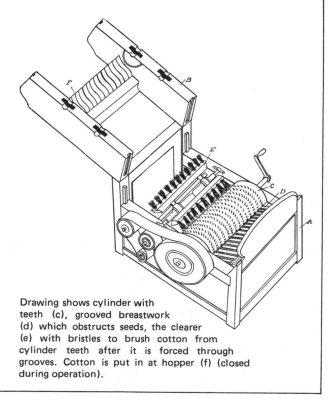

ELI WHITNEY'S COTTON GIN

In 1793, on a plantation outside Savannah, a New Englander named Eli Whitney invented a machine to separate cotton seeds from cotton fibers. It became known as the cotton gin (short for engine).

Although cotton had been grown in coastal Georgia during the colonial years, it was never more than a minor crop. Too much hand labor was required to pick the seed from the fiber.

Whitney's invention changed that. The cotton gin was a simple machine consisting basically of a system of rollers and combs. But the changes it brought to Georgia were far from simple.

When it became faster and cheaper to get cotton ready for making into cloth, the demand for it grew. Rice, corn, and tobacco gave way to cotton as the one crop farmers wanted to grow. The more cotton a farmer could grow and sell, the more profit he could make.

Drawing shows cylinder with teeth (c), grooved breastwork (d) which obstructs seeds, the clearer (e) with bristles to brush cotton from cylinder teeth after it is forced through grooves. Cotton is put in at hopper (f) (closed during operation).

meeting with little else than cotton fields, cotton gins, cotton wagons. . . . I arrived in Augusta; and when I saw the cotton wagons in Broadstreet, I whistled! but said nothing!!! But this was not all; there were more than a dozen tow boats in the river, with more than a thousand bales of cotton on each; and several steamboats with still more. And you must know, that they have cotton warehouses there covering whole squares, all full of cotton; and some of the knowing ones told me, that there were in the place from 40,000 to 50,000 bales. □
[*Georgia Courier,* Augusta, October 11, 1827.]

As cotton grew in Georgia, so did the number of slaves. Slaves in 1790 numbered fewer than 30,000. By 1850, the slave population was over 380,000; by 1860 it was over 460,000. So tied together were cotton and slavery that a Scottish visitor to Georgia in 1844 reported the following:

Such is the superior productiveness to the planter of cotton cultivation, that an acre of cotton will bring ten times the price of an acre of wheat; but it occupies the whole year in its preparation for market. During the high prices of cotton, the planters did not cultivate sufficient grain for their own slaves. Nothing was attended to but the rearing of cotton and slaves. The more cotton the more slaves, and the more slaves the more cotton! □
[George Lewis, *Impressions of America and the American Churches* (Edinburgh: W. P. Kennedy, 1845), pp. 123-24.]

As more and more land was given over to King Cotton, the price of slaves rose. In 1790, a planter had to pay $300 for a good field hand. By 1850, the price was over $1,000, and by 1860 it was up to $1,800. As Georgia planters sank more of their money into slaves, the calls of northern abolitionists for emancipating (freeing) all slaves in the United States sounded more threatening.

Early Anti-slavery Sentiment

Anti-slavery attitudes existed in Georgia since its founding in 1733. The Georgia Constitution of 1798 outlawed the introduction of any more foreign slaves into the state. Even after the development of large cotton plantations, the majority of white Georgians considered slavery an evil. Many wished to find a practical way to get out of it. In 1821 the editor of the *Georgia Journal* in Milledgeville said that no editor in the state would dare argue for slavery.

One effort for getting rid of slavery was the *colonization* movement. It involved establishing in 1822 a colony of ex-slaves in Africa. Named *Liberia,* this territory received thousands of freed blacks from northern and southern states. Some Georgia slaveowners did free their slaves and even helped pay their passage to Africa. But the colonization effort proved very expensive and was soon abandoned.

Forces Line Up on Both Sides of the Slavery Issue

After 1830, anti-slavery attitudes in Georgia were gradually replaced by outspoken defense of slavery. Why?

Several factors strengthened support for slavery: (1) the growth of King Cotton increased the demand and value of slaves; (2) in Virginia, a slave named Nat Turner led a slave revolt that aroused fear that such revolts would spread throughout the South; and (3) abolitionists, on the increase in the North, angered southerners by demanding the immediate freeing of all slaves.

In the 1830s, the abolitionists organized anti-slavery groups, established anti-slavery newspapers, and raised money to wipe out slavery. They also set up an "underground railroad" to smuggle runaway slaves out of the southern states.

Some of the leading abolitionists were ex-slaves. Two such leaders were Frederick Douglass, who edited an abolitionist newspaper, and Harriet Tubman, who risked her life many times leading slaves along the underground railroad. Others were white ministers, authors, teachers, and merchants who felt that slavery was morally wrong—it violated the Bible and the Declaration of Independence. The most famous abolitionist, a Bostonian named William Lloyd Garrison, carried on an almost one-man crusade against slavery through his newspaper, the *Liberator.*

In the North, the abolitionists were not highly popular at first. Then, in 1852, abolitionist Harriet Beecher Stowe wrote a novel, *Uncle Tom's Cabin*, about slave life in the South. The cruelties and suffering portrayed in this book helped swing many northerners to the abolitionist side.

Southerners reacted strongly to the abolitionists' attacks. They resented what they felt were false descriptions of slavery and southern life. They also objected to the open defiance of state and federal laws by abolitionists who helped slaves escape from their "rightful masters."

So outraged were Georgians by Garrison's attacks in the *Liberator* that the General Assembly passed a resolution providing $5,000 reward for his arrest and conviction (or for that of any person circulating the *Liberator* in Georgia). In 1835, the General Assembly made conviction for circulating in Georgia any paper which might incite blacks to revolt punishable by death!

This, then, was the bitter hostility that the slavery question caused between North and South. What was slavery in antebellum Georgia really like?

Plantation Life

How important was slavery in Georgia in 1860? Statistics from the 1860 census provide some clues.

Total White Population 591,550
Total Slaveowners 41,084

Occupations of Whites (in categories totaling over 2,000):
Farmers. 67,718
Farm Laborers. 19,567
Laborers 11,272
Servants. 5,337
Overseers. 4,909
Clerks 3,626
Carpenters. 3,219
Merchants 3,195
PLANTERS. 2,858
Factory Hands. 2,454
Seamstresses 2,411
Teachers 2,123
Physicians 2,004

Most white Georgians did not own slaves. The vast majority of Georgia farms, over 31,000, had less than 100 acres. Only 3,564 had more than 500 acres. Only 6,363 farms or plantations had 20 or more slaves.

Only 2,858 Georgians were classified as planters. But those who did own large plantations with many slaves were the wealthy, educated people who dominated the state's business and government. By and large, this small minority spoke for Georgia.

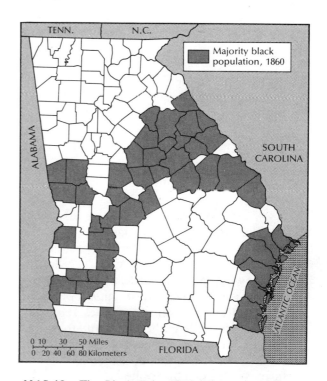

MAP 19. *The Black Belt, 1860. The name "black belt" was given to an area with large slave population and high cotton production. It stretched through several southern states.*

Sources of Information on Slave Life

Many kinds of primary sources provide evidence of slave conditions in antebellum Georgia. The Slave Code (see page 40 in Chapter 4), revised several times, still regulated slavery in the state. Other acts of the General Assembly relating to slaves and masters also provide clues to conditions. Newspapers of the times contain many articles about slavery, reports of happenings on plantations, notices of runaways, and advertisements of slave sales. Also, many visitors to the state reported their observations and opinions in letters and diaries.

The following four sources are all by Georgians. They present very different views of slavery written down over a hundred-year period.

Thomas R.R. Cobb, a prominent Georgia lawyer in the 1850s, helped found the first law school at Athens. He was a leader in the move to have Georgia leave the Union.

THINK ABOUT IT

1. According to Cobb, why was slavery necessary in Georgia?
2. How did blacks benefit, according to Cobb, from the slave system?

 A Patriarchal Social System

. . .[S]lave labor is the only effectual, and therefore cheapest, labor which the Southern States can use in the production of their staples. Experience, in the South, has shown this to be true in the building of railroads. Slave labor must be used successfully on uniform work, requiring physical strength without judgment or discretion. Wherever such work can be found in the Southern climate, slave labor is the cheapest that can be applied.

As a social relation negro slavery has its benefits. . .That the slave is incorporated into and becomes a part of the family, that a tie is then formed between the master and slave, almost unknown in the relation of master and hireling [hired worker]. . . that the old and infirm are thus cared for, and the young protected and reared, are indisputable facts. Interest joins with affection in promoting this unity of feeling.

To the negro, it insures food, fuel, and clothing, medical attention, and in most cases religious instruction. The young child is seldom removed from the parents' protection, and beyond doubt, the institution [slavery] prevents the separation of families, to an extent unknown among the laboring poor of the world. It provides him with a protector, whose interest and feeling combine in demanding such protection.

To the master, it gives a servant whose interests are identical with his own, who has indeed no other interest, except a few simple pleasures. . . .

So long as climate and disease, and the profitable planting of cotton, rice, tobacco, and cane, make the negro the only laborer inhabiting our Southern savannas and prairies, just so long will he remain a slave to the white man . . . ☐

[Adapted from Thomas R.R. Cobb, *An Historical Sketch of Slavery* (Philadelphia: T & J Johnston & Co., 1858), pp. 217-21.]

Charles Henry Smith was a major in the Confederate States Army. His stories of the war appeared in the *Atlanta Constitution* and other newspapers. These stories, supposedly written by someone named "Bill Arp," were very popular through the early 1900s. In 1893, Smith published a textbook for use in Georgia schools. The following excerpt is taken from that book, written almost 30 years after slavery ended in Georgia.

THINK ABOUT IT

1. What is Smith's attitude toward plantation owners (aristocrats)? toward black slaves? toward poor whites?

2. According to Smith, what was the relationship between aristocrats and slaves?
3. For whom was Smith writing his book?

 Aristocrats and Slaves

. . . There was no happier race of people upon the earth than the negroes of the South. They had all the necessaries of life and many of its comforts. . . .

Young negroes grew up to manhood with the children of their master, frolicked with them by day and hunted with them by night. They had their corn-shuckings, their harvest suppers and their Christmas dances, and their merry laugh was always heard, in the field by day and at the fireside by night. The masters were almost universally kind—kind from good policy if nothing else. It was as much to their interest to keep their slaves in good condition as it was to protect and nourish their horses and cows. It was rare to see a puny, sickly negro child, or one that was malformed or diseased. . . .

Never did a race increase faster than the slaves of the South. Nowhere was such ripe old age found among the parents. Good food was abundant on the plantation and comfortable clothing came from the homemade loom and spinning-wheel. . . . Simple medicines and good physicians were near at hand. The marriage relation was enforced among them and divorces were unknown. . . .

Of course there were many bad negroes, and bad negroes had to be punished, and they were sometimes put upon the block and sold, but as a rule families were kept together. . . . In the main, the relation of master and slave was one of tenderness and humanity. . . .

. . . The aristocrats were generally gentlemen of education, refinement, manners and a sentiment of adjusting personal conflicts by the code of honor. . . .

His house was not a palace, but it was large and roomy, having a broad hall and massive chimneys and a verandah or-namented with tall Greek columns. It was set back 100 or 200 yards from the big road, and the lane that led to its hospitable gate was lined with cedars or lombardy poplars. . . .

Not far away were the negro cabins and the orchard and the big family garden, and all around were fowls and pigs and pigeons and hound dogs and pickaninnies to keep things lively. . . .

Most of these old-time gentlemen kept what was called open house, and all who came were welcome. The old gentleman called for Dick or Jack or Caesar to come and take the horses, put them up and feed them. . . . There were plenty of trained servants to do all the work while the lady of the house entertained her guests.

How proud were these family servants to show off before the visitors and display their accomplishments in the kitchen and dining room. They shared the family's standing in the community and had but little respect for what they called the "poor white trash" of the neighborhood. □

[Adapted from Charles H. Smith, *A School History of Georgia* (Boston: Ginn & Company, Publishers, 1893), pp. 125-27.]

Slave Accounts

The next two sources are examples of *oral history*. They are taken from interviews with ex-slaves, conducted in the 1930s by persons working in the Federal Writers' Project, a program of the United States government.

It is important to keep in mind that the persons being interviewed were very old and were asked to remember back 70 years or more. Also, the people who interviewed them may have allowed their own notions about slave life to influence the way they conducted or recorded the interviews.

Nevertheless, these interviews are important sources of information about slave life in antebellum Georgia.

THINK ABOUT IT
1. What do the accounts of Brown and Womble reveal about how slaves were controlled?
2. What do their accounts reveal about the relationship between master and slave?

 Julia (Aunt Sally) Brown (Interviewed by Geneva Tonsell in Atlanta, Georgia, June 1939)

I was born four miles from Commerce, Georgia, and was 13 years old at surrender. My mamma belonged to the Nash family—three old maid sisters—and my papa belonged to General Burns who was an officer in the war. There was six of us chilluns: Lucy, Nelvina, Johnnie, Callie, Joe and me. We didn't stay together long. I was give away when I was just a baby, and I never did see my mamma again. The Nashes didn't believe in selling slaves. If they got rid of any, it was giving them away.

I was give to the Mitchell family, and they done everything mean to me they could. I was put to work in the fields when I was five years old, picking cotton and hoeing. And I slept on the floor nine years, winter and summer, sick or well. I never wore nothing but a cotton dress and my shimmy and drawers. I had such a hard time. That Mistress Mitchell didn't care what happened to us. . . . She used to lash us with a cow-hide whip. When she died I went from one family to another. All the owners was pretty much the same.

We wasn't allowed to go around and have pleasure. We had to have passes to go wherever we wanted. When we'd get out there was a band of white men call the "patty rollers" [slave patrol]. They'd come in and see if all us had passes and if they found any who didn't have a pass he was whipped, given fifty or more lashes. . . .If they said a hundred, you got a hundred. We was afraid to tell our masters about the patty rollers because we was scared they'd whip us again so we was told not to tell. . . .

I worked hard always. You can't imagine what a hard time I had. I split rails like a man. . . . I helped spin the cotton into thread for our clothes. I worked from sun up to sun down. . . .

Some of the white folks was very kind to their slaves. Some didn't believe in slavery and some freed them before the war and even give them land and homes. Some would give the Niggers meal, lard, and things like that. . . .

Sometimes the slaves would run away. Their masters was mean to them and that caused them to run away. Sometimes they'd live in caves. How'd they get along? They got along all right—what with other folks slipping things into them. And then they'd steal hogs, chickens, and anything else they could get their hands on. Some

"Old Sarah." This photo was made in the 1850s. Sarah was brought to Georgia from Virginia. She worked as a slave for five generations of masters.

white people would help, too, for there was some white people who didn't believe in slavery. ☐

[*Georgia Narratives,* Vol. IV, Part 1 (Federal Writers' Project, 1941), pp. 142-47.]

 George Womble (Interviewed by Elizabeth Driskell in Columbus, Georgia, January 1937)

I was born in the year of 1843 near the present site of what is now known as Clinton, Georgia. The names of my parents were Patsy and Raleigh Ridley. I never saw my father as he was sold before I was old enough to recognize him as being my father. I was still quite young when my mother was sold to a plantation owner who lived in New Orleans. As she was being put on the wagon to be taken away I heard her say, "Let me see my poor child one more time because I know I'll never see him again." That was the last time I ever saw or heard of her.

. . . My master, who was Mr. Robert Ridley, had me placed in his house where I was taught to wait tables and to do all kinds of house work. . . .

When Marse Robert died, I was still a small boy. Several months after his death Mrs. Ridley gave the plantation up and took her share of the slaves (ten in number) and moved to Talbot County near the present location of Talbotton, Georgia. The other slaves and the plantation were turned over to Marse Robert's relatives. . . . I was sold to Mrs. Ridley's brother, Enoch Womble. He paid his sister $500 for me.

The slaves all got up long before day and prepared their breakfasts and then, before it was light enough to see clearly, they were standing in the field holding their hoes and other implements—afraid to start work for fear that they would cover the cotton plants with dirt because they couldn't see clearly due to the darkness. An overseer was hired by the master to see that the work was done properly. If any of the slaves were careless about their work, a sound whipping was administered. Field hands also got whippings when they failed to pick the required 300 pounds of cotton daily. . . .

During rainy weather the slaves shucked corn, piled manure in the barns, and made cloth. In the winter season the men split rails, built fences, and dug ditches. . . . The women did the weaving and the making of cloth. Those slaves who were too old to work in the field remained at home where they nursed the sick slaves and attended to the needs of those children who were too young for field work. . . .

At the end of the week all the field hands met in the master's backyard where they were given food for the week. Such an issue was made up of three pounds of fat meat, one peck of meal, and one quart

Atlanta Slave Dealer. This photo was made during the Civil War. Does it suggest that the buying and selling of slaves was much different from trade in tobacco, glass, china, and other goods?

of black molasses. If their food gave out before the time for another issue they waited until night and then one or two of them would go to the millhouse where the flour and meal was kept. Sometimes when they wanted meat they either went to the smoke house and stole a ham or else they would go to the pen where the pigs were kept and take a small pig out. . . .None of this stolen meat was ever fried because there was more danger of the odor of frying meat going farther away than the odor made by meat being boiled. . . .

The younger children were fed from a trough that was 20 feet in length. At meal time each day the master would come out and supervise the cook whose duty it was to fill the trough with food. For breakfast the milk and bread was all mixed together in the trough by the master who used his walking cane to stir it with. At dinner and supper the children were fed pot liquor and bread and sometimes milk that had been mixed together in the same manner. . . .

Most of the sickness on the Womble plantation was due to colds and fever.

For the treatment of either of these ailments the master always kept a large can filled with a mixture of turpentine and castor oil. When anyone complained of a cold a dose of this oil was prescribed. The slaves also had their own homemade remedies for treatment of different ailments. A doctor was always called when anyone was seriously ill. He was always called to attend those cases of childbirth. Unless a slave was too sick to walk, he was required to go to the field and work. . . .

I heard my master say that he would not have a slave that he could not rule. He even went so far as to make all the slaves pay their respects to the newly born white children on the day of their birth. At such a time they were required to get in line outside the door. Then one by one they went through the room and bowed their heads as they passed the bed and said, "Young Marster" or if the baby was a girl they said, "Young Mistress." □

[*Georgia Narratives*, Vol. IV, Part 4 (Federal Writers' Project, 1941), pp. 179-91.]

ACTIVITIES FOR CHAPTER 8

Discussion

A. Southerners, Northerners, and Westerners often differed on the proper role of the federal government. How would each of these groups agree or disagree with the following statements?

   a. "The federal government must build roads and canals so people can market their products."

   b. "The federal government must pass tariffs to protect our economy from foreign competition."

   c. "The federal government has no authority to prohibit slavery in western territories."

   d. "The federal government is superior to the states."

B. Said a historian: "War had to come because the Southerners were determined to leave the Union if Northerners didn't treat them as equals. Also, the fanatics on both sides were unable to compromise on slavery."

   1. Could the historian use the statements by Davis and Seward, page 88, to back up his argument? How?

   2. Do you think the war could have been avoided? What evidence in this chapter supports your opinion?

9 The Civil War

A story often told about the Civil War goes something like this:

At the end of a hardfought battle, after the enemy had fled, a Confederate officer rode slowly over the battlefield. He came upon one of his men carefully digging a grave. Next to the shallow hole the blue-clad body of a Union soldier was laid out.

"Why are you taking such care to bury a Yank?" asked the puzzled officer.

The rebel looked up from his work, tears rolling down his boyish face, and replied, "He's my brother, sir."

This story illustrates that the war Americans fought from 1861 to 1865 not only split the nation, but also split states, communities, and even families. Friends, neighbors, and brothers faced one another in opposing armies. What caused such a terrible conflict to develop?

CAUSES OF THE WAR

In searching for the causes of the Civil War,* it is useful to think of two kinds of causes: fundamental and immediate.

---

*This war has also been known in the South by several other names, the most popular probably being "The War Between the States."

Fundamental (or underlying) causes develop over a long time. The differences between North and South over economics, federal-state relations, and slavery grew over many years. These causes, described in the last chapter, made it possible for a major conflict to occur.

Immediate causes come into being just before the major event itself occurs. Abolitionist John Brown's raid at Harper's Ferry, Virginia, in 1859 and Abraham Lincoln's election as president of the United States in 1860 happened shortly before the war began.

Fundamental causes are wound together like a fuse leading to a keg of powder. Immediate causes are like sparks used to light that fuse. The powder keg—in this case, the Civil War—blew up early in 1861.

Lincoln's Election and Secession

In 1854 the Republican Party was born. Its founders were from the North. They favored protective tariffs for industry and free land in the West. They opposed the extension of slavery into U.S. territories. A few were outright abolitionists.

For the presidential election of 1860, the Republicans nominated (named) Abraham Lincoln of Illinois to be their candidate. The older Democratic Party, whose southern and northern members had managed until then to hold the Union together, now split apart. Southern Democrats nominated John Breckinridge of Kentucky as their candidate; northern Democrats backed Stephen Douglas of Illinois. A third party, the Constitutional Union, organized and nominated John Bell of Tennessee.

Many southerners felt that Lincoln, if elected, would represent only northern interests. Some feared he would attempt to free all slaves and force whites to accept them as social equals. "If Lincoln is elected," these southerners said, "we will be forced to leave the Union." Lincoln won the election.

Reaction in Georgia

Lincoln's election sent shock waves through Georgia. The General Assembly voted $1 million to defend the state. Gov. Joseph Brown called an election for delegates to a special state convention.

On January 16, 1861, the delegates met in Milledgeville. They were sharply divided over what to do. U.S. Sen. Robert Toombs, former U.S. Secy. of the Treasury Howell Cobb, his brother Thomas R.R. Cobb, and Governor Brown favored immediate secession (withdrawal) from the Union.

Alexander Stephens, who had served in Congress and knew Lincoln well, argued that his election could not by itself harm Georgia. Georgians should wait and see what Lincoln would do as president before they took action. Stephens's views were supported by former Gov. Herschel Johnson and by Benjamin Hill, who had run against Brown for governor.

For three days the debate went on. Then, on January 19, 1861, the convention adopted, by a vote of 208 to 89, an "Ordinance of Secession." It stated that the people of Georgia repealed their 1788 ratification of the U.S. Constitution and that "the Union now subsisting between

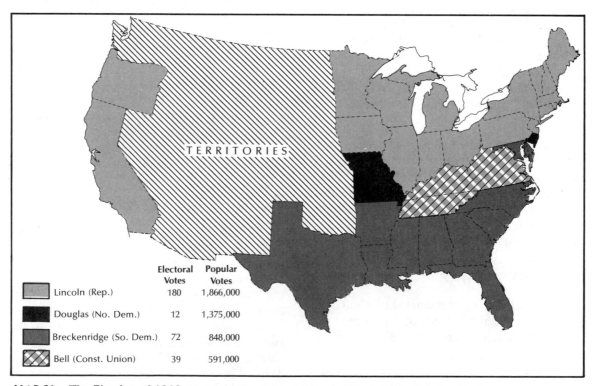

	Electoral Votes	Popular Votes
Lincoln (Rep.)	180	1,866,000
Douglas (No. Dem.)	12	1,375,000
Breckenridge (So. Dem.)	72	848,000
Bell (Const. Union)	39	591,000

MAP 20.   The Election of 1860. How did the states line up in this presidential election? What happened to the Democratic Party?

the State of Georgia and other States, under the name of the 'United States of America' is hereby dissolved. . . ."

Georgia officials resigned from positions in the federal government. Likewise, military officers from Georgia resigned from the U.S. Army and Navy. Throughout the state, most of the white population celebrated secession. To the black people of Georgia it meant little at the time. Changes in their lives would come later.

Not all white Georgians welcomed secession, however. Some prominent citizens, such as Judge Garnett Andrews of Washington in Wilkes County, were strong Union supporters. As Georgia seceded, the judge warned, "Poor fools! They may ring bells now, but they will wring their hands— yes, and their hearts, too—before they are done with it."

Now that Georgia was out of the Union, state leaders joined with those of other Deep South states to form a new government.

THINK ABOUT IT

1. Which states seceded from the Union? Which slave states remained in the Union?
2. What was Lincoln's attitude toward the slave states? What action did he take after his inauguration?
3. How did the Confederacy and the Union compare in terms of war resources? in terms of population?

The Confederacy and the Union

On February 4, 1861, delegates from Georgia and five other seceding states— South Carolina, Alabama, Florida, Mississippi, and Louisiana—met in Montgomery, Alabama, to form a new government. They named it the "Confederate States of America." (Texas delegates, overcoming the fierce opposition of Gov. Sam Houston, arrived later.)

The Constitution of the Confederacy* was written largely by T.R.R. Cobb of Georgia. It was modeled after the U.S. Constitution, but it provided that the individual states would be more powerful than the Confederate government. Also, the Confederate Congress could not pass protective tariffs or any laws opposing slavery.

The delegates elected Jefferson Davis of Mississippi as president of the Confederacy. He had served in the U.S. Army and the U.S. Senate. Alexander Stephens of Georgia was chosen vice-president. The new government began work, raising money and preparing for war, with Montgomery its capital.

Although seven states had declared themselves out of the Union, Lincoln was determined not to let them go. On March 4, 1861, at his inauguration (swearing in) as president of the United States, he stated that "no state . . . can lawfully get out of the Union." Hoping to persuade southern leaders to rethink their actions, he announced that he was not inclined "to interfere with the institution of slavery in the States where it exists." Nevertheless, he warned them, he had a solemn oath to "preserve, protect, and defend" the national government.

On April 12, Confederate forces opened fire on the U.S. Army's Fort Sumter in the harbor at Charleston, South Carolina. The next day, the Fort surrendered.

In response, Lincoln called on the states still in the Union to provide 75,000 men to put down the Confederacy. Also, he declared a naval blockade of its ports.

Army volunteers in the free states answered Lincoln's call. Would the men of the slave states still in the Union do likewise?

Forced now to choose between the

---

*The central government set up by the seceding states was officially named the Confederate States of America. However, it was usually referred to as the "Confederacy." The United States of America was usually referred to as the "Union." In the Civil War, southern troops were called "Confederates," sometimes "rebels" or "rebs." Northern troops were called "Federals," or "Yankees" or just "Yanks."

Augusta, April 1861. The war was just beginning when a Georgia unit, nicknamed the "Oglethorpe Infantry," turned out for this photo. Note the onlookers.

Confederacy and the Union, four states—Virginia, Arkansas, North Carolina, and Tennessee—joined the southern states' new government. The Confederate capital was then moved to Richmond, Virginia.

In four slave-holding states—Delaware, Kentucky, Maryland, and Missouri—most people did not favor secession. These "border states" stayed in the Union. Non-slave-holding western counties in Virginia seceded from that state and, in 1863, joined the Union as West Virginia.

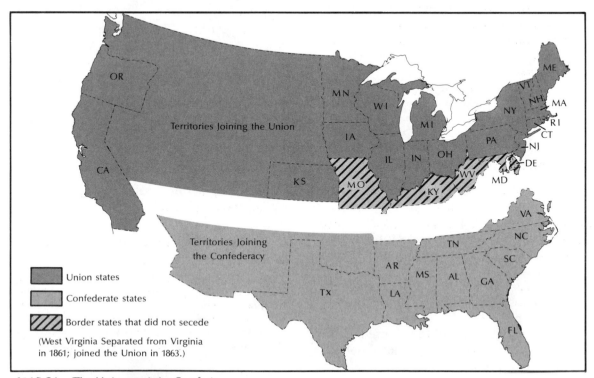

MAP 21. The Union and the Confederacy.

In 1861, neither southern nor northern leaders expected that war, if it came at all, would last very long. Southerners tended to believe that the people of the North would have no stomach for fighting and wouldn't support Lincoln. For their part, northerners were convinced that their huge advantages in resources would mean the swift military defeat of the South. Both sides were wrong. The Civil War would last four years. The cost would be staggering: over 600,000 southern and northern soldiers would be killed and another 400,000 wounded.

How *did* the two sides compare? Figure 2 shows some of the factors which influenced the course, and the outcome, of the war.

FIGURE 2. Northern and Southern Resources Compared, 1860

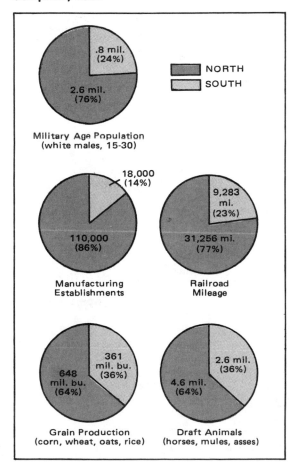

Military Age Population
(white males, 15-30)

.8 mil. (24%)

2.6 mil. (76%)

NORTH

SOUTH

Manufacturing
Establishments

18,000 (14%)

110,000 (86%)

Railroad
Mileage

9,283 mi. (23%)

31,256 mi. (77%)

Grain Production
(corn, wheat, oats, rice)

361 mil. bu. (36%)

648 mil. bu. (64%)

Draft Animals
(horses, mules, asses)

2.6 mil. (36%)

4.6 mil. (64%)

GEORGIA IN THE WAR

THINK ABOUT IT

1. Where was most of the fighting through 1863?
2. Why was Atlanta a special target of the Union forces in 1864?

For two years, the major fighting of the Civil War was far from Georgia's soil. Nevertheless, the people of Georgia very quickly felt the effects of war.

First, the Union Navy's blockade of southern ports prevented the export of cotton, the Confederacy's main source of income. Unable to sell cotton to Great Britain and other countries, the South had little money to buy military supplies and food. As the blockade tightened, Georgians faced food shortages and sky-high prices.

Second, when the Confederate government called for army volunteers, the state's young men (white only) eagerly signed up. (Blacks couldn't be armed, but slave labor was used to build fortifications and repair railroads.) On battlefields in Virginia and other states, thousands of Georgians were killed or wounded. One was Gen. T.R.R. Cobb, killed at the battle of Fredericksburg in 1862.

While Georgians fought elsewhere, the state itself became one of the Confederacy's most important sources of supplies. Farmers switched from growing cotton to raising corn and other foodstuffs needed by the southern armies.

Georgia, with more industry than any other southern state, supplied the Confederacy with rifles, cannons, gunpowder, sabres, wagons, railroad cars, tools, saddles and harnesses, clothing, and other military equipment. Atlanta, Augusta, Columbus, Macon, and Savannah were the main manufacturing centers. Also, thousands of small operations, some in private homes, turned out uniforms, shoes, bandages, and other supplies.

Georgia had over 1,400 miles of railroad, the best system in the Deep South.

This system, with Atlanta its hub, was vital in supplying and transporting Confederate troops.

Georgia's strategic location, its rail network, and its ability to supply southern armies with sorely needed food and equipment, made it the "heart of the Confederacy." Therefore, destruction of Georgia's resources would be fatal to the Confederate war effort.

War Comes to Georgia

At first, fighting in Georgia was minor. Federal naval forces raided the coast, capturing Fort Pulaski in Savannah harbor, and burning Darien. Other raiders tried to wreck the W & A Railroad in 1862.

---

excerpt from—

The Emancipation Proclamation

. . .I do order and declare that all persons held as slaves within [states in rebellion] are, and henceforward shall be, free; and that the Executive Government of the United States, including the military and naval authorities thereof, will recognize and maintain the freedom of said persons. . . .

Abraham Lincoln, January 1, 1863

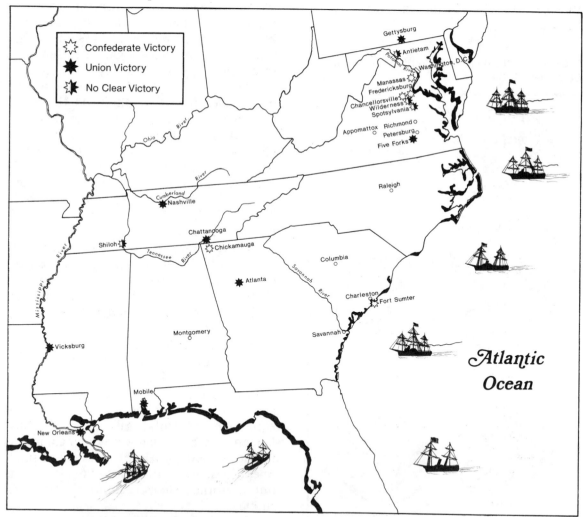

MAP 22. *Major Battles of the Civil War. What might account for the concentration of fighting in Virginia? What was the aim of the naval blockade?*

In 1863, a large Union force, 1,500 strong, rode in from Alabama to cut off the W & A. Near Rome, a Confederate commander with only 500 soldiers tricked the Federals into surrendering.

Alarmed that real fighting had come so close, Atlanta's government leaders took action to protect the city from Union raiders. However, when fighting did come to Atlanta, it was no mere raid. In late 1863 a fierce battle at Chickamauga, on the Tennessee border, provided a hint of things to come.

During the Civil War, Atlanta became the focus of Union military strategy. Other cities, such as Savannah, were larger, and Milledgeville was the capital of the state. But Atlanta, with its industrial and transportation resources, was the heart of the state. (The growth of Atlanta as a major railroad center is described in Chapter 6.) It was the most important city in Georgia.

Sherman Invades Georgia

The story of Atlanta's destruction begins early in 1864. A Union army of 99,000 men, commanded by Gen. William T. Sherman, was at Chattanooga, Tennessee. Thirty miles south at Dalton, 62,000 Confederates, commanded by Gen. Joseph E. Johnston, were dug in.

On April 4—from Washington, D.C.—the commander of U.S. armies, Gen. Ulysses S. Grant, wrote to General Sherman:

> You I propose to move against Johnston's army, to break it up, and get into the interior of the enemy's country as far as you can, inflicting all the damage you can against their war resources. □

In the late spring, the armies of Sherman and Johnston battled at Dalton, Resaca, and New Hope Church. Sherman relentlessly pushed south toward Atlanta. Greatly outnumbered, Johnston would dig in and then retreat down the W & A, not allowing Sherman to break up or encircle his army.

On June 27, at Kennesaw Mountain, Sherman recklessly attacked head on. Johnston taught him a lesson: 3,000 Federals were killed, only 800 Confederates were lost. But again, Johnston's men had to fall back and dig their defensive trenches—this time to defend Atlanta.

Unhappy with General Johnston's retreating, the Confederate government in Richmond replaced him with Gen. John B. Hood. As expected, Hood attacked, but was thrown back several times.

For 40 days, Sherman's artillery pounded Atlanta. Hood, fearing his army would be trapped, evacuated the city on September 1. The next day, the mayor of Atlanta rode out under a white flag to surrender the city. Within a week, Sherman ordered all civilians to leave.

A Georgia Soldier's View

Written correspondence (letters) is one of the best sources of information about

A Confederate Soldier, Wilkes County, Georgia. Name unknown.

the past. Letters provide clues to the private thoughts and attitudes of people who lived long ago.

John W. Hagen was a sergeant in the Twenty-ninth Georgia Volunteer Infantry. The following letter, written to his wife, Amanda, at home in Berrien County, is an example of private correspondence. That is, the writer did not intend for it to be published.

THINK ABOUT IT

1. What does Hagen's letter tell you about his spirit or morale? the morale of Confederate troops in general? of Union troops?
2. What does Hagen spend most of his time doing?
3. What does he think of the Confederates' chances of success in fighting off Sherman's army?

 Letter of John W. Hagen

In Line of Battle, Georgia, July the 4th 1864

My Dear Wife,

. . . We have given up our works & fell back 3 or 4 miles from Marietta, leaving it to the mercy of the Yanks. . . .

We thought this morning being the 4th of July we would have a hopping time with them, but they seem to keep their proper distance. Our men was up on the look out & on the march all night. When we got here we went to work in an open field & worked all day & all night & is yet at work & is about ready to receive them. Our skirmishers are now having a plenty to do & if we stay here we may have something to do in the way of fighting from our works.

We are in the breastworks [temporary fort] now in an open field & they are in line of battle in a hill in another old field about one mile off, but we can see all they do. I do not know whether they will attack us or not, but I hope they will for I am

wore out marching and building breast-works.

The reason we had to leave Kennesaw mountain was because the Yanks was flanking us on the left & we was forced to fall back. The Yankees' army is so much stronger than ours that they can put a force in our front to compete with ours & then they have a corps or two which they can send on either flank & then we have to fall back to prevent them getting in our rear. . . .

Our generals say when we reach the river 8 miles from Atlanta that they will then be forced to fight us in our works. They say the Yanks can not flank us any further, but I do not know. It seems we have a strong position here, but I feel doubtful about their attacking us. But they will roll up their artillery & keep up an incessant shelling.

The Yankees seems to be in fine spirits playing their bands and hallowing. I am now sitting in full view of their line of battle & their wagon trains bringing supplies. They seem so cheerful and full of fun. Some of our troops grow despondent, but it is only those who are always despondent. All good soldiers will fight harder the harder he is pressed, but a coward is always ready to want an excuse to run or to say they or we are whipped....

You must not think strange at this scribbled letter for I am writing in a hurry for I never know how soon a shell may order men to the breast works, etc. . . .

Tell James to think of us when he is eating butter & drinking buttermilk & eating many good things. We get tolerable plenty of meat & bread now, but we want something in the way of vegetables. You must send us something if you get a chance to send it safely.

I must close for the shells is bursting too near me. Give my love to all. . . .

I am as Ever your affectionate husband
J.W.H. □

[Adapted from Bell Irvin Wiley (ed.), *Confederate Letters of John W. Hagen* (Athens, Georgia: University of Georgia Press, 1954), pp. 46-48.]

Atlanta Destruction, 1864. The W & A Railroad Depot is in the background to the right.

Sherman's army occupied Atlanta until mid-November. Then, still following Grant's original plan, he gave orders for the city's destruction. A Union soldier described it this way:

On the night of November 15th, the torch was applied to the railroad shops, foundries, and every one of the many buildings that had been used in fitting out the armies of the enemy in this vast "workshop of the confederacy," as Atlanta was called. The flames spread rapidly, and when morning came, it is doubtful whether there were a score of buildings remaining in the city, except in the very outskirts. □

[Fenwick Y. Hedley, *Marching Through Georgia* (Chicago: R. R. Donelly & Sons, 1885), p. 257.]

Sherman's March to the Sea

After sending part of his army north after Hood, Sherman began his "march to the sea."

On its march, the army was to live off the land and destroy the state's resources.

In his order to his troops, Sherman included the following:

...gather, near the route traveled, corn or forage of any kind, meat of any kind, vegetables, cornmeal, or whatever is needed...

Soldiers not to enter the dwellings of inhabitants, or commit any trespass, but during a halt, or in camp, to be permitted to gather turnips, potatoes and other vegetables, and to drive in stock within sight.

To corps commanders alone is intrusted the power to destroy mills, houses, cotton-gins, etc. . . .

Horses, mules and wagons belonging to the inhabitants, to be appropriated [taken] freely and without limit by cavalry and artillery; discriminating, however, between the rich, who are usually hostile, and the poor and industrious, usually neutral or friendly. . . . □

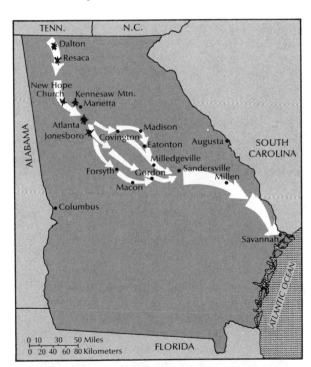

MAP 23.   The March to the Sea. Sherman's army moved over a 60-mile wide path between Atlanta and Savannah. Which areas escaped destruction?

On December 21, 1864, Sherman's army entered Savannah. The general telegraphed President Lincoln: "I beg to present you as a Christmas gift the city of Savannah, with one hundred fifty guns and plenty of ammunition, also about twenty-five thousand bales of cotton."

General Sherman reported that he had destroyed $100 million worth of food and other resources on his march through Georgia. Within a few months, the war was over.

In the spring of 1865, the Civil War ended with the surrender of the southern armies. Holding its last official meeting in Washington, Georgia, the Confederate government collapsed.

The war settled two issues: a state could not leave the Union, and slavery was abolished.

A few days after the end of the war, Abraham Lincoln was assassinated.

Georgians View the End of War

How did Georgians react to the end of what some called the "War for Southern Independence" and the end of slavery?

Eliza Frances Andrews, a daughter of Judge Garnett Andrews of Washington, Georgia, kept a day-by-day diary of the last months of the Civil War. In it she recorded the hardships Georgians suffered as the Confederacy collapsed and her own views of events. Below are excerpts from her diary.

THINK ABOUT IT

1. What are Andrews's emotions regarding the final events of the war?
2. How did she view the South's present condition? The future?

 A War-Time Journal

April 21, Friday. . . .Confirmation of Lee's surrender, and of the armistice [truce] between Johnston and Sherman. Alas, we all know only too well what that armistice means! It is all over with us now, and there is nothing to do but bow our heads in the dust and let the hateful conquerers trample us under their feet. There is a complete revulsion in public feeling. No more talk now about fighting to the last ditch; the last ditch has already been reached. . . .

. . . Somebody thrust his head in at the window and shouted: "Lincoln's been assassinated!" We had heard so many absurd rumors that at first we were all inclined to regard this as a jest. . . . But soon the truth of the report was confirmed. Some fools laughed and applauded, but wise people looked grave and held their peace. It is a terrible blow to the South, for it places that vulgar renegade, Andy Johnson, in power, and will give the Yankees an excuse for charging us with a crime which was in reality only the deed of an irresponsible madman. . . .

May 5, Friday. It has come at last—what we have been dreading and expecting so long—what has caused so many panics and false alarms—but it is no false alarm this time; the Yankees are actually in Washington, [Georgia]. Before we were out of bed a courier came in with the news that Kirke—name of ill omen—was only seven miles from town, plundering and devastating the country. Father hid the silver and what little coin he had in the house, but no other precautions were taken. . . .

I have not laid eyes on one of the creatures myself, and they say they do not intend to come into town unless to put down disturbances—the sweet, peaceful lambs! They never sacked Columbia, [South Carolina]; they never burnt Atlanta; they never left a black trail of ruin and desolation. . . .

May 15, Monday. . . .The streets are so full of idle negroes and bluecoats that ladies scarcely ever venture out. We are obliged to go sometimes, but it is always with drooping heads and downcast eyes. A settled gloom, deep and heavy, hangs over the whole land. . . .

Ah, we'll bide our time. That's what all

the men say, and their eyes glow and their cheeks burn when they say it. Though the whole world has deserted us and left us to perish without even a pitying sigh at our miserable doom, and we hate the whole world for its cruelty, yet we hate the Yankees more, and they will find the South a volcano ready to burst beneath their feet whenever the justice of heaven hurls a thunderbolt at their heads. We are overwhelmed, overpowered, and trodden underfoot. . .but "immortal hate and study of revenge" lives, in the soul of every man. . . .□

[From Eliza Frances Andrews, *The War-Time Journal of a Georgia Girl* (New York: D. Appleton and Company, 1908), pp. 171-73, 212-13, 254.]

Georgia Baker and Alice Green were slaves during the Civil War. In the summer of 1938, they were interviewed in Athens, Georgia, by Sadie Hornsby, a worker in the Federal Writers' Project. Their recollections of the end of the war and freedom follow. (Keep in mind that these interviews were conducted many years after the events under study.)

THINK ABOUT IT

1. How did Baker and Green react to the arrival of Yankees?
2. Did all slaves seem to react the same way to freedom? Why might they have had different reactions?

 Georgia Baker Interview

I remember just as good as if it was yesterday what Mammy Mary said when she told us the first news of our freedom. "You all is free now," she said. "You don't none of you belong to Mister Lordnorth nor Mister Alec [Alexander Stephens] no more, but I does hope you will stay on with them, because they will always be just as good to you as they has done been in the past."

Me, I warn't even studying nothing about leaving Marse Alec, but Sarah Ann and Aunt Mary, they throwed down their hoes and just whooped and hollered because they was so glad.

Whilst Marse Alec was President or something, he got sick and had to come back home, and it warn't long after that before the surrender. Allen was appointed to watch for the blue coats. When they come to take Marse Alec off, they was all over the place with their guns. Us Niggers hollered and cried and took on powerful because us sure thought they was going to kill him on account of his being such a high up man on the side what they was fighting.

Us sure did have the best master in the world. If ever a man went to Heaven, Marse Alec did. I sure does wish good old Marster was living now. □

[*Georgia Narratives,* Vol. IV, Part I (Federal Writers' Project, 1941), pp. 49-57.]

 Alice Green Interview

One day us chillun was playing in the sand pile and looked up and seed a passel of Yankees coming. There was so many of them it was like a flock of bluebirds. Before they left some folks thought they was more like blue devils.

My mammy was in the kitchen and Ole Miss said: "Look out of that window, Milly. The Yankees is coming for sure and they's going to free you and take you and your chillun away from me. Don't leave me! Please don't leave me, Milly."

Them Yankees swarmed into the yard. They opened the smokehouse, chicken yard, corn crib, and everything on the place. They took what they wanted and told us the rest was ours to do what us pleased with. They said us was free and what was on the plantation belonged to us, then they went off and us never seed them no more.

When the war was over Ole Miss cried and cried and begged us not to leave her, but us did. □

[*Georgia Narratives*, Vol. IV, Part 2 (Federal Writers' Project, 1941), p. 45.]

ACTIVITIES FOR CHAPTER 9

Discussion

A. In 1864 Georgia became the scene of some of the fiercest fighting and worst destruction in the Civil War.

　1. Why was Georgia so important to both sides?

　2. What was the Union Army's aim in invading Georgia?

　3. Did the burning of Atlanta and the "March to the Sea" fit that aim? How?

B. The fundamental causes of the Civil War were the issues that divided the United States from the 1820s through the 1850s.

　1. Did the Civil War settle any of those questions? Which ones?

　2. Do you think they would have been settled differently if the Confederate states had won? How?

Writing Project

Not all Georgians favored secession and going to war, but all were affected by the war. How some Georgians viewed events is reflected in the primary sources in this chapter. Their views were influenced by their frame of reference—their backgrounds and their positions.

Assume you were a Georgia civilian during the war. (You might be a cotton planter, a non-slaveholder dairy farmer, a free black laborer, a shipping merchant, a wife and mother, a preacher, a hospital nurse, or someone else.) As Eliza Andrews did, write diary entries for the days you hear news of the following events: Georgia's secession, the fall of Fort Sumter, the beginning of the blockade, the battles of Chickamauga and Gettysburg, the Emancipation Proclamation, Sherman's capture of Atlanta, the end of the war, and Lincoln's assassination.

10 Reconstruction Begins

The time for destruction was over. War-weary Confederate and Union soldiers headed home. The U.S. government gave its men $235 and a free ride home. The Confederates had to trudge home, penniless.

In that spring of 1865, the Georgia soldier returned to ruin and chaos. About 40,000 persons had been killed or were missing. Across the countryside, blackened chimneys—"Sherman's sentinels"—marked the locations of once prosperous plantations. "Sherman's neckties" (rails twisted around trees) and burned depots and bridges were all that remained of the state's railroads. Cotton gins, mills, factories—all lay in ruin.

Farmers and business people faced a bleak future: no stock, no supplies, no equipment, and no money.

In rural areas, bands of ex-slaves or army deserters roamed about taking what little there was from unprotected farms. Thousands of homeless blacks and whites flocked to the cities, seeking rations and shelter. Food shortages brought riots in some cities.

State government had broken down. Federal troops had fanned out across the state arresting Governor Brown and other leaders. Gradually military authority took hold. Under it, city and county governments resumed operation.

Thus, in the spring of 1865, began an era known as Reconstruction.

THINK ABOUT IT

1. What did the war do to the land, labor, and capital (money) on which Georgia's economy was based?
2. What part did northern money play in economic reconstruction?
3. In what ways did the Freedmen's Bureau help people after the war?
4. Why might white Georgians have opposed the work of the Freedmen's Bureau and northern missionary groups?

ECONOMIC RECONSTRUCTION

The Civil War destroyed much of Georgia's agriculture and industry. This destruction forced changes in the social and economic patterns of the people. The old pre-war agricultural economy had been based on three main resources: land, labor, and capital. After the war, the typical planter had plenty of land, but no more slave labor to work it. The freed blacks had their own labor, but no land. Neither had any money. Whites and blacks had to find new ways of working together to make a living.

Land. Many plantation owners sold off some of their land for cash. In this way they raised money to buy the equipment, livestock, seed, fertilizer, *and labor* needed to rebuild.

So much land was available and landowners were so desperate for cash that land sold for a fraction of its pre-war value. It became "dirt cheap." As a result, many more small farms came into being in Georgia. In some cases, blacks as well as poor whites became landowners through aid from the Freedmen's Bureau (see page 116).

Some plantation owners did not have to sell off their lands. But they usually were in need of labor.

Labor. One cause of the labor shortage was the loss of 25 percent of Georgia's white males, killed or disabled in the war. Still others left the state after the war, seeking better luck in Texas, Mexico, and even Brazil.

Of course, the South had lost its vast pool of slave labor. At the war's end, some blacks stayed with their former masters, but thousands left their old plantations. Many needed to find work for pay but didn't know how.

The ex-slaves could now sell their labor—and would have to do so to survive. But few blacks had ever worked for money. They faced new questions: How much is a day's labor worth? How often should a worker be paid?

For white landowners, most of them short of cash, it was often difficult to hire workers. How could blacks, always testing their new freedom, be kept at their jobs? Who was responsible for supplying them with food and housing? How would disputes between employers and employees be settled?

Devising a new "working arrangement" between whites and blacks was not easy. And, because of the shortage of money to pay workers, various arrangements came into use. The black Georgians who wanted to work could either work for wages, rent land, or "sharecrop" with a landowner. (See Chapter 11 for discussion of sharecropping.)

Capital. Usually, "it takes money to make money." For example, to make money growing cotton, a planter needed money (or capital) to buy work animals, plows, seed and fertilizer, and labor.

In 1865, Confederate money became worthless and very few farmers had any U.S. money. The only way to get money (other than by selling off land) was to borrow it. But Georgia's banks had collapsed with the Confederacy; little credit was available. The shortage of capital would make Georgia a poor state for decades.

Rebuilding Begins

Not every aspect of economic life in Georgia was bleak. Even though it would take Georgia a long time to rebuild, some bright spots marked the start of new growth.

For example, in the parts of the state that had escaped war damage—the northeast and the southwest—farm production had resumed. And, in 1865-1866, a worldwide shortage of cotton helped the South revive. Demand for cotton by New England and European textile manufacturers was so great that Georgia farmers who could produce cotton could sell it at a high price. Northern banks, and a few new Georgia banks, began lending money to Georgia cotton producers. Slowly Georgia agriculture improved, but it was tied as ever to cotton.

Other parts of Georgia's economy began to benefit from investments by northern bankers and businessmen. Money from the North helped get the mills going and the trains running again. It helped new companies get started.

Carpetbaggers and Scalawags

Along with northern money came northern opportunists, looking for a way to gain from the South's economic and

Georgia's best-known poet, Sidney Lanier, was born in Macon in 1842. The following poem, written around 1869, is set in Jones County in middle Georgia. In the years following the Civil War, thousands of Georgians pulled up stakes and moved to Texas and other western areas. Lanier speaks about that migration in his poem.

 Thar's More in the Man than Thar Is in the Land

I KNOWED a man, which he lived in Jones,
Which Jones is a county of red hills and stones,
And he lived pretty much by gittin' of loans,
And his mules was nuthin' but skin and bones,
And his hogs was flat as his corn-bread pones,
And he had 'bout a thousand acres o'land.

This man—which his name it was also Jones—
He swore that he'd leave them old red hills and stones,
Fur he couldn't make nuthin' but yallerish cotton,
And little o'*that*, and his fences was rotten,
And what little corn he had, *hit* was boughten
And dinged ef a livin' was in the land.

And the longer he swore the madder he got,
And he riz and he walked to the stable lot,
And he hollered to Tom to come thar and hitch
Fur to emigrate somewhar whar land was rich,
And to quit raisin' cock-burrs, thistles and sich,
And a wastin' ther time on the cussed land.

So him and Tom they hitched up the mules,
Pertestin' that folks was mighty big fools
That 'ud stay in Georgy ther lifetime out,
Jest scratchin' a livin' when all of'em mought
Git places in Texas whar cotton would sprout
By the time you could plant it in the land.

And he driv by a house whar a man named Brown
Was a livin', not fur from the edge o'town,
And he bantered Brown fur to buy his place,
And said that bein' as money was skace,
And bein' as sheriffs was hard to face,
Two dollars an acre would git the land.

They closed at a dollar and fifty cents,
And Jones he bought him a waggin and tents,
And loaded his corn, and his wimmin, and truck,
And moved to Texas, which it tuck
His entire pile, with the best of luck,
To git thar and git him a little land.

But Brown moved out on the old Jones' farm,
And he rolled up his breeches and bared his arm,
And he picked all the rocks from off'n the groun',
And he rooted it up and he plowed it down,
Then he sowed his corn and his wheat in the land.

Five years glid by, and Brown, one day
(Which he'd got so fat that he wouldn't weigh),
Was a settin' down, sorter lazily,
To the bulliest dinner you ever see,
When one o' the children jumped on his knee
And says, "Yan's Jones, which you bought his land."

And thar was Jones, standin' out at the fence,
And he hadn't no waggin, nor mules, nor tents,
Fur he had left Texas afoot and cum
To Georgy to see if he couldn't git sum
Employment, and he was a lookin' as hum-
Ble as ef he had never owned any land.

But Brown he axed him in, and he sot
Him down to his vittles smokin' hot,
And when he had filled hisself and the floor
Brown looked at him sharp and riz and swore
That, "whether men's land was rich or poor
Thar was more in the *man* than thar was in the *land*."

Macon, Georgia, 1869.

[Sidney Lanier, *Poems* (New York: Charles Scribner's Sons, 1901), pp. 180-82.]

Back at Work, 1865. As soon as the fighting ended, Georgians began rebuilding. In Atlanta, tracks were relaid amid the ruins of this locomotive roundhouse to get the trains running again.

political turmoil. Some gained control of businesses or bought land cheaply to sell later at a profit. Others used their money and influence with federal authorities to gain high positions in Reconstruction governments.

Because these persons often carried traveling bags made of carpet material, they were dubbed "carpetbaggers" by white southerners. The carpetbaggers were likened to vultures preying on southerners' misfortune.

Likewise, white southerners who worked with the carpetbaggers received their own nickname—"scalawags." The scalawags were despised by most of their white neighbors.

Help for the People

In March 1865, the United States government set up the Bureau of Refugees, Freedmen, and Abandoned Lands. Popularly known as the "Freedmen's Bureau,"

this federal agency issued food, clothing, fuel, and other supplies to needy white refugees and black freedmen.

At first the Freedmen's Bureau helped thousands of poor whites. Soon, however, it became an agency mainly to help blacks function as free persons. Under slavery, blacks had been denied any education, given few responsibilities, and prevented from making decisions for themselves. Suddenly they were free and responsible for their own lives.

Many blacks were unsure about going back to work on plantations, fearing that white landowners would treat them badly. To overcome these fears, the bureau helped blacks and white landowners draw up labor contracts. Written contracts were designed to guarantee the workers a fair wage and job security and the employers a stable work force.

Because most blacks could neither read nor write, education was a primary concern of the Freedmen's Bureau. The bureau set up schools and assisted charity groups in doing the same. It also helped blacks set up their own churches.

Finally, the Freedmen's Bureau tried to act for blacks in legal matters and encouraged them to take part in politics.

Help for blacks also came from northern missionary and charitable groups, sponsored mainly by the Congregationalist, Methodist, and Baptist churches. Between 1865 and 1873, these groups sent 367 teachers—80 percent of them women—to Georgia. These teachers set up schools across the state and taught both children and adults to read and write. They also stressed the virtues of hard work and good citizenship.

Such groups helped start the first colleges for black students in Georgia. In 1867, Atlanta University, sponsored by the American Missionary Association, was established. In Augusta, the American Baptist Home Missionary Society founded Morehouse College (later moved to Atlanta). The northern Methodist Episcopal Church founded Clark College.

Negative Reactions

White Georgians did not always appreciate the activities of the Freedmen's Bureau and northern missionary groups. At the time, many whites were suffering the same poverty as blacks and receiving little help. Also, Congress had imposed heavy taxes, making it difficult for owners of small farms as well as large plantations to rebuild their lives.

To many white southerners, the "Yankee schoolmarms" seemed set on raising blacks to a position of social equality with whites. Often, agents of the Freedmen's Bureau seemed to care more about helping the Republican party in state politics than about helping people in need. In fact, the bureau did become involved in "political reconstruction."

POLITICAL RECONSTRUCTION

THINK ABOUT IT

1. What was Lincoln's attitude toward the defeated South? What view did the radical republicans hold?
2. What actions of post-war white-run governments angered the radicals?
3. What were the aims of the 13th, 14th, and 15th amendments?
4. How did blacks get to be involved in Georgia government?

A Freedmen's School. This picture, from Harper's Weekly, *June 23, 1866, shows adults as well as children learning to read and write. Why would this be the case?*

In late 1863, President Lincoln began planning for reuniting the nation once the fighting was over. Lincoln saw reconstruction as a healing, not a punishing, process. He expressed this view in March 1865, in his second inaugural address.

With malice toward none, with charity for all, with firmness in the right as God gives us to see the right, let us strive to finish the work we are in, to bind up the nation's wounds....

Lincoln had a plan for reconstructing the South. He wanted southerners (except Confederate government and military leaders) to be pardoned and given back their full citizenship rights. They would simply have to take an oath of allegiance to the United States. When 10 percent of the voters of a former Confederate state had taken the oath, the president would recognize as legal the state government they set up.

On April 15, 1865—only six days after the war ended—Abraham Lincoln was dead, victim of an assassin's bullet. His vice-president, Andrew Johnson, had been the only southern U.S. senator not to resign his seat in 1861. He assumed the presidency determined to carry out Lincoln's plan.

Under this plan, white Georgians took the oath, wrote a new state constitution (which included abolition of slavery), and held elections. Then they began operating state government much as they had before the war.

In December 1865, the Georgia General Assembly ratified the 13th Amendment to the U.S. Constitution (see box, page 123) and adopted state laws recognizing the rights of free blacks. However, these laws—usually called "Black Codes"—prohibited blacks from testifying in court against whites, from serving on juries in cases involving whites, and from marrying whites.

Certain that Georgia was being restored to the Union, the General Assembly chose the state's two U.S. senators—Alexander Stephens and Herschel Johnson.

CONGRESSIONAL RECONSTRUCTION

While the General Assembly was meeting in Milledgeville, the U.S. Congress was meeting in Washington, D.C. Some of its

Gen. John B. Gordon. Georgia's best known soldier, took the oath of allegiance to the United States in September 1865. Why was this probably important to Gordon? His post-war political career is taken up later in this chapter.

United States of America.

GEORGIA,
FULTON COUNTY.

I do solemnly swear, or affirm, in the presence of Almighty God, that I will henceforth faithfully support, protect, and defend the Constitution of the United States and the union of the States thereunder, and that I will, in like manner, abide by and faithfully support all laws and proclamations which have been made during the existing rebellion with reference to the emancipation of slaves—SO HELP ME GOD.

Sworn to and subscribed before me at ....
this 75th day of .... 1865.

I DO CERTIFY that the foregoing is a true copy of the original oath administered by me to the foregoing deponent, the date and day above written.

Atlanta Intelligencer Print.

Republican members—called the "radical republicans"—had strongly opposed Lincoln's plan for Reconstruction. They wanted the South treated as a conquered nation. The radicals distrusted Andrew Johnson, a former Democrat from Tennessee. Moreover, Johnson had gone beyond the original plan and had given pardons to many former Confederate officials.

Radicals in Congress were angry when they learned that the new southern state governments were being run just by whites, mostly ex-Confederates. Also, the southern states had passed "Black Codes" limiting the freedom of the former slaves. To the radical republicans, this was defiance.

Congress refused to approve the new governments or seat their representatives in Congress. President Johnson lacked Lincoln's political skill and gradually lost control of Reconstruction to Congress.

In 1866, in reaction to the "Black Codes," Congress passed the 14th Amendment. It made clear that blacks were citizens of the U.S. and of the state in which they lived. Also, it guaranteed all citizens *equal protection of the law.* That is, it made the federal government the protector of all citizens' rights, regardless of the state in which they lived.

This amendment did not expressly give blacks the right to vote. It did provide, however, that if a state denied any portion of its citizens their rights, it would lose its representation in Congress. Georgia and the other former Confederate states, except Tennessee, refused to ratify the 14th Amendment.

In the elections of 1866, the radicals gained complete control of Congress. Early in 1867, they passed an act that divided the 10 states refusing to ratify the 14th Amendment into five military districts. (Georgia was placed in the Third Military District along with Florida and Alabama.) A U.S. Army general, backed by troops, was put in charge of each district. Once again, Georgia was under military occupation.

Under this new setup, the first task was to register voters. All adult males—black as well as white—who took the oath of allegiance to the United States could register. Certain classes of ex-Confederates were denied this right.

In each state, the new voters were to elect delegates to write new state constitutions (which had to be approved by Congress). When new legislatures were elected, they had to ratify the 14th Amendment. Only after the southern states had done these things would they be freed of military occupation and readmitted to the Union.

Many white Georgians resented this plan. About 10,000 were not allowed to register, but many more than that number boycotted the 1867-68 elections.

Alexander Stephens and His Servant, Aleck Kent Stephens. The former Confederate vice-president, although in poor health and often confined to a wheelchair, worked hard to get Georgia back in the Union. In this 1882 photo, he is on his way to be sworn in as governor of Georgia.

The First Vote. This event was carried on the front page of the news magazine, Harper's Weekly, *November 16, 1867. Freedmen go to the ballot box supervised by federal officials.*

BLACKS IN GEORGIA POLITICS

In the 1867 election for constitutional convention delegates and in the 1868 election for state and federal offices, blacks voted for the first time.

Of 169 convention delegates elected, 37 were black. When the black delegates were denied rooms in Milledgeville hotels, the Third District military commander had the convention moved to Atlanta. (This led to Atlanta becoming the state capital.)

The Constitution of 1868 gave more rights to more citizens than previous Georgia constitutions. Black males gained full civil rights, including the vote. All married women were guaranteed control of their own property. Imprisonment for debt was abolished. And, for the first time, Georgia was to have a free public school system for *all* children. (Public schools opened in 1871.)

In April 1868, following adoption of the constitution, 32 black Republicans were elected to the Georgia General Assembly. Of 172 representatives, 29 were blacks; of 44 senators, 3 were blacks. In the same election, a white Republican, Rufus Bullock, defeated a popular hero, ex-Confederate Gen. John B. Gordon, to become governor.

The participation by blacks (many of them former slaves, but some formerly free blacks from other states) in politics was not easily accepted by most whites. While the newly elected legislature ratified the 14th Amendment, many of its white members looked for ways to remove the black members. Over the protests of the black members, the white majority, in September 1868, voted to expel 28 blacks. (The light-skinned members retained their seats.) The argument for doing this was that the right to vote didn't necessarily mean the right to hold public office.

The summer and fall of 1868 also witnessed the rise of the Ku Klux Klan (KKK) in Georgia. Did the Klan's activities affect black voters? Some clues to the answer appear below in selected county results for two elections held in 1868.

THINK ABOUT IT

1. In which counties did the Republican vote decline between April and November 1868? In which counties did the total vote decline?
2. In which counties is it likely that blacks switched from Republican to Democratic voting?

The activities of the KKK and other such organizations alarmed the radical republicans in Congress. Therefore, in 1868-69 and again in 1871, Congress set up committees to investigate the activities of secret organizations.

The following primary sources are from government documents. They contain testimony of two persons, John B. Gordon and Alfred Richardson, called to appear before a congressional committee in Washington, D.C.

John B. Gordon was Georgia's out-

ELECTION RESULTS, 1868

County	Percent Black Population 1860	Registration to Vote 1867		Vote for Governor* April 1868		Vote for U.S. President** November 1868	
		White	Black	Dem.	Rep.	Dem.	Rep.
Clarke	50%	995	1,156	836	1,068	1,197	1,186
Oglethorpe	over 60%	830	1,158	557	1,144	849	116
Morgan	over 60%	630	1,229	455	1,202	635	1,046
Greene	over 60%	1,002	1,528	808	1,632	1,001	1,200
Taliaferro	over 60%	392	558	346	627	519	187
Warren	over 60%	751	1,219	544	1,124	881	188
Columbia	over 60%	669	1,859	457	1,222	1,120	1

*John B. Gordon (D) vs. Rufus Bullock (R)
**Horatio Seymour (D) vs. Ulysses S. Grant (R).

standing Confederate commander. General Gordon led troops in some of the most important battles of the war, including the final battle under General Lee, at Appomattox, Virginia. Defeated for the governorship in 1868, Gordon later served one term as governor and two terms as U.S. senator. Reputed to be the leader of the Georgia KKK, he was called to testify in 1871.

Alfred Richardson was among the blacks elected to, and later expelled from, the General Assembly in 1868. A representative from Clarke County, Richardson spoke out for black rights. Twice the Klan attacked his house. After being beaten and shot in the second attack, during which he killed one of the attackers, his own death was widely reported. But evidently Richardson didn't die. He was reelected to the General Assembly in 1870 and testified before a congressional committee in 1871.

THINK ABOUT IT

1. What seemed to be the main purpose of the Ku Klux Klan in 1868?
2. Do the testimonies of Gordon and Richardson support each other in any way? How do they differ in their description of the KKK?

 Testimony of Alfred Richardson

Question. . . . Are there many cases like yours, in which you think the attack was for political reasons?

Answer. . . . Every man they whipped they asked him how he voted. Sometimes the men would say they did not vote at all; they were afraid to tell the party they did vote for. Sometimes they would say they voted for the Republican party, and then the men would say, "If you ever do it again, we will kill you."

Q. The advice these disguised men give is to vote the Democratic ticket?

A. Yes sir; they say, "If you vote any other sort of ticket besides the Democratic ticket, we will kill you when we come again." They say they have just come from the grave; that they were killed at Manassas, and are just out of the grave. . . .

Q. Does what these disguised bands say to these people about voting have any effect upon the colored people?

A. Yes, sir. Several of them say that excepting they can get protection against these disguised men going about, they do not intend to vote any more. . . .

This engraving, titled "Two members of the Ku-Klux Klan in their disguises," appeared in Harper's Weekly, December 19, 1868.

Q. Do these bands ever whip women?

A. Yes, sir.

Q. Why do they whip women? They do not vote.

A. Many times, you know, a white lady has a colored lady for cook or waiting in the house. . . . They have some quarrel, and sometimes probably the colored women gives the lady a little jaw. In a night or two a crowd will come in and take her out and whip her.

Q. For talking saucily to her mistress?

A. Yes, sir.

Q. Does that state of things control colored labor down there? Do these bands make the negroes work for whomever they please?

A. Do you mean the Ku-Klux?

Q. Yes, sir.

A. Well, they go sometimes as far as this: When a man is hired, if he and his employer have any dispute about the price, and there are hard words between them about the amount of money to be paid, they whip the colored man for disputing the white man's word, or having any words with him.

 Testimony of John B. Gordon

Q. What do you know of any combinations in Georgia, known as Ku-Klux, or by any other name, who have been violating the law?

A. I do not know anything about any Ku-Klux organization, as the papers talk about it. . . . [B]ut I do know that an organization did exist in Georgia at one time. I know that in 1868—I think that was the time—I was approached and asked to attach myself to a secret organization in Georgia . . . .

Q. Tell us about what that organization was.

A. The organization was simply this—nothing more and nothing less: it was an organization, a brotherhood of the property-holders, the peaceable, law-abiding citizens of the State, for self-protection. The instinct of self-protection prompted that organization; the sense of insecurity and danger, particularly in those neighborhoods where the negro population largely predominated.

The reasons which led to this organization were three or four. The first and main reason was the organization of the Union League, as they called it, about which we knew nothing more than this: that the negroes would desert the plantations, and go off at night in large numbers; and on being asked where they had been, would reply, sometimes, "We have been to the muster;" sometimes, "We have been to the lodge;" sometimes, "We have been to the meeting." These things were observed for a great length of time. We knew that the "carpetbaggers" . . . were organizing the colored people. We knew that beyond all question. . . .

There was this general organization of the black race on the one hand, and an entire disorganization of the white race on the other hand. We were afraid to have a public organization; because we supposed it would be construed at once, by the authorities at Washington, as an organization antagonistic to the Government of the United States. It was therefore necessary, in order to protect our families from outrage and preserve our own lives, to have something that we could regard as a brotherhood—a combination of the best men of the country, to act purely in self-defense, to repel the attack in case we should be attacked by these people. That was the whole object of this organization. I never heard of any disguises connected with it; we had none, very certainly. □

[Testimony taken by the Joint Select Committee to inquire into the Condition of Affairs in the Late Insurrectionary States, Georgia (Washington, D.C.: 1872).]

THE END OF RECONSTRUCTION

In 1869, Congress again put Georgia under a military commander, who ordered the General Assembly to reseat the expelled black legislators.

To be admitted back into the Union, said Congress, Georgia must ratify another amendment to the Constitution—the 15th. The General Assembly did so. Federal troops once more withdrew from Georgia.

In 1871, Georgia's U.S. senators and representatives were sworn in at Washington, D.C. Included was Rep. Jefferson Long of Macon, a black man. After 10 years, Georgia was back in the Union.

Once federal troops withdrew from Georgia, the administration of Republican Gov. Rufus Bullock was doomed. During his term in office, he and his aides had recklessly spent public funds. Newspaper columns charged that Bullock's friends were filling their pockets with much of this money.

As proof of corruption mounted, Georgians elected a solidly Democratic legislature that began looking into the financial dealings of the "carpetbagger" government. Facing impeachment (removal from office), Governor Bullock resigned. In a special election to fill the governor's office, Democrat James M. Smith was elected.

Meanwhile, in Washington, D.C., the radical Republicans were losing their strength and their enthusiasm for either punishing the South or helping the southern blacks. In 1872, Congress passed an amnesty act, making all but 500 former

---

The 13th, 14th, and 15th Amendments

Amendment 13: Passed by Congress February 1, 1865. Ratified December 18, 1865.
  "Neither slavery nor involuntary servitude . . . shall exist within the United States, or any place subject to their jurisdiction."

Amendment 14: Passed by Congress June 16, 1866. Ratified July 28, 1868.
  "No State shall make or enforce any law which shall abridge [limit] the privileges or immunities [or rights] of citizens of the United States; nor shall any State deprive any person of life, liberty, or property, without due process of law; nor deny to any person within its jurisdiction the equal protection of the laws."

Amendment 15: Passed by Congress February 27, 1869. Ratified March 30, 1870.
  "The right of citizens of the United States to vote shall not be denied or abridged by the United States or by any State on account of race, color, or previous condition of servitude."

Confederates eligible to hold office. The Freedmen's Bureau was abolished the same year.

In 1872, Governor Smith was easily reelected. Only four blacks were elected to the General Assembly. With the state firmly controlled by white Democrats, the *Atlanta Constitution* noted the passing of "the long night of Radical rule."

That rule is ended. The darkness is succeeded by light. Thank God Georgia is redeemed.

ACTIVITIES FOR CHAPTER 10

Discussion

A. The Civil War not only made Georgia's black people free, but also it left them on their own.

  1. What special problems did black people face after the war?
  2. What kinds of help did they get?

B. Reconstruction caused much controversy among the people who lived through it. It later caused controversy among historians who studied it. Some thought it was fair, others thought it was unfair.

  1. What were the main differences between Lincoln's reconstruction plan and congressional (or radical) reconstruction?
  2. What parts of radical reconstruction do you think were good or helpful?
  3. What parts do you think were bad or harmful? Explain your conclusions.

Writing Projects

Reread the poem by Sidney Lanier. What message was Lanier trying to get across? We don't know if the poem influenced any people to stay on as farmers in middle Georgia, but it could have.

To get Lanier's message across to more people, use some other medium (form of communication). Possibilities are posters, cartoons, song lyrics, sermons, speeches, letters to the editor, slogans, or even another poem. In any case, be sure to point up the difference between a Jones and a Brown. Or, present proof that there is more in the man than there is in the land.

UNIT V
1870 - 1920: Fifty Years of Struggle

11. **Economic Life of the People**
12. **Change at the Turn of the Century**

GEORGIA EVENTS	DATE	EVENTS ELSEWHERE
Public school system begins operation	1871	
Department of Agriculture created	1874	Woman's Christian Temperance Union formed
Henry Grady joins *Atlanta Constitution*	1876	Alexander G. Bell invents telephone; Custer defeated at Little Big Horn
Constitution of 1877 adopted	1877	Thomas A. Edison invents phonograph
Atlanta's first cotton exposition held	1881	Booker T. Washington founds Tuskegee Institute
Georgia Tech started	1885	Benz develops gasoline engine for cars
Coca-Cola developed	1886	American Federation of Labor organized
New capitol building opened	1889	Oklahoma Territory opened to whites
General Assembly passes first "Jim Crow" laws	1891	Populist Party formed
Booker T. Washington speaks at Cotton States Exposition	1895	Roentgen discovers X-ray
	1896	Supreme Court upholds "separate but equal"
	1898	Spanish-American War; U.S. annexes Hawaii
	1903	Wright brothers' first successful flight
Blacks lose the vote	1906	Congress passes Pure Food and Drug Act
Statewide prohibition passed	1907	
	1909	National Association for the Advancement of Colored People (NAACP) founded
Girl Scouts organized	1912	Titanic sinks
Child labor law passed	1914	World War I begins in Europe
Compulsory school attendance law passed	1916	Albert Einstein presents Theory of Relativity
	1917	U.S. enters World War I; Revolution in Russia
Peak of cotton production	1918	World War I ends
	1919	18th Amendment (Prohibition) adopted
	1920	19th Amendment gives women right to vote

11 Economic Life of the People

In the late 1800s and early 1900s most Georgians had to struggle just to make a living. From their efforts new forms of economic life emerged in the state. These people—the farmers, the factory workers, the storeowners—are the main focus of this chapter.

Their story begins in 1867, as told by Celestine Sibley, a writer for the *Atlanta Constitution.*

 Morris Rich and the New Atlanta

Morris Rich was born in the ancient and strife-ridden city of Kashau, Hungary, in 1847, the same year a little frontier town across the sea changed its name from Marthasville to Atlanta. When he was 12 years old, Morris joined the heavy migration of Europeans to the New World.

In America, Morris and his brothers held a variety of jobs. In 1865, he gave up his job in a Chattanooga store and turned to peddling, with the entire state of Georgia as his territory. For a year and a half Morris traveled through the Georgia countryside, taking to their doors goods the like of which war-starved citizens hadn't seen since long before Sherman's march to the sea.

When he stopped in Atlanta something

about the little war-scarred, determinedly rebuilding town must have appealed to Morris. For, in 1867, he decided to stay.

He borrowed $500 from his brother William and rented a rough little building down by the railroad tracks. It had a number, 36 Whitehall Street.

Little more than two years had passed since the Battle of Atlanta, when the most utter desolation ever visited on an American city by war had leveled the little town. But, all around him that spring of 1867 Morris saw Atlanta's energy at work.

The population had already surpassed that of pre-war Atlanta, reaching a total of 20,288 persons, of whom, sadly enough, 928 were the widows and orphans of Confederate soldiers. The city limits had been extended to enclose a circle three miles in diameter. The city treasury, down to $1.64 at the end of the war, was burgeoning with $29,000, and the city directory estimated the number of stores on business streets at 250—"mostly brick buildings."

Morris's little store was not brick but a crude 20- by 75-foot structure thrown together from rough-hewn pine boards. There were plenty of others like it, hastily built stores and houses and "calico" fences woven from odds and ends to keep wandering livestock out of gardens that were now needed more than ever.

Once when he was an old man Morris recalled for an interviewer that the day he opened his store it had been raining and Whitehall Street was a mire. He went out and laid boards over the red clay mud to protect the footwear of the customers he hoped would come.

That was May 28, 1867.

And the customers did come. Young Morris and a cousin, who had come to work for him, put in long hours in the store. Their strong sellers were 50-cent corsets and 25-cent stockings, for the women of Atlanta had little money for finery in those days. Even those who had been accustomed to nice things were now lucky to get the practical necessities.

Morris accommodated himself to the times, selling for money when he could get it and cheerfully taking chickens and eggs and corn in exchange for drygoods when barter was necessary.

Many a night the gas street lights, newly restored to the city, would be burning when Morris left the store and walked toward William's house, gingerly bearing a basket of eggs or a mess of turnip sallet from the day's receipts.

There were several drygoods stores bigger and finer than Morris's little beginning. Merchants who had operated in Atlanta before the war were back and operating again. Up Whitehall Street there were hardware stores, gun shops, and other businesses. Several banks had also been founded.

Hotels were going up, and many houses were emerging from rubble and mud. Fire protection was restored and the *Daily Intelligencer* reported that horses, instead of men, had been obtained to pull the fire steamer for Mechanic Fire Company No. 2.

In spite of the little city's preoccupation with building, there was trouble. Crime was a problem. Bands of rowdies roamed the streets. Robbery and murder happened frequently.

Morris, although young, set the course which his family and his enterprise were to follow for a hundred years. He chose to be a part of Atlanta and to share what he had—and he expressed it in his merchant's way by extending credit to those who needed it, probably worse in 1867 than they ever would again. It wasn't easy because he had little capital to work with, but he accepted the time-honored custom of letting country people settle up their bills once a year—"when the cotton comes in"—and he went on from there.

When Morris Rich had been in Atlanta 10 years the railroads had recovered from the ministrations of Sherman's men. By 1877, old roads had been mended and new ones were advancing in all directions. Atlanta was booming as a marketing and distribution center, a natural crossroads between the grain- and stock-raising regions of the north and the cotton-, tobacco-, and rice-raising regions to the south.

Rich's Store. Store employees lined up for this photo taken in the 1880s. How does the street compare to streets shown in the photo on page 116?

Morris Rich, now 30 years old, had prospered. He had already expanded sufficiently to move twice—to 43 Whitehall Street and then to 65 Whitehall at the corner of Hunter. Each move brought a bigger store and a bigger stock and was heralded by a lively volley of advertising. . . .

Best of all, Morris's South Georgia brothers, Emanuel and Daniel, had disposed of their store in Albany, brought their stock to Atlanta to pool it with his, and were coming into the store with him. Both started as clerks and in February 1877 Morris took an ad in the *Constitution* to announce a new partnership.

The little store was no longer "M. Rich" but "M. Rich & Bro." . . . .

Within two years all three bachelors had married.

For years the three Rich brothers walked home together for midday dinner and a nap or rode *The Dummy,* a steam engine-drawn streetcar, which ran down Pryor Street.

While the brothers were establishing homes and families, things were flourishing down on Whitehall Street. In the Sunday *Constitution* of July 2, 1882, they offered for rent "one of the best stores in the city"—the one they occupied at 65 Whitehall.

"They only move," said the advertisement, "because they want more room, which they will get in their new store, 54 and 56 Whitehall Street."

The new store opened the following September, after a series of removal sales at the old building. The *Constitution* saluted the new store as "a bazaar of fashion. . . emporium of fashion and design."

That story shows how Atlantans had in a brief 15 years progressed from the grim situation of the postwar days and how Morris and his brothers had earned the affection and respect of the town. . . . □
[Adapted from Celestine Sibley, *Dear Store, An Affectionate Portrait of Rich's.* Copyright ©1967. Reprinted by permission of Doubleday & Company, Inc.]

INDUSTRIALIZING GEORGIA

Morris Rich was but one of thousands of Georgians, natives and newcomers alike, who were willing to invest, to take a risk, in building a "new South." The idea of a new South—its future prosperity based on manufacturing and other industry, not just agriculture—appealed to many Georgia leaders.

The best known of these leaders—sometimes called the "bourbon redeemers"*—were ex-Confederate officers John B. Gordon and Alfred E. Colquitt, and ex-Governor Joseph E. Brown. From the governor's office in Atlanta and in the U.S. Senate in Washington, they worked to bring industry to Georgia. Their main problem was to get the investment capital, that is the money, to flow from North to South. In this effort, they were assisted by a young man from Athens, Georgia—Henry Grady.

In the 1870s and 1880s, Henry Grady became the best known spokesman for the new South. From New England to Texas, he made speeches urging businessmen to invest their money in southern manufacturing. From his desk at the *Atlanta Constitution*, he fired off articles painting a bright future of an industrialized South. Here is an example of Grady's writing.

THINK ABOUT IT
1. What was Grady's aim in his speech?
2. What was the second paragraph's message?

 The New South

A few years ago I told, in a speech, of a burial in Pickens County, Georgia. The grave was dug through solid marble, but the marble headstone came from Vermont. It was in a pine wilderness, but the pine

---

*The name "bourbon" referred to the old ruling family of France that returned to power after the French Revolution. "Redeemer" referred to remaking Georgia after the years of Reconstruction.

coffin came from Cincinnati. An iron mountain overshadowed it, but the coffin nails and screws and the shovels came from Pittsburgh. With hard woods and metals abounding, the corpse was hauled on a wagon from South Bend, Indiana. A hickory grove grew near by, but the pick and shovel handles came from New York. The cotton shirt on the dead man came from Cincinnati, the coat and breeches from Chicago, the shoes from Boston; the folded hands were encased in white gloves from New York, and round the poor neck, that had worn all its living days the bondage of lost opportunity, was twisted a cheap cravat from Philadelphia. That county, so rich in undeveloped resources, furnished nothing for the funeral except the corpse and the hole in the ground, and would probably have imported both of those if it could have done so. And as the poor fellow was lowered to his rest, on coffin bands from Lowell [Massachusetts], he carried nothing into the next world as a reminder of his home in this, save the halted blood in his veins, the chilled marrow in his bones, and the echo of the dull clods that fell on his coffin lid.

There are now more than $3,000,000 invested in marble quarries and machinery around that grave. Its pitiful loneliness is broken with the rumble of ponderous machines, and a strange tumult pervades the wilderness. Twenty miles away, the largest marble-cutting works in the world put to shame in a thousand shapes its modest headstone. Forty miles away four coffin factories, with their exquisite work, tempt the world to die. The iron hills are gashed and swarm with workmen. Forty cotton mills in a near radius weave infinite cloth that neighboring shops make into countless shirts. There are shoe factories, nail factories, shovel and pick factories, and carriage factories, to supply the other wants. And that county can now get up as nice a funeral, native and home-made, as you would wish to have. ☐

[Henry W. Grady, *The New South* (New York: Robert Bonner's Sons, 1890),pp. 188-91.]

Henry Grady didn't live to see his vision of a new South come true. This brilliant speaker and writer died suddenly from pneumonia at the age of 38. By the time of his death in 1889, however, Henry Grady's message had caught on.

RISE IN MANUFACTURING

THINK ABOUT IT

1. During what period did employment in manufacturing and value of goods manufactured in Georgia begin to rise sharply?
2. What was the purpose of holding "expositions" in the 1880s and 1890s?
3. How would an investment such as Captain Tift's eventually help many people?

The rise of manufacturing in Georgia between 1870 and 1910 was dramatic. In 1870 only about $14 million was invested in manufacturing establishments. By 1890, that figure had risen to almost $57 million, and by 1910 it would exceed $202 million. The graphs that follow tell more about the growth of industry. The rise in number of employees is shown in Figure 3. The increased value of manufactured goods is shown in Figure 4.

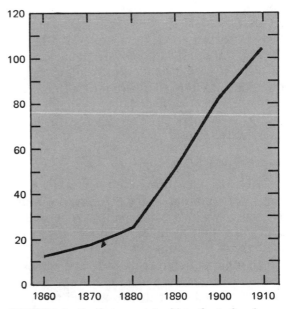

FIGURE 3. Employment in Manufacturing in Georgia, 1860-1910 (in thousands)

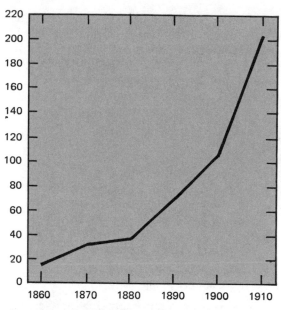

FIGURE 4. Value of Manufactured Goods in Georgia, 1860-1910 (in millions of dollars)

The Cotton States and International Exposition, 1895. How were people dressed for their visit to the exposition's midway?

Textile Manufacturing

Cotton mills had existed in Georgia since 1829. Before the Civil War they were small mills, located mainly along the fall line where water power was plentiful. In those days, Georgians had to buy almost all their manufactured goods, including cotton cloth, from outside the state.

But Georgia had the potential to manufacture cotton goods on a large scale. Many Georgia business and government leaders thought it would be a way to industrialize the state. After all, Georgia had lots of cotton. It had enough labor available. All that was needed was heavy investment in large textile plants.

Boosting the State

In 1881, Atlanta staged a World's Fair and Great International Cotton Exposition. The idea was to bring people to Georgia and show them why they should invest in industry in the state.

In one popular feature at the exposition, cotton growing in a field in the morning was picked, ginned, woven, and tailored into a suit all in one day. Governor Colquitt donned the cotton suit and then

made a speech and toured the fairgrounds in it.

The 1881 fair was such a success that Atlanta held another, the Piedmont Exposition, in 1887. The president of the United States, Grover Cleveland, attended. The fairgrounds later became Piedmont Park.

Then, in 1895, the city put on its biggest show, the Cotton States and International Exposition. On display were the resources and achievements of Georgia and the other cotton-producing states. Booker T. Washington, a black educator, spoke on the role of black people in the South's economic life as he saw it.

By 1900, Georgia had become an important state in textile manufacturing.

Other Industry

Georgians and investors from other states put their money into many kinds of industries. Iron, coal, gold, and clay were mined. Granite and marble quarries were developed. New factories and mills, steam-powered as well as water-powered, turned out a variety of products, such as cotton-seed oil, fertilizer, construction materials, and furniture. Wherever the resources and the railroads were available, manufacturing plants might spring up.

In time, new towns grew up around the mills and factories.

Tifton: From Sawmill to City

Forest products became an important part of Georgia's new economy. Georgia's forests, especially the pines on the Coastal Plain, had been a valuable resource since early colonial days. In the late 1800s, all over the South, newcomers invested money and energy in the pinewood industry. New industries and new towns grew up around this resource. Tifton was one of these towns.

In 1872, a Connecticut Yankee named Henry Harding Tift arrived in Berrien County. There, on the Brunswick and Albany Railroad, he built a sawmill. Captain Tift, formerly a steamship engineer, had paid $10,000 for 4,900 acres of piney woods and wiregrass.

At first, Tift cut timber and sawed logs into lumber to be hauled away on the railroad. Soon he began producing naval stores—turpentine, pitch, and resin.

As Tift employed more workers, he built houses for their families. Then he built a commissary (a general store owned by an employer) where workers could buy food, clothing, and other supplies. The village that grew up there—Tifton—attracted other businesses, including saloons. Rough, hard-working men had money to spend.

On land cleared of timber, the captain, as he was known to all the people, experimented with growing cotton, tobacco, peaches, and grapes. A cotton mill was started. Later, pecans and livestock were added to Captain Tift's interests.

By the early 1900s, Tifton became a commercial center for southwest Georgia. Railroads extended in several directions. Farmers drove in from miles around to sell their cotton and other products and to buy supplies.

The saloons and the rough and tumble life gradually gave way to a more civilized society. With financial support from the captain, schools, churches, and a hospital were raised. Tift gave the state of Georgia hundreds of acres to build an agricultural college and an experiment station for con-

Rabun County Sawmill. Around 1900, lumbering was important in north Georgia as well as south Georgia. What kind of power did these men have to help them in their work?

ducting research to improve farming methods.

Tifton was but one of dozens of Georgia cities that developed around an industry. Some began as "railroad towns"; they were simply stopping places on the line.

SOCIAL CHANGE

As more industry came to Georgia, the lives of many of its people changed. For some people, industrialization meant more income and better lives. The whole state benefited from increased tax money. Government could provide better schools, roads, and other services.

But not everyone was thriving. Some people began to criticize the treatment of workers in the factories and mill villages of the state. Newspapers and magazines carried articles describing the "evils" of industrialization.

Following are two primary sources describing the lives of persons working in Georgia cotton mills.

Life in the Mill Village

Clare De Graffenried was born in 1849 in Macon, Georgia. Upon her graduation from Wesleyan College in 1865, she made a graduation speech attacking the federal troops camped nearby and nearly got the college closed down.

After teaching school for many years, she went to work as a special investigator for the U.S. Department of Labor. Her job was to look into the working and housing conditions of women and children employed in mills and factories.

The following reading is from an 1891 article she wrote for *Century Magazine*, one of the country's most popular magazines.

THINK ABOUT IT

1. For many "cracker" families, industrialization meant switching from farm work to mill work. What kinds of family problems came along with this switch?
2. What contributed to the bad health of mill workers?

Docks at Brunswick, 1890. How were the naval stores shown in the photo probably brought to the ships for loading? How important was barrel manufacturing in 1890?

3. According to De Graffenried, what did the mill owners do to help their workers?

 The Georgia Cracker in the Cotton Mills

The name coined to specify the native folk that spin or weave in the villages and towns is—"Crackers." The term embraces hundreds of thousands of non-slaveholding whites in antebellum days and their present descendants.

No colored people are employed in textile industries. Their labor market is limited to the cotton fields and farms of the country. . . .

The operatives [mill workers] live to some extent in houses belonging to the corporations. Only a small proportion own their own homes. . . .

Around country mills the provision for housing the wage-earners is often inadequate. It is at serious risk to life and health that the operatives in remote settlements are forced to lodge in rotting, neglected habitations, even though they be rent free.

The choicest of these rickety abodes was described by a girl whose only home it had been for fourteen years: "I reckin hit 'll set up thar a right smart while yit, but hit 's pow'ful cold en leaky. . . ."

. . . Not a clock or watch is owned in the settlement. Life is regulated by the sun and the factory bell, which rings for rising, breakfast, and work. The hours of labor vary from seventy to seventy-two a week.

The workers were "borned in the country," and seldom visit even the neighboring town. In complete isolation and ignorance their lives run out. Now and then a traveling minister enlivens the little church on the hilltop. At intervals a Sunday-school furnishes the only religious instruction. There is no regular school.

All purchases are made on the order system at the "company's store." Though it is not compulsory to deal there, there is no competition. The wages of each member of the household are put together. Women often work a lifetime without touching a cent of their pay. One forlorn old maid lamented: "I hain't seed er dollar sence Confed money gave out. Hit 'u'd be good fur sore eyes ter see er genewine dollar...."

The hardships everywhere disastrous to textile workers fail to account for the wrecked health of so many of the Southern workers. Malaria, lurking about the stream, invades the houses close to the bank. Drainage is neglected and epidemics are common.

The use of snuff is a withering curse. Habitual users smoke and chew tobacco, and dip snuff and "lip" the powder. The weed is applied with a softened twig dipped into the snuff and rubbed on the teeth. All down the alleys of the factories are women and little girls with the inevitable stick in their mouths. Excessive use of this stimulant often creates the desire for a stronger one, and among the older women drunkenness is not uncommon.

The weakness and sickness of the operatives also stems from the early age at which work in the mills is begun. When five or six years old the juveniles follow the mothers to the mills, where they are incarcerated till premature old age. Unmarried women of thirty are wrinkled, bent, and haggard. Mothers seem to carry the weight of a century on their bowed backs.

Take a little maid whose face is buried in her sunbonnet, and who, when asked her age, responds, "I'm er-gwine on ten." Push back her bonnet, hoping to find a face of vigor and joy. A sad spectacle reveals itself. Out of unkempt hair look glassy eyes ringed with black circles reaching far down her yellow cheeks. Her nose is pinched, the yellow lips furrowed with snuff stains. The skin is cadaverous.

"When do you go to school, my child?"
"Hain't never been thar," she responds.
"Never at school! Can't you read?"
"No, 'm; but Lizy kin."
"Who is Lizy?"
"Me 'n Lizy's sisters."
"Where is your father?"

"Him done dade."

"And your mother?"

A backward motion of the thumb toward the mill is the only response.

"What is your name?"

"Georgy Alybamy Missippy Kicklighter."

"What do you do all day, Georgy?"

"Wuks." The same backward turn of the thumb.

"How long have you been working?"

"Ev'ry sence I was mighty nigh er kitten."

Asked to state at what age work began, she guessed:

"Seven year."

"What do you do in the mill?"

"Pieces ainds." Then she recollects, "But I hain't been nowhar 'cep'n' in mill he'pen maw sence I was five year ole."

"And were you never put at school?"

"Teacher done sont fur us, but me 'n' Lizy nary one didn't git thar, fur hit broke [quit]."

"You look sallow. Does anything ail you?"

"I be pow'ful weak."

"What does the doctor give you?"

"Don' give me nothin'. Maw, she gimme groun' pease. She 'low them's better 'n doctor's truck."

This is the product of three generations of mill workers, the grandmother, mother, and child drudging side by side. None of them could read or write, none had ever been four miles from their shanty and the factory. "Lizy" was the freak of nature, the genius of the family, having learned her letters at Sunday-school.

Though the public are indifferent, mill officials as a rule oppose child labor as utilized in the South. Often a wholesale dismissal takes place, quickened by protests of labor unions. But, under various pretexts, the gnome-like toilers creep back, especially into the country and suburban mills because of the scarcity of hands. A most powerful factor in this abuse is that the fathers will not work and the little ones must. Year after year bills to prevent the employment of children under ten and twelve are defeated in the legislature. □

[From Clare de Graffenried, "The Georgia Cracker in the Cotton Mills," *Century Magazine*, Vol. XLI, No. 4 (February 1891), pp. 483-98.]

The Cotton Mills of Georgia: Another View

In 1917, 26 years after De Graffenried's article came out, another writer looked at mill village life. The article by J. Archie Willis on the facing page comes from an advertisement two pages long published in the *Atlanta Journal*. The mill at White Hall was well known throughout Georgia and is still in existence (under different ownership). However, the mill village no longer exists. The houses were sold off to workers many years ago.

THINK ABOUT IT

1. According to Willis, what did the mill owners do to help their workers?
2. In what other ways does Willis's picture of life in a mill village differ from De Graffenried's?

The Fulton Cotton Mill and Company Houses, 1880s. This mill was much larger than most of those found in Georgia.

GEORGIA'S FIRST COTTON MILL IS DOING UPLIFT WORK ON A MAGNIFICENT SCALE

The Mill's Employees. There are one hundred and twenty operatives employed in the mill, seventy-five of this number being males and only forty-five women and young ladies. As is the rule, in instances of this kind, and they are numerous among the cotton mills of Georgia, the large number of men and the few women is an indication that the heads of the families make a sufficient wage to support their homes, without the wives and mothers having to leave their children and go into the mill to aid in the support of the family. . . .

There are probably half the number of operatives working in the Georgia Factory who have been with the mill since they were little children. Many of them were born and raised in the village, taking their places in the mill as they became old enough to do the work. And practically all the people of the village have been with the mill for many years.

There is a reason for these mill operatives' loyalty to their factory, and it is that reason which will form the most interesting feature of this article. When 500 people continuously, year after year, remain in the employ of one corporation, there is a compelling force back of their service which is unusual. And when that force is love, the love of the entire population of five hundred souls or the spirit back of the organization, the story of it is interesting as well as unusual.

The Mill Village. The mill village of the Georgia Factory and the village of the White Hall Yarn Mill . . . form the little town of White Hall on the Central of Georgia Railroad, five miles from Athens. . . .

The houses which the mill furnishes for its operatives are good—they are better buildings, in fact, than one will find in most country communities, and they are comfortable. They range in size from two to five rooms, all are ceiled [have ceilings], newly painted, and are set away in the groves that stud the hills rolling back from the Oconee. . . .

A garden is furnished with every home, and every family is planting that garden this year . . . . The rich river bottom on which these gardens are laid off produce vegetables enough and to spare. . . .

The Mill School. The mill has built a school house, adequate for the needs of the children of the operatives. And, this school is in charge of a competent young lady teacher. She has an enrollment of fifty young boys and girls, ranging in ages from 6 to 16 years.

Church and Sunday School Work. There are two churches at White Hall. The mill built the Baptist church and turned it over to the people of the village for their use. The Methodist church, while built by the members, was aided by the mill when it was built.

There is a fine Union Sunday school at White Hall, the members of the Methodist and Baptist denominations coming together in a hall built by the mill. There is an average attendance of more than 125 each Sunday, and the interest which the people of the village take in the Sunday school work is an indication of the high morals of its people.

Sports among the Operatives. A good baseball diamond has been provided for the operatives, and the young men of the village have an excellent baseball team. The entire population takes an active interest in the sport.

In addition . . . there is fine fishing in the Oconee river that runs through the village and everyone has the privilege of catching all the fish that he may have the time and patience to get . . . .

The Mill Store and Low Prices. The mill operates a big general merchandise store, where everything that comes under the head of necessities is kept, and it sells these things to the operatives at much less cost than the same things could be bought for elsewhere. . . . The store is not run for the purpose of making money off the operatives and their families, but is conducted for the convenience of the village and its people.

No Sickness at White Hall. The little town of White Hall is one of the healthiest places in the state of Georgia, there being, always, very little sickness among the five hundred people who make up its population. In fact, there has only been one case of typhoid fever in the village during the last seven years! And that case, . . . was brought to the mill from another town in the state.

This is a remarkable record . . . . The cleanliness of the place is, I presume, in large measure, responsible for the small amount of sickness to be found here.

From J. Archie Willis, advertisement in *Atlanta Journal,* April 22, 1917, pp. 6-7.

AGRICULTURE

The Black Belt's Riddle

To whom does the cotton belong: to the tenant who grew it? to the landlord who "furnished" the tenant? or to the banker who financed the landlord?

Although industry became more important to Georgia's economy in the late 1800s, the state remained mainly agricultural. Most Georgians continued to live in rural areas. In 1870, almost 92 percent of the people lived in the country; by 1900 that figure had decreased, but only to about 84 percent.

During this period, Georgia farmers tried to *diversify*, that is, to get away from the same crop—cotton—they had always produced. Some tried truck farming—growing fresh vegetables for nearby markets. They also raised peaches, pecans, corn, cattle, and hogs.

Cotton, however, remained "king." In fact, more cotton was produced than in the antebellum years.

As it was in antebellum days, the "Black Belt" was the heart of Georgia agriculture. In counties where huge plantations once operated with hundreds of slaves, black residents often outnumbered white residents.

The three main population groups who had inhabited this region during its pre-war prosperity were still there, each having certain resources and certain needs.

The main questions faced by persons in agriculture were:

1. How could the land (which was plentiful) be divided up so that it would be farmed most efficiently?
2. How could the labor supply (which was plentiful) be distributed so that needed work would be done and paid for?
3. How could the capital (which was scarce) be obtained to put the land into production?

In the post-war years, Georgians struggled to find answers to these questions. However, the solution that developed only created more problems. In the long run, it helped to keep Georgia a poor state for 75 years after the Civil War ended. The "solution" was called *sharecropping*.

Sharecropping: A New Approach

THINK ABOUT IT
1. How did renting and sharecropping differ?
2. Why was credit so important to farmers? Where did they usually get it?
3. In order to get a loan, what possession did a farmer have to put up as security?

Sharecropping began when planters divided their land into small parcels and settled individual families on them. The sharecropping system attracted labor to the former plantations where it was needed. It gave blacks some measure of being on their own. Each sharecropper family worked its part of the land as if it were a separate farm. The family paid for use of the land by giving a share of the crop it raised to the landowner.

Not all farm workers were sharecroppers. A visitor to Georgia around 1880 would have found that the people working the land fell into four groups: owners, wage laborers, renters, and sharecroppers.

Owners generally had more income than the other three groups. Some worked their small farms by themselves. Others had renters, sharecroppers, and wage laborers (or hands) working their land. Most owners were white.

Wage laborers were farm hands who came on the owner's land as needed (such as at cotton-picking time) to work for cash. Owners usually had little cash to pay wages, so this group was small in number. Wage laborers were the poorest farming group because their employment was so unsteady.

Renters and Sharecroppers ('croppers for short) lived with their families on a part

Picking Cotton, Gwinnett County. Tenants and landowner posed for this photo around 1910. Children often worked alongside parents and grandparents.

of an owner's land and raised a crop on it. Renters and 'croppers were also known as tenants. Various kinds of deals were worked out between landlords and their tenants for dividing up the costs of raising a crop and the income from selling the crop.

The chart below compares two examples of such deals.

A Confusing System

Landowners and tenants had many disputes over "who owed what to whom." Finally the Georgia Supreme Court settled the issue. In a major decision, it said that sharecropping was merely a form of laboring, that the 'cropper's share of the crop was a form of wages. This meant that the

Two Forms of Tenancy*

		Renting	Sharecropping
A.	What the owner furnishes:	Land House	Land House Tools (e.g., plow) Work stock (e.g., mules) Feed for stock Seed Fertilizer
B.	What the tenant furnishes:	Labor Tools Work stock Feed for stock Seed Fertilizer	Labor
C.	What the owner receives:	Fixed amount of cash or part of crop	One-half of crop
D.	What the tenant receives:	Entire crop less fixed amount	One-half of crop

*These two forms of tenancy had many variations. For example, the owner and tenant might each supply part of the fertilizer. Or, a sharecropper might supply his own mule. Sometimes, then, a crop might be divided one-third to the owner, two-thirds to the tenant.

sharecropper was not an independent farmer because he raised his crop under the owner's authority.

Preference for Renting

The renter was not under the owner's direct supervision. The renter was responsible for managing his part of the owner's land. This kind of independence appealed to many tenants, black and white.

However, there were drawbacks to renting. The renter had to know *how* to farm. He had to make his own decisions about buying seed, using fertilizer, and raising and selling his crop. He took all the risks, not the landowner. If the renter mismanaged his farm or lost his crop because of bad weather, he suffered all the loss—not the owner who still was due his rent.

The renter who made no money off one year's work soon found himself in debt. To pay off what he owed, the renter might have to sell his mules, plows, and other tools. Next year, he would likely be a sharecropper.

Credit

To make money, a farmer had to have money. Unless he could sell something, the only way the Georgia farmer could get money was to borrow it.

Owners and tenants were rarely able to borrow money from the few Georgia banks in business after the Civil War. Often they bought goods "on credit" from local merchants.

Whether they borrowed money from a bank or bought on credit from a merchant, farmers had to put up security. That is, they had to possess something of value the lender could have in case they couldn't pay off their debt. The loan security that bankers and merchants demanded was the farmer's cotton crop. The crop always had more value than anything else the Georgia farmer might possess. To protect lenders, Georgia law required that the merchant or bank be paid off *first* when the farmer sold his cotton.

What happened if farmers raised a crop too small to pay off their debts. Or, if the price they got for their cotton was too low? Obviously, merchants could easily fall into debt as well. They too borrowed money—often from northern banks—to set up their businesses. They also bought on credit the supplies they sold to farmers. They had bills to pay.

Often a merchant had to take the owner's land or the tenant's work stock and sell it to pay off his own debts. Usually, however, he chose to carry the farmer's debts another year. He would often extend more credit and hope that next year's crop would bring enough to pay off two years worth of debt.

By 1900 Georgia was still a farming state, a one-crop state. The system of agriculture involved thousands of families sharecropping or renting small farms and living on a local merchant's credit. What was it like to be part of this system?

The following story provides a glimpse into the lives of three families—owner, 'cropper, and merchant—who might have lived anywhere in Georgia's "Black Belt" in the late 1800s or early 1900s.

THINK ABOUT IT

1. In what ways did the three families depend on each other?
2. What role did credit play in each family's efforts to make a living?
3. In a sense, each family was stuck in a situation. How did each of them get there? How would they like things to be different?

A Story of Three Families and One Crop

The flop-eared little mule, its ribs and hip bones sticking way out, leaned into the traces one last time and quit.

"No use," sighed Jake Farmer, squinting at the big house still 50 yards up the steep hill. "Y'all wait here." Jake shuffled up the dusty road, leaving Millie and their four children in the wagon with the family's few belongings.

They had started at sun-up and spent most of the day bumping along the county roads. Millie pulled a torn blanket around herself and the baby to protect them against the early March wind. "Three houses in four years," she thought. "I hope this one 's better."

As Jake started up the steps, a stern-faced woman came out on the porch. "Ma'am, is Mr. Land about?" Jake asked, his hat in his hand.

"Who are you?" The woman eyed Jake suspiciously.

"Jake Farmer, ma'am. Them 's mine," he added, pointing down the hill. "Mr. Land told me to come on. We're goin' on shares."

"What d' you say your name is?" the woman demanded.

"Jake Farmer. Everyone in the south county knows me. Used to own a place down there, but couldn't meet my debt after the big drought and lost it. Then I rented from Mr. James Harvey and. . . ."

"You wait down there," she nodded toward the wagon. "He'll be back directly." Then Mrs. Land turned and went back in the house.

The wind was blowing colder by the time Edward Land drove up in his buggy. "Ma'am," he smiled and touched his hat brim. "Jake, turn around that poor excuse for a mule. Y'all's house is back down this road 'bout half a mile."

"Haw, Little Un," Jake shouted. The mule started plodding after Mr. Land's high-stepping horse and buggy.

As they reached their new home, the older children jumped off to inspect it.

"See that," said Mr. Land, pointing to fields of stubble stretching beyond the tenant house, "before the war, my daddy had 2,000 acres in cotton, a lot in corn, and even a few in wheat. He sold off about half of it in '65. No more hands to work it."

The Farmers Find a New Home. This drawing is by the same artist as the one of the Settlers (page 35). How has the artist expressed the difference in spirit between the two families?

An 1890s Hardware Store in Americus. How many different items for sale can you identify in this photo?

The little house had no paint or window panes and the roof sagged. "Don't look like much, but it don't leak bad and the fireplace works," said Mr. Land.

"Sure beats the place we been livin' in." Millie looked into the two dark and musty rooms. "Mr. Land . . . about furnishing us some provisions, we be mighty hungry. Them kids is been whinin' so; them not havin' hardly nuthin' to eat more 'n a week now," Millie's voice cracked and she began coughing.

"Main thing's gettin' you some med'cine," Jake put his arm around his wife.

"I don't furnish croppers food or tobacco or soap; nothing like that," replied Mr. Land. "Now Mr. Seller at the store will advance you some when I tell him you're on shares with me. He's fair; never cheated a body I know of. 'Course, if y'all need something to eat tonight, come fetch some meal and fat meat up at the house."

*   *   *

Edward Land put down the *Southern*

Cultivator and rubbed his eyes. "Can't read no more tonight, Selma," he sighed, getting up to throw another log on the fire.

"No sense readin' it," his wife muttered, not looking up from her knitting. "You can't buy any of that new-fangled equipment in it, anyhow."

"One of those new gangplows* and some better cotton planters sure would help." Mr. Land stared into the fire. "But fertilizer cost this year is gonna be 'bout $10 an acre." He paused, then said more cheerfully, "I talked to Leroy Seller this mornin'. He expects cotton will bring two, three cents [a pound] more this year."

"Said that last year, didn't he?" his wife asked.

Her husband continued, ignoring the question. "If he's right, and we get two bales to every three acres like we did before, and I can plant 900 acres, I figure I can clear $2,000 easy this fall."

"Not with the tenants we have now. Ed, you're always having to tell 'em when to plant and where to plant; how to fertilize, and chop and pick. If you don't keep up with 'em, they work your mules to death, tear up your tools and equipment and . . . oh, how I wish we still had cash renters on the place and no croppers."

"So do I, Selma, but there's not another tenant in this county who can meet his own expenses in raising a crop, who's got tools, and good mules and . . . "

"I know, Ed, seems like things just keep getting worse."

*   *   *

Jake Farmer tied Little Un in front of "Leroy Seller—General Merchandise and Ginning Co." Several men were standing around the doorway talking and smoking.

"Mornin' Mr. Jake."

Jake turned to a smiling round-faced

---

*A gangplow had several plow blades while earlier plows usually had only one. It could turn more than one furrow at a time, so a farmer with a gangplow could plow more in a day than a farmer with a single plow.

Cotton Gin in Floyd County, 1890s. Often farmers had to wait in line for hours to get their cotton ginned. Note the sign: "Positively No Smoking Allowed in My Gin Yard."

black man. "Asbury! How are ya? Must be two, three years. Makin' any money?"

"Fine, Mr. Jake, fine. I'm still rentin' from Mr. Joel Parks. Got me a good Tennessee mule and off 'n fifteen acres, made 'most ten bales last year. Got out of debt and cleared 'bout $180."

Jake sighed, "Wish I could just pay rent and be on my own. I lost 'most everythin' two years back, after my crop failed. When I couldn't pay James Harvey his rent, he took my stock, all my tools, even some old furniture that belonged to my ma and pa. Asbury, I got no way to meet expenses to plant even five acres. And Little Un there 's too poor to plow more 'n a potato patch."

"Sure is," agreed Asbury, appraising the skinny mule dozing in the warm sun.

In the store, Jake arranged with Leroy Seller to get provisions. Seller set a limit— a weekly credit allowance. Also, Jake had to agree to bring his cotton to Mr. Seller to be ginned.

As Seller's son gathered up Jake's order, the merchant marked in an account book what Jake would have to pay when he sold his cotton in the fall. It included a 10 percent interest charge.

Jake whistled as he drove Little Un home. In the wagon were fatback, meal, flour, molasses, dried peas, coffee, salt and pepper. There was soap, some cough syrup for Millie, and the first "store bought" dress his six-year old daughter would have. Jake also bought—on credit—shells for his shotgun, some seed to plant a garden patch, and a sack of feed for Little Un.

*   *   *

Leroy Seller took his account books home with him that night. After supper, he and his oldest son sat down with the account books at Seller's desk.

"Son, I just don't know how I can let you go. Look at all these past due accounts I'm having to carry. Some of these debts go back four years. Last year we had a fair crop in this county, but cotton brought only eight and a half cents a pound. Most of these people didn't make nearly enough to settle up," he said flipping some pages.

John Seller slumped in his chair. "Pa, maybe I can enter in the middle of the term, after the crop is in and sold, after Christmas. What about that?"

"Son, right now I don't see the money coming in," replied the merchant.

"Pa, we were so busy today, I'm plum worn out from getting up orders. It looked to me that money was coming in." John stopped, sensing his father getting angry.

"Boy, what you don't understand is that selling on credit, lending money on a crop yet to be planted, isn't the same as cash coming in. Sure I'm selling more. Take fertilizer. I have to be generous selling on credit to folks who need that fertilizer. You can't make a crop around here anymore without tons of fertilizer. But I have to pay my Yankee suppliers almost 10 percent more for it than I did last year. If cash doesn't come in, I can't pay my bills.

"Pa, you make it sound so bad, but I know you just picked up three farms to settle debts. Now they are. . . ."

"Next to worthless, they are!" The merchant slammed a book on his desk. "I made a mistake making loans with only land put up as security. Now I'm stuck with a lot of eroded fields that nobody in his right mind would pay five dollars an acre for."

"Pa, you see why I want to go up to Athens to school? There's no future here."

"Enough! You'll stay here and help me . . . at least another year. Then, maybe, if the price of cotton gets back up where it once was, and we have a good crop in this county, and folks pay off their debts . . . ." Leroy Seller waved an account book at his son, "Maybe then we can let you go off to the university to be a lawyer." □

A Tenant Shack, Lowndes County, 1905. Not all sharecroppers lived in houses this run-down, but thousands did.

HELP FOR THE FARMER

The sharecropping system meant years of poverty and debt for thousands of Georgia farmers. Dissatisfied with their lot, many of them organized to improve the situation.

THINK ABOUT IT

1. What kinds of self-help did the farmers try?
2. What kinds of help did state government provide?
3. What part did racism play in the failure of the Populists in Georgia?

Farmers and Politics

The Grange, a nationwide "self-help" farmer organization, came to Georgia in 1872. It set up cooperative stores—stores run by and for farmers—where members could buy supplies directly from producers. Its aim was to cut out the merchant's markup and get supplies at lower

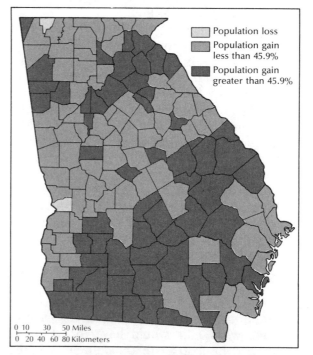

Population loss

Population gain less than 45.9%

Population gain greater than 45.9%

0 10 30 50 Miles
0 20 40 60 80 Kilometers

MAP 24. Population Change, 1860-1880. In general, which areas grew at a greater rate than the state average of 45.9%? Compare with the map on page 95. Was the black belt growing in population?

cost. By 1876, about 18,000 Georgia farmers had joined the Grange.

In 1874, Georgia Grangers and other farmers pressed the General Assembly to create a Department of Agriculture (the first of its kind in the nation). The department's purpose was to improve agriculture by distributing information about new seed, how to use fertilizer, control insects, and market crops.

About the same time, the University of Georgia established a College of Agriculture. The state also set up agricultural experiment stations to determine what plants and animals could be most profitably raised on Georgia farms.

By and large, however, the state government was not very concerned with the problems of small farmers. Industry was more important.

Many farmers felt this favoritism toward industry was helping to keep them in debt. In northwest Georgia they organized a challenge to the regular Democratic Party. Their champions were Dr. William H. Felton of Cartersville and his wife, Rebecca Latimer Felton. As an "Independent Democrat," Dr. Felton was elected three times to the U.S. Congress on a campaign to help the farmer. Mrs. Felton made speeches, wrote articles, and bombarded newspapers with letters outlining the injustices farmers and other 'little people" were suffering.

Although the independent movement died out after 1880, a new self-help organization appeared. In 1887, the Farmers' Alliance came to Georgia. Those who joined the Alliance could borrow money at lower interest rates. The Alliance also set up farmer "co-ops" and organized boycotts of suppliers who charged too much.

The Alliance also grappled with the railroads. Farmers had no choice of transportation facilities. They had to pay whatever rate the railroad charged to transport their produce to market. Often, the railroad charged the small farmer higher rates than the large shipper. The rates changed frequently and from place to place. The Farmers' Alliance fought for laws requiring railroads to post their rates in the railroad stations and charge the same rates per mile for all shippers.

By 1890, 100,000 Georgia farmers had joined the Alliance. It called for tighter regulation of the railroads, changes in state tax laws to ease the burden of farmers, better schools, and better roads. Democratic candidates for the General Assembly noted the strength of the Alliance. They agreed to support its demands. For two years, a "farmer's legislature" passed laws that helped the farmers.

Tom Watson

The new champion of farmers was Thomas E. Watson from Thomson, Georgia. In 1882, McDuffie County's small farmers—black and white—had combined to send this fiery 26-year-old lawyer to the General Assembly.

Watson did not share Henry Grady's dream of an industrialized Georgia. He hated it. He saw that industrial prosperity did little to help the majority of Georgians who toiled in the cotton fields. He lashed out at those he saw as the farmers' enemies: the bankers who charged high interest rates, the railroads with their high freight rates, and the politicians who supported the banks and railroads.

In 1890, with Alliance support, Tom Watson was elected to the U.S. Congress. In Washington, he won a big victory for farming people. He sponsored and pushed through a law providing for RFD—rural free delivery. No longer would farm families have to travel miles to town to pick up their mail.

About this time, a new political party, the People's Party (sometimes called "The Populists"), was growing in the United States. Many Democrats, including Tom Watson, joined it. The Populists were for political equality and called on all farmers, black and white, to unite.

In the election of 1892, Tom Watson ran for Congress as a Populist. The Democrats fought back fiercely. They charged that voting for a Populist would mean the end of white supremacy; blacks would again hold political office. They scared many white voters and bought off some black ones. Watson was defeated.

Tom Watson ran again and again as a Populist, but never won. With each defeat he became more bitter. Although he became well known and wealthy from publishing magazines and books, he wound up a sick, hateful man. More of his story appears in the next chapter.

ACTIVITIES FOR CHAPTER 11

Discussion

A. Under the sharecrop system of agriculture, Georgia remained a poor state for 75 years following the Civil War.

  1. How did post-war conditions give rise to the sharecrop system?

  2. How did the system involve people other than farmers?

  3. How were people trapped by the system?

B. Henry Grady and the bourbon redeemers saw industrialization as the key to Georgia's future prosperity.

  1. How did they think industrialization would bring prosperity to the people?

  2. How successful were their efforts?

  3. What were some negative, or unwanted, effects of industrialization?

Writing Project

What was life in a mill village really like? The accounts on pages 133-35 present conflicting information—a problem that historians often face.

Write an article, like one you might find in a magazine, on "cotton mill life." It should be as accurate as possible, but not too long.

12 Change at the Turn of the Century

As the nineteenth century ended and the twentieth century began, life in Georgia was undergoing some big changes. New technology changed the ways people worked and carried on their daily lives. Social changes affected Georgians' values, how they looked at life, and how they related to one another.

Technological Change. Developments such as electric power and the internal combustion engine helped make manufacturing more efficient. With new power-driven machinery, factory workers could produce goods at a faster rate than in the past.

New technology changed daily lives, too. In 1900, Georgians and their goods were transported mainly by the railroads and the river steamers. For short trips, most people still relied on a horse or mule to pull the family wagon. But early in the century, automobiles began appearing on the streets of major United States cities.

Typical Georgia homes had kerosene lamps and a fireplace or woodstove for light and heat. A well was in the front yard, an outhouse in the back. However, in Atlanta, Savannah, and a few other places, some people had electricity and gas in their houses. Some well-off families were getting indoor plumbing and even a telephone.

New food products began appearing in Georgia homes, too. While cured meat, cornbread, and molasses remained big in the diets of most Georgians, the stores began offering packaged cereals, canned vegetables, and bottled soft drinks.

Social Change. Another kind of change was going on. New attitudes, different outlooks on life, and more diverse lifestyles were emerging.

Some social change was related to problems brought on by technological change. For example, as the abuse of child workers became widely known, people began to call for limits on child labor.

Social change was also influenced by advances in technology, by improved economic conditions, and by new ideas that people read or heard about.

Compared to technological change, social change came more slowly and caused more controversy. Many Georgians resisted such change.

This chapter looks mainly at several big areas of social change. It also provides a few glimpses of daily life at the turn of the century.

BLACK GEORGIANS AND SOCIAL EQUALITY

The Civil War wiped out laws governing race relations, but it did not erase racial attitudes and customs that had grown up over 200 years in America. Racial segregation continued.

The Constitution of 1868 called for Georgia's first real system of education "to be forever free to all children of the state." It did not say that children should be segregated in school. Yet, when the schools opened in 1871, the white majority made sure that blacks and whites were in separate buildings.

During the Reconstruction years, many whites became convinced that the radical Republicans were trying to force black "social equality" on the South. They became more determined to uphold white supremacy, to keep blacks "in their place." This meant keeping blacks from voting, from working in cotton mills or other industries, from eating in restaurants or staying in hotels that served whites. In general, whites refused to associate with blacks as equals.

Not all white Georgians felt the same about the proper "place" of blacks in Georgia society. Two prominent men of the times, Robert Toombs and Atticus G. Haygood, held very different views.

THINK ABOUT IT

1. What role does Toombs see black people playing in the government of "new South" Georgia?
2. How does Haygood's view of black Georgians' place in society differ from that of Toombs?
3. According to Haygood, how should whites help educate their black neighbors?

Two White Georgians View the Blacks' Place in Society

Robert Toombs was born and lived most of his life in Washington, Georgia. Before the Civil War, he had served Georgia in both the U.S. House of Representatives and the U.S. Senate. Toombs was briefly Confederate secretary of state and later a brigadier general in the Confederate Army. He was known as the "unreconstructed rebel" because he openly opposed Reconstruction and refused to take an oath of allegiance to the Union. Toombs was a delegate to the 1877 convention which replaced the "carpetbagger constitution" of 1868 with a new constitution.

The following excerpt is from a speech Robert Toombs made to the convention.

 Who Are the People?

One of the foundation stones of this government is that the people are sovereign, and the other that it has a republican form of government, where the officers controlling its powers are elected by the people . . . . Who are the people? It is those in society who are strong enough to form civil government, and to administer its powers. They are not anybody. . . .

The federal government, the conqueror and public enemy of my country, has injected into the social organization and political body 500,000 savages, who, whatever their rights, are not fit to exercise the powers of government . . . .

These people are a kind, affectionate people. But shall we forget the history of this people in their attempts to establish a government in Africa, where they have been, according to Jewish account, 6,000 years, and, according to those people who call themselves "scientists," as much as 60,000 years. They have not been able to do it and cannot do it.

They were put upon us by those people in the north who intend to make good government impossible in the south for all time to come. . . . □

[Robert Toombs, Speech before the Constitutional Convention, in Samuel W. Small (Reporter), *A Stenographic Report of the Proceedings of the Constitutional Convention Held in Atlanta, Georgia, 1877* (Atlanta: Constitution Publishing Company, 1877), pp. 223-24.]

Atticus G. Haygood was born at Watkinsville, Georgia in 1839. He served as a chaplain in the Confederate States Army and later became a bishop of the Methodist Church. At the time he wrote *Our Brother in Black* he was president of Emory College, Oxford, Georgia. The following is an excerpt from that book.

 ## Our Brother in Black

The problem before us, the Northern and Southern people together, and the Southern people in particular, is the right education and elevation of our black brother, the free negro, in our midst. Do not, beloved white brother, scare at this word "elevation." Nothing is said about putting the "negro above the white man." Let me whisper a secret in your ear: *That cannot be done unless you get below him.* Think of this, and if you find yourself underneath blame yourself.

The negro cannot rise simply because he is black; the white man cannot stay up simply because he is white. A man rises, not by the color of his skin, but by intelligence, industry, and integrity. . . .

Let the white man rise as high as he can, providing always that he does not rise by wrongs done to another. And let every other man rise to his full stature, the white, the black, the red, the yellow. No honest man, with brains in his head, doubts for one moment that it is God's will that every man he ever made of every race, should make the most of the "talents" his Creator gave him . . . .

This new citizen is a voter, and, unhappily for all, he is not ready for his responsibilities. Voting means choosing, and wise choosing means intelligence [education]. Woe to the land where those who hold the balance of power are in ignorance. This tremendous engine of political power, the ballot, must be in hands that know what they are doing. This voter *must be educated.*

But we must go beyond the mere voter. His wife, his daughter, must be educated also, else the race will not be educated; the need is to *teach the race.*

In what ways, now, can we of the white race help our colored neighbor to be what he ought to be as a member of the community? . . .

I must teach the negro to respect my rights; I do this best by respecting his. I must teach him to respect and keep his contracts; to do this I must respect and keep mine. I must teach him to obey the law and to respect authority; to do this I must set him the example. I must teach him to speak the truth; to do this I must speak the truth to him. . . .

If we of the South are to make progress with our problems, if we are to become the people Providence designs us to be, if we are to do our duty to God and man, then let us understand distinctly, once and for all, that in the administration of law the negroes shall receive, not only in theory but in practice, fair dealing and justice. □

[Adapted from Atticus G. Haygood, *Our Brother in Black: His Freedom and His Future* (New York: Phillips & Hunt, 1881), pp. 129-43, 182-94.]

Separate but Equal

Whose attitude, Toombs's or Haygood's, do you think represented the feeling of most white Georgians? Let's look at laws passed later by the Georgia General Assembly.

In 1891, the Georgia General Assembly passed the state's first "Jim Crow" laws. The term "Jim Crow"—taken from an old minstrel song titled "Jump, Jim Crow"—referred to written laws and unwritten customs which kept blacks and whites separated. One law passed in 1891 required railroads to provide separate passenger cars for blacks and whites. Another law stated that black and white prisoners were to be segregated in convict camps.

Gradually, local governments joined the state in enforcing segregation. Atlanta and Savannah segregated streetcars. Soon Georgia cities had by law segregated theaters, elevators, water fountains, and park benches. "White only" signs appeared in train station waiting rooms, restaurants, and other public facilities.

Blacks protested strongly. But in the 1890s and early 1900s blacks who boycotted segregated streetcars gained little support from their white neighbors. Segregation became an accepted way of life.

In the North as well as throughout the South, attitudes of white supremacy took hold. "De facto" segregation (segregation existing *in fact*) if not "de jure" segregation (segregation existing *by law*) became commonplace. Certain neighborhoods, schools, and beaches became "off limits" to blacks. Certain jobs and other opportunities were closed to them.

Even the federal government accepted segregation as lawful and proper. It continued to maintain separate military units for black and white soldiers even after the Civil War.

Then, in 1896, the U.S. Supreme Court delivered a stunning blow to the blacks' struggle for equality. In the case of *Plessy v. Ferguson*, the Court upheld the Louisiana conviction of a black man who tried to ride in a train car reserved for whites. This ruling put the federal courts in support of the so-called "separate but equal" doctrine. If equal public facilities were provided for both races, the Court ruled, then they could be legally separate.

Blacks had no power, however, to make sure such facilities as schools and parks were equal. In fact, black facilities (if they existed at all) were usually far inferior to those provided for whites.

How did blacks respond to this situation? Just as whites differed on how blacks should be treated, so did blacks differ on what they should do for themselves.

THINK ABOUT IT
1. What did Booker T. Washington suggest blacks should do to improve their lives?
2. Why might this message have gained support from whites?

3. How were the positions of Hope and DuBois different from those of Washington?

Black Leaders Differ

Perhaps the best known black leader in the 1890s and early 1900s was Booker T. Washington. Washington built Tuskegee Institute in Alabama into a leading center of education for blacks. There he stressed technical training, learning a trade, and agriculture. Washington made many speeches around the country, calling on whites to support this kind of education for blacks. White audiences liked his views. Tuskegee grew to over a thousand students.

In 1895, Booker T. Washington made one of his most famous speeches at the Cotton States and International Exposition. Many whites and blacks agreed at the time with his message, which quickly became known as the "Atlanta Compromise." The following is a brief excerpt from the speech.

 Up From Slavery

[This exposition] will awaken among us a new era of industrial progress. Ignorant and inexperienced, it is not strange that in the first years of our new life we began at the top instead of at the bottom; that a seat in Congress or the State Legislature was more sought than real estate or industrial skill; that the political convention or stump-speaking [campaigning] had more attraction than starting a dairy farm or truck garden. . . .

Our greatest danger is that in the great leap from slavery to freedom we may overlook the fact that the masses of us are to live by the productions of our hands, and fail to keep in mind that we shall prosper in proportion as we learn to dignify and glorify common labor, and put brains and skill into the common occupations of life . . . .

No race can prosper till it learns that

there is as much dignity in tilling a field as in writing a poem. It is at the bottom of life we must begin, and not at the top. Nor should we permit our grievances [complaints] to overshadow our opportunities. . . .

The wisest among my race understand that the agitation of [fighting over] questions of social equality is the extremest folly, and that progress in the enjoyment of all privileges that will come to us must be the result of severe and constant struggle rather than of artificial forcing. . . .

It is important and right that all privileges of the law be ours, but it is vastly more important that we be prepared for the exercises of these privileges. The opportunity to earn a dollar in a factory just now is worth infinitely [much] more than the opportunity to spend a dollar in an opera house. . . . □

[Booker T. Washington, *Up From Slavery, An Autobiography* (New York: Doubleday, Page, & Co., 1901), pp. 218-25.]

While many blacks followed Washington's line of thinking, some did not. Two black leaders who did not agree with the "Atlanta Compromise" were John Hope and William E.B. DuBois.

For many years, Dr. John Hope was one of the nation's leading educators. He was president of Morehouse College in Atlanta and later president of Atlanta University. In 1896, a year after Booker T. Washington had presented his views, Hope challenged them.

Why Not Equality

If we are not striving for equality, in heaven's name for what are we living? I regard it as cowardly and dishonest for any of our colored men to tell white people or colored people that we are not struggling for equality.

If money, education, and honesty will not bring to me as much privilege, as much equality as they bring to any American citizen, then they are to me a curse, and not a blessing. God forbid that we should get the implements with which to fashion our freedom, and then be too lazy to fashion it. Let us not fool ourselves or be fooled by others. If we cannot do what other freemen do, then we are not free.

Yes, my friends, I want equality—nothing less. I want all that my God-given powers will enable me to get—then why not equality? Now catch your breath, for I am going to use an adjective: I am going to demand *social* equality. In this Republic we shall be less than freemen if we have a whit less than that which thrift, education, and honor afford other freemen. If equality—political, economic, and social—is the boon [reward] of other men in this great country of ours, then equality—political, economic, and social—is what we demand. □

[Quoted in Ridgely Torrance, *The Story of John Hope* (New York: The Macmillan Company, 1948), pp. 114-15.]

Atlanta University, 1890s. How would this sewing class fit Booker T. Washington's stress on vocational education?

William E.B. DuBois was born in 1868 in Massachusetts. In the same year that Washington spoke at the Atlanta exposition, DuBois became the first black student to earn a Doctor of Philosophy degree at Harvard University.

Like Dr. Hope, Dr. DuBois was associated with Atlanta University, teaching and studying the problems of black people living in America. He was an outspoken, controversial leader in the fight for black civil rights. In 1903, his book *The Souls of Black Folk* made it clear that all black leaders did not agree with Washington's views.

In 1905, in New York, DuBois organized the Niagara Movement, the first big effort to end Jim Crow laws. Four years later, he helped found the National Association for the Advancement of Colored People (NAACP) and edited its magazine, *The Crisis.*

Below are the major aims of the Niagara Movement as drafted by DuBois.

 Niagara Movement Aims

These are the things we as black men must do:

Stop the curtailment of our political rights.

Urge Negroes to vote intelligently and effectively.

Push the matter of civil rights.

Organize business co-operation.

Build school houses and increase the interest in education.

Open up new avenues of employment . . . .

Distribute . . . information in regard to laws of health.

Bring Negroes and labor unions into mutual understanding.

Study Negro history.

Increase the circulation of honest newspapers and periodicals.

Attack crime among us by all civilized methods . . . . □

[Adapted from W.E.B. DuBois, "The Niagara Movement," *The Voice of the Negro,* Vol. II, No. 9 (September 1905), pp. 619-22.]

A year after DuBois launched the Niagara Movement in New York, race relations were getting worse in Georgia. In a bitter campaign for the governorship, one candidate for the Democratic Party nomination called for taking away the vote from blacks. A month after the primary election, a race riot in Atlanta left twenty-five blacks and one white dead.

Blacks Lose the Vote

Since the days of Reconstruction, many white Georgians had bitterly opposed black participation in politics. Ku Klux Klan terror was intended to scare black voters away from the polls. After the Klan died down in the 1870s, whites used other means to prevent black voting.

Although Georgia's new Constitution of 1877 did not directly disfranchise (take away the vote of) blacks, it did provide that only men who had paid up all their taxes could vote. This rule disfranchised thousands of poor blacks—and poor whites.

In the 1890s, the populists' success in uniting poorer black and white farmers alarmed the white Democratic party leaders of Georgia. So, they took steps to keep blacks from voting.

In 1900, the Georgia Democratic Party ruled that only white men could vote in its primary.* The party argued that a primary is a private affair—for members only. The Republican and Populist parties were by then all but dead in Georgia. Therefore, the Democratic primary, not the general election, became the only real political contest. Blacks could still vote in

---

*A primary is a first election held to choose a party's candidate to run in the election for office (usually called a "general election") against another party's candidate.

the general election, but that hardly mattered. There was usually only one candidate for each office—a white Democrat.

Other states had already enacted laws to prevent blacks from voting. Mississippi had passed laws which required paying a poll tax and passing a literacy test in order to vote in its general elections. Men who couldn't read and explain the state constitution (to the satisfaction of white election officials) or pay their poll tax couldn't vote. These requirements worked against uneducated whites as well as blacks.

Louisiana had inserted a "grandfather clause" into its state constitution. This allowed a man to vote, even if he failed to pass the literacy test, as long as his father or grandfather had been eligible to vote on January 1, 1867. Few blacks could meet this requirement because their fathers and grandfathers had been slaves.

In 1908, Georgia adopted a grandfather clause, a literacy test, and property ownership [40 acres or valued at $500] as qualifications for voting. For the following 30 years, practically no blacks would vote in Georgia.

Racial Violence Continues

The Atlanta race riot in 1906 was not an isolated incident of racial violence. By then, Georgia had gained an unwanted reputation for lynching. The victims of this form of murder—carried out by unruly mobs—were mostly blacks. In the worst year, 1899, 27 black men were lynched for alleged crimes ranging from "inflammatory language" and "resisting arrest" to "robbery and murder."

As Jim Crow laws were passed and blacks were denied the vote, racial hatred took on a new status. For instance, Tom Watson, the man who spoke up for blacks in the 1880s, preached race hatred and violence after 1900. He had learned that the votes of poorer, less-educated whites could be won by playing on their fears of black social equality. Eventually Watson told the readers of his newspaper that Jews

and Catholics were also their enemies.

In 1915, a lynch mob, urged on by Watson's editorials, took Leo M. Frank from the state prison and hanged him. Frank, a white Atlanta factory manager, was a Jew. His lynching gained national attention. In the same year, the Ku Klux Klan was reborn at Stone Mountain.

PUBLIC EDUCATION

Georgia's first constitution had called for public schools in each county, but the General Assembly never set aside the money to develop them. Before the Civil War the state made several attempts to educate the poor white children, but it never started a permanent school system. Usually, children from wealthy families went to private academies.

The Constitution of 1868 set the stage for the public schools of today. It provided for a "thorough system of general education to be forever free to all children of the state."

Two years later, the schools got their real start. The General Assembly created the office of state school commissioner (later renamed state superintendent of schools) and the State Board of Education. In 1871, with an appropriation of $174,000 from the legislature, the public schools of Georgia enrolled about 31,000 children. Schools were to open three months of each year.

At first, public support for the schools was meager. Some whites disapproved of public education for blacks, even though black and white pupils were to be segregated.

Then, in 1872, Gustavus J. Orr was appointed school commissioner. Almost single-handedly he built a permanent system of public education for Georgia. For 15 years he traveled through the state, often at his own expense, pointing out the benefits of schooling. He encouraged citizens to tax themselves to pay for schools. He helped county school boards make the most of the little money available for education. Commissioner Orr is remembered as the "father of the common school system" in Georgia.

Attitudes toward the Schools

Through the early 1900s, public education was mostly a local—not a state—effort. Local property taxes furnished most of the money for the schools. Georgia was a poor state, so these funds were not easy to raise.

According to the Constitution of 1877, state funds could be used for "common schools" (the elementary grades) and for the state university, but not for high schools. If a community wanted to have a high school, it had to pay for it on its own.

What was the public's attitude toward education in the early 1900s? Items from two newspapers provide some clues.

THINK ABOUT IT

1. What clues do the two articles provide about how important public education was to the people around 1900?
2. Why was the editor of the *Ledger* opposed to tax support for the high school?

 ### The School's Big Attendance

The Public School opened Monday with over 200—the largest enrollment in years. The school is in fine shape for a successful year.

The *Enterprise* agrees with a number of our citizens . . . that the number of teachers employed in our Public Schools is too small, and that the number should be increased. However proficient and well-qualified a teacher may be, the teacher cannot do herself or [her] pupils justice when the room is crowded as some are in the school here. We understand there are 65 children in one room and 52 in another. This number is too large and it is impossible for any teacher to devote as much time to the pupil, as should be; and the *Enterprise* would be glad to know that another teacher would be elected at an early date.

It would mean better order in the school room, and a more thorough training.

Education is one thing that cannot be curtailed, and when you put upon a teacher more than the teacher can do, you seriously cripple the school, dwarf the minds of the children, and hinder them in the pursuit of knowledge.

It is a question that should strike a responsive chord in the hearts of parents who patronize the school. This question should be insisted upon and the sooner proper provision is made, the better. □
[*The Georgia Enterprise*, Covington, Georgia, September 7, 1900, p. 1.]

 ### The High School

The recommendation of Mayor Chappell that the High School be made self-supporting is on the right line. Only a small percentage of the children who attend the public schools go through the High School and graduate from that institution. In most cases, those who go through the High School are children of parents who are amply able to pay for their education.

It is a fact that the children of the [ordinary] man have [to go to] work before they get through the High School. Their parents can not afford to send them to school for the long term of years necessary for them to get through all the various grades of the public schools and to graduate from the High School. A poor man, with four or five children, certainly can not afford to keep them all in the schools until they graduate.

The High School, of necessity, while it is open to all benefits but few, and those few should pay their own way through this school. It is costing the city a good deal of money to run the public schools. While this is true, there are a great many children in Columbus who do not attend the schools at all. Such money as the city of Columbus may be able to pay on account of schools should certainly go toward supporting grades lower than those taught in the High School.

The *Ledger* is not opposing the public schools, but if there is to be a High School, we agree with Mayor Chappell that it should be made self-supporting, and we believe that the taxpayers endorse this view of the matter. □

[*The Columbus Ledger,* Columbus, Georgia, December 17, 1903, p. 4.]

In 1912 Georgia voters approved amendments to the state constitution that included high schools in state funding. They also gave counties the authority to levy taxes for their support. As a result, by 1920 Georgia had 169 high schools.

Meanwhile, the Georgia General Assembly had recognized that all children needed some education. In 1916 it passed the state's first compulsory school attendance law. The law said that all children age 8 to 14 had to attend school for at least four months of the year. However, if a child lived more than three miles from the nearest school, he or she could be excused from attending. A child could also be excused for seasonal labor in agriculture.

In rural areas, schools usually had only one room with no electricity or water. They were often run-down. In the cities and larger towns, schools had several rooms and were in better condition.

What did students learn in the common schools in the early 1900s? State Superintendent M. L. Brittain set down the following school standards.

The Community School, Brunswick. A horse-drawn school bus brought pupils to this new school in 1915. The building is still in use. In 1982, what differences might you see?

1. Which of the standards might still apply to today's eighth grader?

What an Eighth Grade Pupil Ought to Know

1. How to speak and read the English language with fair accuracy.
2. How to write with fair legibility, in particular, ordinary business letters.
3. How to use the principles of arithmetic in ordinary business transactions.
4. How to spell at least the words used in ordinary business transactions.
5. Enough geography to appreciate current events, and to know something of the nations of the world.
6. The leading facts of American history; to feel a patriotic pride in the deeds of our fathers and to give reasons for opinions as to men and measures.
7. The value of physiology and hygiene—what it means to have a healthy body and hygienic surroundings.
8. To know something of the plants, birds, trees and agricultural life of the vicinity.
9. The civic virtues—to be honest, trustworthy, obedient, truthful and polite. □

[*High School Quarterly*, January 1915, III (2), p. 81. In Oscar H. Joiner (gen. ed.), *A History of Public Education in Georgia* (Columbia, South Carolina: R.L. Bryan Company, 1979), p. 263.]

Georgia Schools Segregated

The Georgia Constitution of 1877 specified segregated education. It stated, "separate schools shall be provided for white and colored children." For nearly a century, Georgia public schools separated students by race.

Black Georgians challenged laws providing for segregated schools. But the courts upheld the so-called "separate but equal" doctrine. As long as blacks were furnished school facilities equal to those of whites, schools could by law be separate.

Under this doctrine, Georgia operated a dual education system: one for whites, one for blacks. This practice applied to state colleges as well as public schools.

Although it was supposed to be equal, the education furnished black children was quite different from that offered to white children. The figures below, taken from the 1908 Georgia Department of Education's *Annual Report*, tell part of the story.

THINK ABOUT IT

1. What do the figures tell about who actually went to school around 1908?
2. If separate education had been really equal how might the figures have looked different?

EDUCATIONAL FACILITIES IN 1908

	White	Percent	Black	Percent
Total school population	386,227	53	349,244	47
Number pupils enrolled	306,891	60	201,512	40
Number pupils in high school	17,253	91	1,697	9
Value of school furniture, etc.	$590,336.00	85	$101,385.00	15
Value of school libraries	77,628.00	99	940.00	1
Average teacher's monthly salary	44.29	69	20.23	31

Source: Dorothy Orr, *A History of Education in Georgia* (Chapel Hill: University of North Carolina Press, 1950), p. 314.

Both state and local tax money went in greater amounts to educate each white child than each black child. As a result, white children had finer school buildings, more books, supplies, and equipment, and better-prepared and better-paid teachers.

SOCIAL REFORM

Across the United States in the years 1890 to 1910, many Americans organized to make life better—especially for those less fortunate. Persons who worked to bring about changes were called "reformers." Their special targets were evils related to the growth of industries and cities.

At the urging of reformers, federal, state, and local governments passed laws on subjects they had not had to consider in earlier years—for example, working conditions.

To protect mill and factory workers, young and old, from accidents and disease, governments passed new laws. They set safety and sanitation standards, regulated working conditions, and limited hours of work.

To protect children, the Georgia General Assembly, passed two laws designed in part to get children out of the factories. In 1914, it passed a child labor law and two years later a compulsory school attendance law. Not everyone agreed such laws were needed. Some parents insisted they had a right to work their children as they saw fit, without any interference from government. For many years child labor and school attendance laws lacked public support, so they were difficult to enforce.

At a time when fewer Americans were raising their own meat and vegetables, governments also passed laws to protect the public against unwholesome food. They set standards of cleanliness and provided for inspection of packing houses, bakeries, and canneries. Other laws were passed to protect against "medicines" containing narcotics, alcohol, and other harmful ingredients.

Ad in the Golden Age, *1906. How does this soft drink ad reflect the movement for social reform? To whom would the ad appeal?*

Many kinds of reform laws were enacted in the "Progressive Era," as it is often called. They covered not only labor and health, but also education, business, morality, and even government itself. Georgians were involved in all these reforms—too many to examine here. Three areas to which they gave their attention were prison reform, prohibition, and women's suffrage.

THINK ABOUT IT

1. How did post-Civil War conditions in Georgia make the convict lease system attractive to state government leaders? To businessmen?
2. What finally brought about the end of the lease system?

Prison Reform

In 1866, the Reconstruction government of Georgia faced a growing problem:

how to handle persons convicted of serious crimes. The government had little money to spend on the care of prisoners. Moreover, the state penitentiary had been almost completely destroyed by Sherman's troops.

To manage prisoners, Georgia set up a convict lease system. This prison system had already been tried in other states, but it was new to Georgia. Under it, state government leased persons convicted of felonies* to railroads and other private companies.

This system transferred the expense of caring for prisoners from the taxpayers to private businesses. At the same time, businesses had a source of cheap labor. Across the state convicts were put to work laying railroad track, mining coal, sawing lumber, making bricks, and distilling turpentine.

As the number of convicts increased in Georgia, the lease system became big business. In 1876, three companies arranged a 20-year lease of almost all the state's prisoners for $25,000 a year. Some of the state's leading men became involved in it. Ex-Governor Joseph E. Brown headed one company, and John B. Gordon owned part of another. In 1879, when the lease began, 1,196 convicts were turned over to them. In 1899, when it ran out, the three companies had 2,201 convicts.

Under the lease system, boys as young as ten, women, old men in their seventies, and those who were sick or insane were all treated alike. It soon became clear to some Georgians that the system was a monstrous evil.

The state had regulations the private companies were supposed to follow, but many abuses occurred. For example, it was against state regulations to work leased convicts on the Sabbath and longer than sunrise to sunset. Yet, some worked as long as 15 hours a day, seven days a week.

---

*Persons convicted of less serious crimes, misdemeanors, were usually sentenced to county-run prison camps.

By day, prisoners usually worked in chains, overseen by "whipping bosses" ready to punish them. At night, some convicts slept chained together or locked in outdoor cages.

In the late 1800s, Georgia's courts were run by whites only. A black person's testimony seldom counted. Georgia's convict population was 90 percent black. The families and friends of black convicts had little influence, so the brutal system continued.

Some well-known Georgians did condemn the system. The Feltons and Tom Watson fought to have it abolished. Ten years after he himself had leased convicts, John B. Gordon, as governor, spoke out against the lease system. He told the General Assembly that it "makes possible the infliction of greater punishment than the law and the courts have imposed. . . .[and] it reduces to minimum the chances for reformation."

However, it would be another decade before the efforts of reformers would bring change. They published articles, made speeches, and held mass meetings to arouse the public.

Mrs. Selena S. Butler, a teacher at Morris Brown College in Atlanta, made one of those speeches in 1897. An excerpt from it follows.

 The Chain-Gang System

It is those convicts leased to private corporations who suffer miseries which [only] their poor miserable selves and God know. The chain-gang bosses, as a rule, are selected from the lowest element of the white race, and rather glory in their office and the freedom of dealing out misery and cruelty to helpless convicts for small offences, and often for no offence at all. Many of the chain-gang camps are situated in places remote from settlements and public roads, where no one can interfere with the inhuman treatment these poor, helpless creatures receive from beings who would be a disgrace to the brute kingdom. Many of the prisoners have scarcely enough clothing on their uncared for bodies to protect them from the gaze of others, or from winter's cold or summer's heat. . . . The majority of the prisoners in these private camps are poorly fed. . . .

In one camp sixty-one men were found sleeping in a room not more than nineteen feet square and seven feet from floor to ceiling. . . . Many of these convicts know not the comfort of sleeping upon even a cheap mattress or heap of straw, but must wrap about their tired and neglected bodies a blanket much worn and filled with dirt and vermin, and lie down, not upon a wood floor, but the dirt floor of a tent. . . .

. . . Little or no provision is made for the care of the sick; some have been forced to work till they fell upon the ground, dead. □

[Selena S. Butler, *The Chain-Gang System,* read before the National Association of Colored Women at Nashville, Tenn., September 16, 1897 (Tuskegee, Ala.: Normal School Steam Press Print., 1897.)]

In 1897, Governor William Atkinson and the General Assembly took the first steps toward prison reform. They set up a state-run prison farm for all female prisoners, and for male prisoners either under 15 years old or too sick or weak to work.

Finally, in 1908, reacting to harsh criticism from newspapers and the public, the General Assembly thoroughly investigated the convict lease camps. Its findings were shocking. The system was abolished.

Thereafter, prisoners would either be kept on state prison farms or assigned to county prison camps to work on public roads. Although this change meant better living conditions for many prisoners, the chains and brutal treatment lasted for many years.

Agitation for reform continued. In 1915, the General Assembly, recognizing that young people in trouble should not be treated like adults, created the state's first juvenile courts. More reforms were to come in the 1930s and 1940s.

A Chain Gang, 1910. This gang, working on Richmond County public roads, got a rest when this photo was taken.

Prohibition

Another reform of this period was "prohibition." Oglethorpe had banned strong liquor in the Georgia Colony, but many colonists ignored the law. By 1742, the Trustees gave up trying to keep rum out of Georgia.

In antebellum Georgia, drinking hard liquor was widely accepted. However the costs of drunkenness—to individuals, families, and communities—were frequently pointed out, mainly by preachers.

After the Civil War, the Methodist and Baptist churches, and organizations such as the Woman's Christian Temperance Union (W.C.T.U.) and the Anti-Saloon League tried to stop the sale of liquor in Georgia. They convinced the General Assembly to pass laws (called "local option laws") allowing the citizens to vote by county on the question of prohibition. By 1881, almost 50 Georgia counties had voted themselves dry. The "wet" forces fought back and some counties reversed their vote, but by 1906 over 100 had voted out liquor.

After Atlanta's race riot of 1906, which some whites blamed unfairly on drunkenness among black residents, the "dry" forces pushed for statewide prohibition. In 1907, they succeeded. More than a decade later, the whole United States went dry.

On the next page are a W.C.T.U. song and a map used to gain support for prohibition. An account of the day the General Assembly passed a bill (a proposal for a law) to prohibit liquor sales statewide appears below. These documents give some of the flavor of the prohibition movement.

THINK ABOUT IT

1. What evidence does the song, "Make the Map All White," provide about the techniques the prohibition forces used to win their fight?
2. How important was religion in the prohibition cause?
3. Which parts of the state, urban or rural, generally remained wet to the last?

 The General Assembly Votes Georgia Dry

. . . in the corridors and grounds about the capitol there was a surging mass of humanity. White ribbon [the badge of the prohibitionists] was fluttering everywhere. The Fulton County W.C.T.U. served lunches all day in the corridors just outside of the Hall of Representatives. The liquor men offered 13 amendments which were voted down as quickly as they were reached. About 8 o'clock a message filtered through the doors to the praying White Ribboners, that the vote had begun on the bill; instantly the wildest enthusiasm prevailed though no demonstration was made according to promise.

There was a call for Mrs. Armor and when she was found the crowd gathered about her and said: "We are going to march to Henry Grady's monument and hold a jubilee as soon as the bill is passed and we

want you to head the procession." Mrs. Armor enthusiastically agreed.

Suddenly word flashed down the line: "92 votes; the bill is safe," but they had pledged to keep quiet until the voting was over and there they stood holding their breath in intense eagerness for the end to come. In a few moments the official announcement was made: "The bill is passed by a vote of 139 to 39."

The scene was indescribable—grown men sobbed like children, women threw themselves into each others' arms weeping— bells rang, horns blew, whistles screamed.

The great crowd marched through the streets in orderly procession and in a few minutes were a multitude whom no man could number. Laughing, crying, singing, shouting, rejoicing with joy unspeakable and full of glory, they swept on till Henry Grady's monument was reached, where speeches were made . . . .

The last burst of fervid eloquence was made by a little news-boy who cried at the top of his voice: "Good-bye booze! Georgia's gone dry!" □

[Adapted from Lula Barnes Ansley, *History of the Georgia Women's Christian Temperance Union* (Columbus, Georgia: W.C.T.U. of Georgia, 1914), pp. 238-39.]

Women's Rights

"Woman suffrage had its inception in [the] fight against Saloons." These words were spoken by Rebecca Latimer Felton, a leader in the prohibition movement and in the struggle for suffrage—the right to vote— for women.

For many years, Mrs. Felton had fought political battles along with her husband, Dr. William Felton, against the bourbon Democrats, liquor candidates, and "big interests." She saw these groups as working against the hopes of ordinary people. Unlike her husband, however, she could neither vote nor hold political office.

The struggle for women's suffrage was a national one. In the years following the

WET AND DRY MAP OF GEORGIA.

The Counties Which Legalize the Sale of Liquor are Black.

1906

"The church could destroy the liquor business if it would— The liquor business would destroy the church if it could."

Help wipe these foul blots from our State. The women of Georgia appeal to you in the name of God and Home and Native Land.

Mrs. Mary Harris Armor, Pres. Ga. W.C.T.U.

MAKE THE MAP ALL WHITE

O my comrades, have you heard the glorious word that's going 'round?
There'll very soon be no saloon on all Columbia's ground.
There's a wave of prohibition rolling up from every strand,
And all the states it inundates straightway become dry land!
By city, state or country, or by township or by town,
Just let the people have a chance—we'll vote the dramshops down—
    Refrain:
        Till we make the map all white,
        Till we make the map all white,
        We'll work for prohibition
        Till we make the map all white.
The distillery and the brewery and the winery must go;
The saloons can stay no longer, when the people have said "NO!"
So we'll sing them out and pray them out and educate them out,
We'll talk them out and vote them out and legislate them out;
We'll agitate and organize and surely win the fight,
We'll work for prohibition till we make the map all white.
    Refrain:

Source: Ansley, *History of the Georgia W.C.T.U.,* 1914.

Civil War, Susan B. Anthony and Elizabeth Cady Stanton tried unsuccessfully to get the Fifteenth Amendment applied to all women as well as men.

However, at the state level, women were meeting with some success. In 1869, Wyoming (then a territory) granted voting rights to women. By 1900, Colorado, Idaho, and Utah had done likewise.

In Georgia and most other states, however, strong opposition to giving the vote to women persisted. In the following reading, Rebecca Latimer Felton responds to some of the arguments against women's suffrage.

THINK ABOUT IT

1. According to Felton, why should women have the right to vote?
2. In addition to voting rights, what else is she demanding?

 Votes for Women

It is claimed that a woman should not vote, because she does not pay her husband's debts, while he is obliged to pay hers. That is not correct. He can put a little "ad" in the newspaper and nobody will give her credit who sells dry goods or provisions.

It is said that women are represented by their husbands at the ballot box. This is not true of the ten millions of unmarried women who have nobody to vote for them. (But there are eight or nine millions of unmarried men, who vote for nobody but themselves. *And, nobody votes for the drunkard's wife!*)

There are as many widows in this country as widowers. As a rule they manage well their business affairs . . . . They deserve the ballot because their property is taxed to the limit and beyond, and they are not allowed to protest.

Women make fine teachers. But, a callow youth can vote at 21, while his capable teacher, if a woman, is forbidden to vote. Women are the mainstays in public schools. They are not only forbidden the vote, but their pay is reduced because of their sex.

They make superior stenographers, but while their pay may reach $50 a month; the young man in trousers gets from $75 to $100, with no better work—and according to common report, not so reliable as to fidelity and regular work habits.

The more I think about these inequalities and this manifest injustice, the more I am tempted to eulogize [praise] the heathen who lived on the Ganges river, and who drowned the girl babies, because they were unfit to live! □

[Adapted from Mrs. William H. Felton (Rebecca Latimer Felton), *The Subjection of Women and the Enfranchisement of Women* (Cartersville, Georgia: May 14, 1915), pp. 3-8.]

Mrs. Felton and other Georgia "suffragettes" were not successful at the state level. Not until 1920, with adoption of the Nineteenth Amendment to the United States Constitution, would they and all American women gain the same voting rights as men had.

Gwinnett County Suffragettes. Around 1920, these women were campaigning in Dacula for the right to vote.

LEISURE TIME ACTIVITIES

Of course, life in Georgia was not all problems. Around the turn of the century, Georgians did a lot of things for fun.

For many Georgians, the church was the center of social as well as spiritual life. Revivals, singing conventions, camp meetings, Sunday school picnics, and church suppers were special events.

For entertainment, there were minstrel and vaudeville shows, stage plays, band concerts, circuses, and baseball games. Some people enjoyed cameras, music boxes, player pianos, and phonographs.

In those days before radio and television, newspapers and magazines were the main news sources. From them, Georgians learned about local and world events.

In 1903, Georgians read several startling news items in their papers. A man named Ford was developing an assembly line technique for mass producing automobiles. Two men had made the first transcontinental auto trip from New York to San Francisco. The Wright brothers from Ohio had made a much shorter but far more astounding trip, by air, at Kitty Hawk, North Carolina. And, the United States had signed a treaty to build a canal across Panama.

In 1914, the newspapers informed Georgians of the opening of the Panama Canal. But there was bad news as well. A great war had broken out in Europe. Three years later the United States entered World War I.

The newspapers and magazines not only informed the people but also helped shape their attitudes. At the same time, they also reflected what was important in people's lives.

Ad in the Golden Age, *1906. At whom was this phonograph ad aimed? What values did it promote?*

MAGAZINES AND NEWSPAPERS

The following three readings are taken from a magazine and two newspapers published in Georgia shortly after the turn of the century. They provide some clues about the lives and attitudes of Georgians at that time.

THINK ABOUT IT

1. What does the article from Uncle Remus's Magazine tell about Joel Chandler Harris's reaction to the Atlanta race riot of 1906? About his view on race relations in general?
2. Did Christmas and baseball seem to mean the same things to Georgians around the turn of the century as they do today?

Uncle Remus's Magazine

Joel Chandler Harris, the creator of Uncle Remus, was born at Eatonton in 1848. In his early teens he decided to

On the Flint River, 1910. Near Bainbridge, a congregation had gathered for a baptism when the steamboat passed. What other information can you get from this photographic source?

become a journalist. He worked for several newspapers before coming to the *Atlanta Constitution* in 1873. There he became an associate editor, along with Henry W. Grady.

Harris used his evenings to write short stories, based on Afro-American folklore. In the 1880s and 1890s, his "Uncle Remus" stories made Harris world famous.

Later, Harris started his own magazine, called *Uncle Remus's Magazine*. In it, Harris used the fictional Billy Sanders of Shady Dale to present his own views on current affairs. In the following excerpt, Mr. Sanders is giving his opinions in the editor's office of *Uncle Remus's Magazine*.

 Opinions of Billy Sanders of Shady Dale

I hear tell that the preachers are all gittin' together, black and white, an tryin' for to understand one another a little better. It shorely is a preacher's problem, but considerin' what they say they stand for, they've been puttin' it off a mightly long time. You people in the cities, especially right here in Atlanta, have got to set

up in bed an' take notice of a heap of interestin' facts that are wuth rememberin'. I've heard folks say that all niggers look alike to them, but they don't look alike to me, an' they never will, not whilst my eyesight's good. Thar's jest as much difference betwixt niggers as thar is betwixt white folks, an' a heap more if you know the races right well. . . .

Now this is a great big fact that you've got to reckon with. . . . If lynchin' done any good whatsomever, it'd be another thing. But it don't do any good, an' it works harm all round. It makes brutes of good men; it lowers, as you may say, the thermometer of religion, an' civilization, an' law an' order. I know these are mighty big words; but ever'thing that's big ain't holler like a bass drum. These things mean somethin', they stand for ever'thing the white race has worked up to in the course of hundreds of generations; an' if we're gwine to knock out all the props an' go back to whar we started from, instid of playin' the game like sensible men, we deserve all an' more than the trouble we're havin', an' that we're bound to have. ☐

[Adapted from *Uncle Remus's Magazine* (September 1907), pp. 22-23.]

Play Ball, That's What Thomasville Will Do in Future

The Thomasville base ball club has been guyed [made fun of] unmercifully during the past week about the number of games lost recently and they have enough of that sort of business. From now on they will play ball right. Thomasville has as good material as any town of its size if it was properly managed. This the lovers of the game propose to do in the future.

A meeting of ball players and others met on Friday night and organized under the name of the "Thomasville Base Ball Association." The membership includes the best ball players in the city. Any one so desiring can become a member by paying a small initiation fee and monthly dues.

Mittens, breast protectors, bats, balls, etc., were ordered by telegraph yesterday and will arrive in time for the two games which are expected to be played this week with Moultrie and Coon Creek. Uniforms for the players will be procured at once.

The boys say we can safely promise the people of Thomasville some interesting games in the near future. □
[Adapted from the *Daily Times-Enterprise*, Thomasville, Georgia, August 26, 1894, p. 1.]

Pleasant Christmas Day in Columbus

Christmas day 1903 is now a beautiful memory of the past. More people than usual spent the day quietly at home. It rained from early in the morning until about noon. Most of the hunting parties planned were spoiled and only the most courageous ventured into the woods and fields during the day.

Many elaborate Christmas dinners were given at Columbus homes, and the big demand at the fruit and candy stores showed that the children were provided with plenty of all the good things they usually get at Christmas. Their stockings were well filled when they awoke early Christmas morning and yesterday more than one man was

The Siloam Baseball Team, 1902. What evidence is there that baseball was important in this small Greene County town? What later happened to discourage hometown baseball?

heard to say that he was aroused by his children on Christmas morning anywhere from 3 to 6 o'clock.

The day passed in Columbus without being marked by any serious crime or tragedy. There was a good deal of drinking and reckless use of fire works, but the police handled the crowds nicely, making only an occasional arrest.

"I am very proud of the work of the police force during the holidays," said Chief Williams yesterday. The men kept sober and did their work well. The crowds were in a good humor and the police allowed them to enjoy themselves so long as they did not fight or injure property.

The poor of the city were not forgotten on Christmas. A generous spirit of giving was manifested on every hand, many people going directly into the homes of the poor and providing them with the necessaries and comforts in which they stood so badly in need.

The children of the poor were also remembered, toys and good things to eat being provided for their enjoyment. For two days Sanitary Inspector Ledsinger played Santa Claus at his office at the court house. It was announced through this paper some days ago that Mr. Ledsinger would take great pleasure in distributing second hand clothing, food, toys and anything else sent him by the charitable people of Columbus. Scores of children called at his office and each went away carrying a package. □

[Adapted from the *Columbus Ledger*, Columbus, Georgia, December 27, 1903, sec. 3, p. 18.]

ACTIVITIES FOR CHAPTER 12

Discussion

A. Atticus G. Haygood, Booker T. Washington, W.E.B. DuBois, John Hope, and Gustavus Orr were all concerned with education.

  1. What are some ways that education might be related to progress or prosperity?

  2. What are some factors that hindered the development of education in Georgia?

B. Much controversy surrounded the reform movements of the early 1900s. People responded to these reforms in different ways, depending on their values.

  1. Which of the reforms discussed in this chapter—prisons, prohibition, or women's rights—do you think was the most important?

  2. Who might have agreed with you in 1900? Who might have disagreed with you?

  3. Identify some values that might influence a person's attitudes toward each of the reforms.

Writing Project

Life for black Georgians worsened between 1870 and 1920. Gradually, the measures of democracy, equality, and justice they had obtained during Reconstruction slipped away.

What caused this to happen? Some historians have pointed to bitterness left over from Reconstruction, depressed economic conditions, politics, lack of education among poor whites, or just plain human weakness.

Write an essay on what you think the main causes were. If you think there were several causes, explain how they worked together.

UNIT VI
1920-1980: Development of Modern Georgia

13. Boom and Bust
14. Politics and Civil Rights
15. A New Image

GEORGIA EVENTS	DATE	EVENTS ELSEWHERE
Boll weevil ravages cotton fields	1921	
WSB radio goes on the air	1922	Stock market boom begins
Farmers leaving rural areas	1924	American Indians gain citizenship
Warm Springs Foundation opened by FDR	1927	Charles Lindbergh flies across the Atlantic
	1929	Stock market crash; Depression begins
Eugene Talmadge becomes governor	1933	Franklin D. Roosevelt becomes president; New Deal begins
Governor Rivers's "little new deal" for Georgia	1937	
	1939	World War II begins in Europe
Extensive building of war plants and military bases	1941	Bombing of Pearl Harbor; U.S. enters war
Ellis Arnall becomes governor; 18-year-old vote passed	1943	War turns in favor of allies
New state constitution adopted	1945	Atomic bomb dropped; World War II ends
Three governors affair	1947	Jackie Robinson integrates baseball; "cold war" in Europe begins
3 percent sales tax passed	1951	First commercial computers
	1954	Supreme Court rules against segregation in public schools
Southern Christian Leadership Conference (SCLC) founded	1957	USSR launches Sputnik satellite
School integration begins	1961	President Kennedy creates Peace Corps
County unit system abolished	1962	John Glenn orbits earth
	1963	President Kennedy assassinated
Georgia goes Republican in presidential election	1964	Congress passes Civil Rights Act
General Assembly elects Lester Maddox	1967	
	1968	Martin Luther King, Jr., assassinated
Jimmy Carter becomes governor	1971	18-year-olds get the vote, nationwide
George Busbee elected governor; Hank Aaron breaks Babe Ruth's record	1974	President Nixon resigns
	1977	Jimmy Carter becomes president
	1981	Ronald Reagan becomes president

13 Boom and Bust

The 1920s in the United States were later called the "roaring 20s" or the "golden 20s." Those terms conjured up a picture of jazz bands and vaudeville shows, and "flappers" in short skirts dancing the Charleston. They bring to mind big time spectator sports such as baseball and boxing, bootleg whiskey, fast cars and silent movies—in short, high times.

For some Americans, the 1920s really were prosperous and carefree. Generally, the U.S. economy boomed after a brief depression in 1920-21. New industries grew rapidly and the average wage of American workers—except in farming—went up.

Perhaps the most visible sign of the new prosperity was the automobile. Back in 1910 the whole nation had fewer than 500,000 motor vehicles. By 1920 that number had grown to over 9,000,000. By 1930 almost 27,000,000 cars, trucks, and buses traveled on American roads. The automobile gave rise to other new industries. Business boomed for producers and suppliers of gas and oil, tires and fan belts, spare parts and repairs—and paved roads.

Radio was another boom industry of the 1920s. In 1920, when the nation's first regular radio station began broadcast-ing in Pittsburgh, Pennsylvania, fewer than 20,000 Americans had a "wireless." By 1926, over 700 stations were broadcast-ing. By 1930, four of every ten American families could gather around their radios to listen to baseball games, news reports, and music and comedy programs.

Also, telephones, electrical power, and indoor plumbing appeared in more and more American homes. A "well-off" family might even have a washing machine, vacuum cleaner, and refrigerator.

Most American farmers, however, did not share in the prosperity of the 1920s. Since Georgia was primarily a farm state, the 1920s were not so "golden" for many Georgians.

GEORGIA IN THE 1920s

THINK ABOUT IT

1. What caused Georgia farmers to suffer in the 1920s?
2. Where did many go when they left their farms?
3. What were some improvements in the way Georgians lived in the 1920s?

For many Georgians, the end of World War I meant the end of prosperity. The

U.S. economy slumped as the demand for war material disappeared. Suddenly there was surplus of production.

Farmers were especially hard hit in 1920. The figures for cotton, Georgia's big money crop, tell part of the story:

Cotton Production in Georgia, 1918-21

Year	Number of Bales	Price per lb.	Total Value
1918	2,122,405	.28	$291,831,000
1919	1,658,253	.36	296,827,000
1920	1,415,129	.15	108,257,000
1921	787,084	.17	65,328,000

Source: Georgia Department of Agriculture.

The drop in prices was only the first in a series of setbacks that hit Georgia farmers in the 1920s.

The Boll Weevil

In 1914, an insect called the boll weevil appeared in southwest Georgia, having crossed through Texas and the southern states from Mexico. Slowly the winged insects spread north and east. By 1919, they had infested all of the state's cotton lands. The larvae of the weevils that fed on the cotton bolls had enormous appetites. Farmers watched in disbelief as almost overnight their healthy stands of cotton were destroyed. By 1923, the cotton crop was down to 588,000 bales.

Because of the boll weevil, thousands of farm families went hungry. As the farmers lost out, so did the merchants who depended on their business and the bankers who had lent them money.

In 1925, much of Georgia was hit by the worst drought since 1845. Some parts of the state had no rain all summer; even ancient oak trees withered and died from

Broad Street, Augusta, about 1929. The automobile dominates the scene. Painted parking spaces and crosswalks, traffic lights, and traffic jams are already part of downtown.

lack of water. The drought slowed the weevil, but it also reduced the per acre yields of most crops. By the thousands, Georgians abandoned their farms.

One writer described the wholesale exodus from Greene County, Georgia, this way:

> The trains began to make longer stops in the stations at Greensboro and Union Point, Woodville and Carey. The Negro farm folk were climbing aboard with their cumbersome bundles. Many left in the fall of 1922, more in 1923, and still more in 1924 and 1925 as cash and credit resources further dwindled. The Whites, a little less dependent, could weather the depression a little longer. So their migration was smaller and its peak was two years later.
>
> Between 1920 and 1930 Greene's colored population decreased by 43 percent, white by 23 percent . . . .
>
> The number of farmers in Greene dropped from 3,000 in 1920 to 1,557 in 1930. . . .
>
> Nearly 7,000 people left here (Greene County). They were usually headed for distant cities—Birmingham or Detroit, Chicago or Philadelphia, Cincinnati or Washington—to look for work. But most of them stopped in Atlanta or Athens or Augusta, for they had no money to go farther. Farm people left Greene in the middle 1920s as virtual refugees. □

[Arthur Raper, *Tenants of the Almighty* (New York: The Macmillan Company, 1943), pp. 156-57.]

Following is an oral history account by one Georgian, telling about life in the 1920s as he remembers it.

Joel Hurt lived in Oglethorpe County during the 1920s. His account of those years comes from an interview at Lexington in 1981.

My daddy was a school teacher. Didn't have money—that was one of the poorest paying jobs I know of. He worked for $35-45 a month. Taught 10 grades in school. One or two months out of the year sometimes, the trustees didn't have the money to pay him with. . . . didn't get it.

I started doing chores. . . plowin' mules, haulin' lumber, blacksmithin', whatever you could to make a living. I *made* my money. My daddy didn't have any money to give me. We had food and a good house to live in. My mother fed all the children and kept our clothes clean—that's all we had. . . .

I'll tell you something about the preacher. You know what he got for his pay sometimes? Eggs, chicken, butter, spend-the-night, feed-his-horse, put corn in the buggy for his horse another day or two, and two or three bundles of fodder. And, if he went to the right place, maybe a country ham or a side of bacon.

Entertainment? Well, somebody played the fiddle, somebody played the banjo, somebody played the guitar, and just moved everything out of one big room—we loved to go to a dance. We had a good time—and maybe somebody'd have a cake, parched peanuts, somebody'd have a good bunch of apples, and have a good time.

First cars I ever saw—one was a White two cylinder and one was a Buick two cylinder. I thought, "if I could ever in the world get my hands on one". . . and I did get my hands on one when I was 13 years old. My brother-in-law gave me one, in 1916, a secondhand Ford, and I never been without a car since. Gas was five gallons for 75 cents. Later, I took the body off the old car and made a racer out of it. I can remember puttin' a couple or three girls on it and we ride up here to the drugstore—that was a long trip from Maxeys. I'd tell 'em, "there's just a quarter in the crowd now, unless ya'll got some money." See, we'd get an ice cream cone or coke cola a piece, have a nickel for a pack of chewing gum, and go on back home.

Times were hard, wasn't any money. We had a period 1916-1921 when cotton went way up, you know. That was where it broke so many people that had money and big farms, that were holding it [cotton] for the 50-cent margin. The bankers told 'em to hold it, "it was going there." And, it never went there. I sold my little bit I made, 1920-21, I made pretty good little crop, sold mine to pay my debts, an' I come out all right doing that. But the others held theirs when they could have got 30-40 cents. They were holding for 50 cents—and some of 'em finally took 6 cents and 8 cents.

Lot of 'em lost their farms. Hard, sho nuff, hard. Yes, and the insurance company got about a third of the land back out this way when times got so hard. See, they'd borrowed from the insurance company to try to bind over—and it never did go. The boll weevil hit 'em then, hit along in 1921. The dry year got us in 1925—that's when I thought I had a nice crop. But it didn't rain on it from the time it come up to the time I gathered the first bale of cotton and ginned it—and that's all I made.

So, I lit out for Florida the next day to try to make a livin' and pay my debts, too. I had to do something to pay my debts. I was willing to work. I couldn't find work here, an' everybody said, "go to Florida, there's a gold mine in the sky down there." It wasn't quite that way, but I found a job anyway. Put my shirt and britches in an old Dodge car I had and four other men went with me. We all went down there and got jobs. Stayed 20 years, met my wife, raised my family—and then, I decided to come back here.

Many people left. Yes, sir—just as fast as they could get the money to leave. Some of 'em in my town went to Gary, Indiana, to work in the steel factories up there. There was boys leavin' every which way. □

The Brighter Side

Even though times were hard in the state, Georgians shared in the progress of the 1920s. Paved roads crept out from the cities to help farmers bring their produce to market and end the isolation of rural life.

A Famous Georgia Product. By the early 1920s, Coca-Cola was being bottled and sold all over the U.S. Many bottlers, like this one in Cobb County, still used horse-drawn delivery wagons.

Atlanta, the hub of the Southeast's railroad network, added a new dimension in transportation. In 1926, the region's first regular air mail service opened at Candler Field.

The state's people also shared in the good times. In 1922 the first radio station in the South, WSB in Atlanta, went on the air. The "Voice of the South" broadcast weather and cotton market reports and special music programs and story hours for children. On Sundays, Georgians could listen to church services in the morning and baseball games in the afternoon.

Every fair-sized Georgia town had a movie theater; larger cities had fancy movie palaces—the Fox in Atlanta being the grandest of all. Like other Americans, Georgians loved spectator sports. The state had its share of national heroes. In baseball, Ty Cobb from Royston, Georgia, batted over .400 more seasons than any other major league player and was one of the game's all-time greats. About the same time, Atlanta native Bobby Jones was winning one golf tournament after another. Hailed as the world's greatest golfer, he helped to make the game a popular sport in the United States.

In the late 1920s, football grew more popular as the teams of Georgia Tech and the University of Georgia defeated Notre Dame and Yale.

THE GREAT DEPRESSION

THINK ABOUT IT

1. What was the "crash of '29?" What brought it on?
2. How did investors lose their money? How did banks and depositors lose theirs?
3. Why was the depression that began in 1929 so much worse than earlier ones in the nineteenth century?

The American economic prosperity of the 1920s ended with a crash.

The United States had suffered business depressions before. Cycles of ups and downs—prosperity and depression—became common to industrialized nations in the 1800s. Typically, during a depression period, prices would go down as production of goods exceeded the demand for them. Many industrial workers would be out of work as factories slowed production. However, none of these depressions had any long-term effects on American society.

In 1929, though, a depression began that dragged on for a decade. Its effects would be far-reaching: the national government assumed greater power in regulating business and greater responsibility for the welfare of people. The American people,

A Movie Theater in Augusta. During the depression, movie theaters often did a good business. Why might movies be popular during hard times?

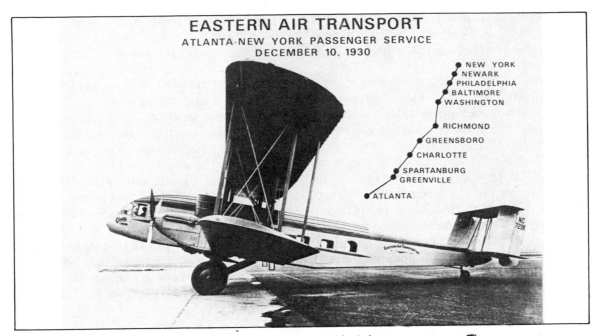

Non-stop service was far in the future when this ad appeared in Atlanta newspapers. The plane carried only 18 passengers.

too, would change. Their attitudes would alter—toward business and its freedom to operate without interference and toward government and its role in their lives. They would even change their ideas about their own rights and responsibilities. How did this Great Depression come about?

The Crash of '29

The beginning of the nationwide depression dates from the "stock market crash"—an enormous drop in stock prices—in late 1929.

During the late 1920s, as American business was booming, many people confidently invested their money in stocks (ownership shares in a corporation). Some hoped to make a fast fortune by speculating.

Speculating involved buying stock at a low price with a plan to sell it soon at a higher price. Stock prices kept climbing as the economy boomed, so speculating seemed like a good thing to many Americans. The favored stocks were in the new rapidly growing industries such as automobiles, aviation, radio, motion pictures, and telephone and other utilities.

As more and more speculators jumped into the market, hoping to "get rich quick," the prices of stocks continued to zoom upwards. The future looked rosy. So, more people were convinced to invest in stocks. They borrowed money from the banks to do it, planning to make their profits before the loans had to be paid back.

Flaws in the Prosperity

The prosperity of the 1920s proved faulty. For example, agriculture had remained depressed since the end of World War I. Farmers had been producing more than consumers demanded, so their crop prices stayed down. Farmers had little money to spend on the goods other Americans were enjoying.

Certain industries, too, such as textiles and mining, were not prospering. Workers in these industries got low wages and had little to spend. Then too, as transportation of goods and people shifted to trucks and cars, the railroads began to suffer.

Americans themselves were going heavily into debt with big mortgages on new houses and installment loans for cars and luxuries.

Some economists and government leaders pointed out that questionable business and banking practices could lead to trouble. However, the national government in the 1920s had a *laissez-faire* policy toward business. Said President Coolidge in 1927, "The business of America is business." He meant the government to keep "hands off." With little regulation from government, corporations and banks were free to operate as they pleased. Sometimes their practices were unsound or unfair; sometimes they were downright dishonest. For example, certain corporations were set up that sold stock but produced nothing. Unsuspecting investors were stuck with worthless stock, while the sellers got away with the money. Banks sometimes took foolish risks with their depositors' money, making loans with little or no security backing them. They, too, sometimes bought worthless stock.

In 1929, many industries found themselves with surplus goods on hand. They had overproduced. To get rid of their huge inventories, they cut prices and cut back on production. Suddenly, investors lost confidence that stock prices would continue to rise. Expecting that prices would drop, they started selling off their stocks. More stockholders joined in the selling. As soon as more stocks were up for sale than people wanted to buy, stock prices dropped. Panic selling set in. Stock prices plummeted.

When investors had to sell their stocks for less than they paid for them, they couldn't pay back their loans. Banks collapsed. People with deposits at those banks lost their savings.

In 1930 and 1931, thousands of businesses cut back production or went bankrupt. Millions of their employees were laid off. Unemployed, and often without any savings, these people had no way to pay off their debts or even to buy necessities. Many families lost their homes,

farms, and cars. By 1932, about one of every four American workers was unemployed. Local governments and private organizations, such as the Salvation Army, set up shelters for the homeless and distributed food to the hungry.

Why was the Great Depression so much worse than earlier depressions? Back when American society was more agrarian, less industrial, the majority of the people were not affected by business cycles. They provided for most of their own needs—working on their own farms, raising their own food, building their own shelters. But, by 1930, the American people had become far more *interdependent*. That is, they depended upon one another—to supply the houses, cars, electricity, paved roads, and the

Poverty in Atlanta, 1936. During the depression, eight families shared one bathroom in this apartment house.

"storebought" food, clothing, and other goods.

Moreover, practically all parts of the United States economy had become *integrated*—linked together. A change in any one part affected other parts. For example, the mining industry was tied to the steel industry tied to the auto industry tied to the tire industry tied to the. . . . So, when the depression set in, it spread to all parts of the economy and affected almost every American.

Georgia in the Depression

As you've already read, for many Georgians the depression began long before the stock market crash of 1929. Many Georgians, not just farmers, barely scraped by. As the economy weakened, government also ran short of money. Government services were cut, and sometimes public employees were not paid on time.

Following are oral accounts of the Great Depression as recalled by two Georgians.

THINK ABOUT IT

1. What were prices and wages like in Georgia during the depression?

2. What were some other signs of "hard times" mentioned in the two accounts?

 Sidney Thurmond lived in Clarke County. Remarks are from an interview at Athens in 1981.

I worked in a grocery store and ran a corn mill. I believe I worked for 50 cents a day, and a lot of people worked for 35. You'd work all week for $3.

At that time, people in the country had their own cows and corn. You could go out in the country and find something to eat. Course you didn't find steak and pork chops, but you found something to eat. People would bring their corn to the mill and sell it and buy coffee or something.

Different from the '20s to the '30s? I tell you the truth. For black people it was hard all the way through. Black people didn't have something to give up, 'cause they didn't have nuthin' to start with. A day's work, that's all they had.

Nobody got no checks, nobody got no handouts or nuthin! During the last Hoover

Chopping Cotton on Rented Land, Greene County. Most men and women in rural Georgia worked hard for low wages during the depression.

days, they would ship carloads of flour to each county and they would give that. That's the first I knew of a handout.

People in general did [get something besides flour] but not me. I had a job—50 cents a day—and that was all day! Sun to sun—workin' around a store and runnin' a corn mill.

Oh Lord, there was lots of folks walkin', beggin'. I've seen a man, a poor wife and four or five children; they just walkin' in the road. Most of the time, they walked the railroad and stop at your house. Saw worlds of 'em.

At the store where I worked, I been down there a many a morning to unlock it, and there'd be a man and his wife and children be done spent the night on that porch. When they'd wake up they want to give the children a drink of water or some crackers or something.

But you didn't find nobody robbin' nobody and they didn't bother nobody. I don't remember anybody robbin' or breakin' in. People didn't harm you. They'd come by and beg you for something. You give it to 'em and they'd take it and go on. If you didn't they'd just go on down the road. No, it wasn't like it is today.

Gas was 15-16 cents a gallon, [but] a lot of people just parked their cars. Had no money. Had to get mules and horses and buggies again. I seen a lot of big men park their car and went to drivin' a horse. People had to change.

People worked for anything—clothes, bread, food. I know a lot of women worked all day and bring home some old suit of clothes they didn't want. What they had left over from dinner, or some milk and butter—that's all she'd get. They didn't have nuthin' to pay 'em with.

My family didn't feel the depression. We saw it, but we were lucky. I always had a job. I could buy a heap with the little money I was making. We saw it, but didn't feel it.

I started workin' for $3 a week and

quit work for $40 a week—same job. I stayed 29 years. □

 Dorsey Crowe lived in Oconee County. These remarks are from an interview at Bogart in 1981.

That's what we called "Hoover days" because he was president and everybody had to blame somebody for the hard times. So, they blamed Hoover. I think it would a been a depression regardless of who was president.

We had old Ford automobiles, weren't able to buy gas for 'em. We'd taken the motors out, taken the body off and made a wagon out of the frame and pulled it with the horses and mules. With them ball bearings, it pulled real easy. We called them "Hoover buggies."

Every little town around here had a bank—was one at Statham, Bogart, Eastville, and Watkinsville. When they went broke, the people lost their money. A few of the banks paid 'em maybe 10 percent or something like that. It was a great loss. For years after that, country people would hide their money—when they'd get a little money—instead of puttin' it in a bank. They were afraid it would go broke again. They put it in jars and buried it around their homes.

I was around 15 years old then. We'd pick a sack of cotton every morning before we'd go to school and when we'd get in from school, we'd go to pickin' cotton. We were out there by daylight—and then pick until dark. Cotton back then, at one time, got down to 5 and 6 cents a pound, [but] cotton was the money crop, only way to make a livin'.

Tenant farmers, in those years, were lucky to pay out of debt. The landlord had to furnish 'em something to eat till fall. Maybe some of 'em work all year and might clear $50—$50 above his eats and all. The landlord had to furnish him something to eat, place to live, had to furnish him wood to burn. To buy clothes, they'd

> *"One interesting thing about one of the local drugstores here in town [Greensboro]: they had a specialty during the depression years that they called the "boll weevil." It was a glass of chocolate milk with a scoop of vanilla ice cream in it. You got that for a nickel. That was a very popular demand of the soda fountain in those days. Since the boll weevil had done so much damage in the county, they called this cheap dessert the "boll weevil." It was about the biggest nickel's worth you could find."*
> —Lila Belle McCommons, from an interview in 1981.

borrow from the landlord till fall.

We planted corn, but used that mostly for feed for the horses, and we made corn meal for corn bread. We always growed wheat, so you had your own flour. There wasn't no money hardly anywhere around. But most farmers had plenty to eat. Just didn't have no money. Carrither's mill up here ground corn into meal and wheat into flour. To pay for grinding, they tolled it—took out so much in toll—no cash passed at all.

Was mighty little fresh meat you had. Course once in a while, a neighbor would kill a cow and peddle it around from house to house in his buggy. Sold roasts for about 5 cents a pound, steak about 10 or 12 cents. But mostly they chunked it up. Didn't cut it up into all kinds of steaks and things. We had plenty of cured pork. You'd raise your own hogs, 'cause you had plenty of corn to raise 'em with. We'd kill in the winter time, and salt 'em down.

Daddy also had a store, built it in '24. I guess we was better off than the average person 'cause of the store he run. People would bring eggs to the store and he'd pay 'em. Every Saturday, he'd go to town [Athens] and take those eggs and sell 'em to a store. Then he'd buy groceries from the store at wholesale price to bring back to his store. He had to give a lot of

credit until fall when people sold their cotton. Back then people would pay you—they paid off their debts. □

THE ROLE OF GOVERNMENT

THINK ABOUT IT
1. How did President Roosevelt differ from President Hoover in his attitude toward government's responsibility in fighting the depression?
2. What were the three main goals of the "New Deal" programs?
3. How did these programs violate the old principle of *laissez-faire*?
4. Which of the New Deal ideas became a permanent part of American society?

Such a depression had never hit the United States before. The question "What should be done?" faced everyone, including government leaders. Did government have a responsibility to do something? Some people thought so, others did not.

The president of the United States from 1929 to 1933, Herbert Hoover, felt that the American economy was basically sound. Hoover, a Republican, believed strongly in *laissez-faire,* the government shouldn't interfere in the economy. Business could take care of itself. In this belief, he was supported by most business leaders. However, as the depression grew worse, pressures to do something mounted. President Hoover and Congress set up government programs to lend money to keep banks and businesses going, and to buy surplus farm products.

In 1932, a presidential election year, many Americans blamed President Hoover for the depression. His Democratic opponent, New York Governor Franklin D. Roosevelt, won by a landslide.

In his campaign, Roosevelt—nicknamed "FDR"—had promised the people a "New Deal." Government, he pledged, would become directly involved in ending the depression and in preventing another one from occurring. As soon as he was inaugurated in March 1933, he began a series of actions that would eventually change the role of the national government in American society.

The New Deal

The government's New Deal programs were aimed at "Relief, Recovery, and Reform." Because there were so many new government agencies (or divisions) set up to administer these programs, they were usually known by their initials rather than their names.

Relief programs were aimed at providing help to the millions of unemployed and their families, many of whom were near starvation. Although some relief programs gave direct handouts of food, clothing, and cash, most programs involved work.

- Civilian Conservation Corps (CCC): Put young men to work in rural and forest areas—planting trees and terracing fields to prevent soil erosion. These men also worked on dams, roads, and forest fire prevention and mosquito control projects. They lived in army-type camps. The government paid them $30 a month—$22 of which was sent to their parents.
- Public Works Administration (PWA): Put about a half-million men to work on public construction projects, such as school buildings, community auditoriums, hospitals, dams, roads and bridges, airports for the military, and ships for the navy.
- Works Progress Administration (WPA): The biggest and most controversial work relief program. From 1935 to 1941, the WPA gave work to almost eight million unemployed men and women, ranging from construction workers to artists, musicians, and writers.* Its 250,000 projects included such widely varying activities as clearing slums, building power plants, and providing free plays and concerts.

---

*The ex-slave interviews you read in Chapter 8 were conducted as part of a WPA effort called the Federal Writers' Project.

Work Relief, Bibb County, 1936. WPA road projects such as this one employed many Georgians and helped get the state "out of the mud."

A WPA Nursery School. What are some reasons schools such as this one in Macon may have been started?

The WPA spent over 11 billion dollars on its projects. Many citizens criticized them as a waste of the taxpayers' money. Others defended the WPA, pointing out that work relief did more than provide people with income, which when spent stimulated business recovery. It also boosted their pride in themselves and gave them hope at a time when the morale of millions was at a low point.

Recovery programs were aimed at helping the economy get back on its feet. One of the main problems was low farm prices because of overproduction.

● Agricultural Adjustment Administration (AAA): Aimed to bring farm income back up to its World War I levels. It paid farmers to produce less cotton, corn, wheat, rice, milk, and fewer hogs. It also bought farm products to distribute to people on relief. The effect was to raise farm prices and thus enable farmers to buy manufactured goods.

● Farm Security Administration (FSA): To relieve rural poverty. Provided loans to almost a million sharecroppers, renters, and farm laborers to buy land, tools, and livestock. It also assisted farmers in trying new crops and taught them soil conservation, livestock raising, and farm management.

● National Recovery Administration (NRA): To help business, industry, and their employees. Attempted to have business operate according to strict codes of conduct. The codes specified how much certain businesses would produce, the prices they would charge, and the wages they would pay. Their goal was to control production and raise prices. The codes outlawed such practices as unfair advertising and price discrimination. The codes also set minimum wages and maximum working hours for each industry. Child labor was prohibited.

- Federal Deposit Insurance Corporation (FDIC): A recovery program to help restore confidence in the nation's banks. Deposits in an insured bank (which had to meet certain federal regulations) were protected against loss up to $5,000.

Reform programs were aimed at making changes in the way Americans worked and did business so as to prevent future hardships like the ones they suffered in the 1930s.

- Securities and Exchange Commission (SEC): Set up to oversee the buying and selling of stocks. To protect investors, and the corporations themselves, the SEC set rules against the wild speculation and shady dealings that had led to the 1929 crash.
- National Labor Relations Board (NLRB): To protect workers who wanted to organize unions. Under the NLRB, employees were guaranteed the right to choose representatives to bargain collectively with employers over wages and working conditions.
- Rural Electrification Association (REA): A major reform effort to provide electrical power to rural areas of the country.
- Tennessee Valley Authority (TVA): The biggest single project under REA. Built dams and operated power plants to provide electricity to people in seven states. Brought power to millions of farm families through cooperatives.
- Social Security Act: Began to provide government pensions, or retirement pay, to older citizens. It also provided federal money to state governments for helping people who were unemployed or unable to work.

DEPRESSION POLITICS IN GEORGIA

In the late 1920s, the General Assembly spent more money than was available from taxes. By 1930, state government couldn't pay its bills. It owed public school teachers alone about $4 million in back pay.

In 1930, Richard B. Russell, Jr., was elected governor on a promise to reorganize state government and straighten out its finances. With the cooperation of the General Assembly, Russell did provide Georgia with a more efficient government. Under Russell, the office of governor gained more power—especially over the spending of money.

In 1932, in the depths of the depression, Governor Russell was elected to the United States Senate. At the same time, the voters chose Eugene Talmadge to be governor.

THINK ABOUT IT

1. What appeal did Eugene Talmadge have to rural voters in 1932?
2. What was Governor Talmadge's attitude toward New Deal programs?
3. How did the majority of Georgians view the New Deal?

Talmadge had been Georgia's Commissioner of Agriculture. He had admired Tom Watson and took some of the same populist views, championing the small farmer and preaching the ideals of thrift, hard work, and rugged individualism. Talmadge was popular with rural white Georgians. He knew the hardships farmers were suffering and promised to help them as governor. Like Watson, Talmadge was a speaker who could move his audience. He would, he said, cut the fee for all auto tags to $3, reduce property taxes, lower utility rates, and cut spending. He won easily.

When Eugene Talmadge took office, he found the General Assembly and other state officials opposed to the measures on which he had campaigned. The governor insisted that a promise to the voters was

Gov. Eugene Talmadge makes a point to listeners in a country store. When he spoke at political rallies, his rural supporters would often drive long distances to hear him.

sacred. He took several steps to meet his promises. He pressured some officials, threatened to withhold the salaries of others, and suspended still others. He even imposed martial law and had the national guard remove certain officials from their offices.

Talmadge used the powers of the governor—especially his control of finances—as no one before him had done. Many Georgians were outraged by the governor's high-handed actions. Newspapers attacked him, but many voters applauded his strong actions.

Governor Talmadge and the New Deal

At first, Talmadge supported the Roosevelt administration's efforts to com-bat the depression. Then he began to see the New Deal as threatening to "the Georgia way of life." For example, he opposed work relief programs, especially their minimum wage requirements, saying:

Some of the opposition want the state of Georgia to pay a boy who drives a truck, or a negro who rolls a wheelbarrow, a minimum of 40 cents per hour, when a hardworking white woman in the cotton field, right beside the road where they are, is picking cotton from sunup to sundown. If you put a minimum of 40 cents per hour on picking cotton this year in Georgia, the present price of lint and seed would not pay the pick bill. □

[Eugene Talmadge, *The Statesman*, Hapeville, Georgia, August 14, 1934.]

Governor Talmadge opposed work relief programs for two reasons. He believed they (1) undermined private enterprise by paying too high a wage and (2) undermined white supremacy by giving blacks equal pay with whites.

When the General Assembly passed laws to enable Georgia to participate in other New Deal programs, the governor vetoed them. For instance, he vetoed social security retirement benefits and unemployment insurance for Georgia.

By 1936, Governor Talmadge openly denounced President Roosevelt as a socialist and said he would run against him for the presidency. (At that time, the state constitution prohibited a governor from serving more than four years in succession.)

Many Georgians had mixed feelings: they held many of the values that Talmadge preached, but they also appreciated the help Roosevelt was giving them. Furthermore, since the late 1920s, FDR, a victim of polio, had come regularly to Warm Springs, Georgia, for treatment. As president, he established there his "Little White House," which made him special in the eyes of many Georgians.

Following is an oral account of the arrival of the New Deal in Georgia.

 Lila Belle McCommons lived in Greene County. She was interviewed at Greensboro in 1981.

I came directly from college to Greensboro to teach in the high school in 1928.

I well remember when President Roosevelt came into office and how everybody sat by the radio to listen to his fireside chats. They thought he was just wonderful. I didn't hear a single person in this area criticize him. No, he wasn't that popular everywhere else, but in most small towns and rural areas, they thought he had really come to turn the country around. He would tell us over the radio that things were getting better all the time and that all we had to fear was fear itself. He would say not to be uneasy about the future, that it was going to get better all the time.

We benefitted in this area because it was chosen for a number of the CCC camps—the army of young workers, who worked in forests and fields, stopping erosion. Some people said it was a waste of money. But it kept a lot of young fellows employed. And it resulted in newly planted forest areas that of course led into the sawmill and pulpwood business still flourishing today.

The business people thought it was a good thing because the young men spent money with the local merchants. They not only kept themselves going, but helped their families, their parents, survive those hard years.

Another thing they did was to build beautiful parks. They built one down at Crawfordville, a recreation center with swimming facilities, camping facilities, an open pavilion where young people could go and have a square dance. So, it had many fringe benefits besides giving young unemployed men jobs. The benefits of those programs were far-reaching. □

President Roosevelt at Warm Springs. "He always made sure he did meet other patients, and they felt a closeness to him. To know that a person in his position—the president— shared the facilities, certainly made you feel good that you were part of the set-up."—a former patient.

So, in 1936, Georgians voted for the New Deal. They gave their presidential vote to Roosevelt and elected E.D. Rivers—a Talmadge foe—their governor. At the same time, they re-elected Richard Russell to the United States Senate over Eugene Talmadge, who ran for the Senate instead of the presidency.

With the election of Rivers, Georgia joined the New Deal fully. Public works, such as roads, bridges, courthouses, and school buildings, were constructed. Other programs, from welfare and health to slum clearance and soil conservation were conducted. Georgians could join social security retirement and unemployment programs.

At the same time, the General Assembly upgraded public education by providing funds for free textbooks and a guaranteed seven-month school year.

However, Governor Rivers's "little new deal" ended on a sour note. Refusing to raise taxes to cover all the new expenses, he juggled the state's finances. State government was again in debt.

In 1940, Eugene Talmadge was back, running for governor, while FDR was running for an unprecedented third term as president. Both won.

THE LEGACY OF THE NEW DEAL

When President Roosevelt took office, almost 13 million Americans were out of work—about 25 percent of the nation's labor force. By 1940, over 8 million were still unemployed, almost 15 percent.

The New Deal, then, was not successful in ending the depression. Its programs were experiments. Some worked; some didn't. Still, many people in the 1930s saw that their government was trying. The New Deal gave them hope and helped them get through the hard times.

What were the long-term effects of the New Deal? According to the U.S. Constitu-

tion, one purpose of government is, "to promote the general welfare." The New Deal gave that phrase a new meaning: government has the duty to protect all its citizens.

Since the 1930s, citizens have come to expect various kinds of government protection. They deposit their money in banks without fear of losing it. They approach old age expecting to have an income even when they can no longer work. Working people expect to be paid a minimum wage. They also expect government to support their right to organize a union and bargain with employers. By law, persons who are handicapped, unemployed, or otherwise needy are entitled to certain kinds of government protection.

Americans also pay for these protections. Government is far bigger, costs much more, and is tied in to the daily lives of citizens far more than before the New Deal.

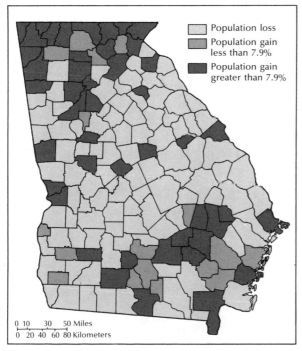

Population loss

Population gain less than 7.9%

Population gain greater than 7.9%

0 10   30   50 Miles
0 20 40 60 80 Kilometers

MAP 25. Population Change, 1920-1940. Average growth for the state was only 7.9%. In general, which areas of the state lost population? Where did the people go? Compare this map with the one on page 142. What was happening to the black belt?

ACTIVITIES FOR CHAPTER 13

Discussion

A. The Great Depression of the 1930s was not the first depression in the United States, but it was by far the worst.

1. What weaknesses in the economy of the 1920s helped bring on the depression?

2. What business and banking practices were also to blame?

3. When the depression came, why was it so far-reaching?

B. The federal government's New Deal brought a revolutionary change in the relationship between government and business.

1. How did presidents Hoover and Roosevelt differ on the proper role of government in meeting the depression?

2. What were the three main goals of the New Deal?

3. What were some objections to the New Deal?

4. What programs of the New Deal are taken for granted in America today?

14 Politics and Civil Rights

. . . it is the purpose of the Nation to build now with all possible speed every machine and arsenal and factory that we need to manufacture our defense material. We have the men, the skill, the wealth, and above all, the will.

—President Franklin Delano Roosevelt, radio address to the American people, December 29, 1940

Within a year of the president's address to the people, the United States was at war. World War II would bring far-reaching changes to Georgia.

Georgia's economy moved into full swing in the early 1940s. Wartime demands for agricultural and manufactured products did what the New Deal had failed to do. Unemployment practically disappeared. Farm income shot up. The state's existing factories operated at full speed. New manufacturing plants were built.

The war also brought thousands of people to the state. Some came to military training centers. Others worked at war production facilities.

All this activity caused the income of Georgians to rise sharply. The average worker made twice as much money in 1945 as in 1941.

But while the state prospered from the wartime economy, 320,000 Georgians went into military service. Seven thousand never returned.

Paratroop Training at Fort Benning, Columbus, 1941. Other military training centers were Camp Gordon at Augusta and Hunter Field near Savannah. Military command headquarters were at Warner Robins Air Base near Macon and at Fort McPherson in Atlanta.

B-29 Bombers Assembled at Marietta. This Bell Aircraft plant was Georgia's largest war production facility. Other plants in Macon and Milledgeville made weapons, and shipyards in Savannah and Brunswick built naval vessels.

THE POST-WAR YEARS

When the war was over, the nation's factories that had been producing tanks, warplanes, and weapons switched over to producing tractors, cars, refrigerators, and other business and consumer goods. In Georgia, too, post-war manufacturing brought continuing prosperity to many people.

Through the 1950s and 1960s, manufacturing in Georgia expanded. Some northern companies moved their operations south where the climate was milder and fuel costs were lower. Other attractions were low taxes and non-union labor.

Most of Georgia's manufacturing was "light" industry, such as clothing, furniture, and carpeting. But, there was some "heavy" industry, including auto assembly plants at Atlanta and paper manufacturing at Savannah.

Before World War II, only a few thousand tractors were in use on Georgia farms. After the war, the tractor rapidly displaced the mule. Tractors, mechanical cotton pickers, and other machines saved human labor as well as animal labor. A farmer with the new machines could produce a crop that formerly required the work of several men with mules.

Mechanization not only made farming more efficient but also changed rural life. First, the sharecrop system of agriculture faded away. If a tenant farmer couldn't

Senator Russell with the Troops in France, 1945. As a U.S. Senate leader in military affairs, Georgia's Richard Russell often made inspection tours of wartime facilities.

The Changing Countryside. In the post-war years, chicken houses such as this one in Barrow County began appearing throughout north Georgia. They were a sign of new prosperity. Poultry soon became one of the state's leading farm products.

buy his own place, he usually headed for the city to find a job in industry. Second, as the tenants left, the number of individual farms dropped—from over 200,000 farms in 1940 to about 100,000 in 1960. At the same time, the average size of farms almost doubled—to about 200 acres.

After the war, cotton was no longer the main crop in Georgia. Many farmers switched to raising crops that brought in more money: peanuts, soybeans, and corn. Others switched to raising livestock or poultry or became "tree farmers," planting pines in the old cotton fields.

Population Changes

Along with these changes in Georgia's economy came dramatic changes in population. First came the big move to Georgia cities. In 1940 two-thirds of Georgia's people lived in rural areas. By 1960 only half the state population lived there.

The largest urban area was around Atlanta. Augusta, Columbus, Macon, and Savannah grew, too, and Albany almost tripled its population between 1940 and 1960.

As the cities grew, suburban areas developed. Houses, shopping centers, schools, and some industries were located just outside cities in formerly rural areas. Increased traffic between city centers and suburban areas created a need for the first expressways, built in the late 1940s and early 1950s.

There were also other population changes in Georgia. The movement of rural black Georgians to northern states, which began in the 1920s, continued. Between 1940 and 1950, Georgia's black population dropped by more than 20,000. At the same time, Georgia's white population increased by over 350,000. In the 1950s, the state's black population did grow, but the white population growth rate was three times higher.

The 30 years, 1940-1970, were years of great change in Georgia. This chapter will touch on some aspects of that change.

CHANGING GEORGIA POLITICS

Since the election of Richard Russell in 1930, state politics had been dominated by strong governors. However, in 1941, as Georgians anxiously followed the events of World War II overseas, an event occurred at home that would bring big changes to state government—especially in the office of governor.

THINK ABOUT IT

1. What reforms did the Arnall years bring to state government?
2. What was the county unit system of vote counting? Why was it outlawed by the U.S. Supreme Court?
3. How did the issue of race relations affect state politics in the 1950s and 1960s?
4. How did actions by the federal government influence politics in Georgia?

Ellis Arnall and Reform

In 1941, Governor Eugene Talmadge got word that a professor at the University of Georgia was in favor of having blacks and whites go to the same college. The governor promised to rid the state colleges of any professor who favored "communism or racial equality." At that time, Georgia laws gave the governor so much power in state government that Talmadge was able to get several professors fired.

Because of the governor's action, the University of Georgia (and later all white public colleges in the state) faced losing its accreditation. This meant that university students' credits and degrees would have no official value. Many citizens were outraged that this political move by the governor had put the university in such a bad position.

At this point, the Georgia attorney general, Ellis Arnall, announced that he would run against Governor Talmadge. In the spring and summer of 1942, college students by the hundreds fanned out across Georgia campaigning for Arnall. It was the only race for governor that Eugene Talmadge would lose.

Arnall Makes Some Changes

Ellis Arnall had promised to reform state government if elected. Change came quickly.

First, Arnall asked for, and the General Assembly passed, laws that reduced the powers of the governor. The governor lost power to remove certain elected officials from office or to strike their salaries from the budget as Eugene Talmadge had done. Another law took away the governor's power to pardon convicted criminals and gave that power to a Board of Pardons and Paroles. The governor also lost his seat on the boards which ran the state's schools

Ellis Arnall Campaigns for Governor, 1942. Here Arnall speaks to a crowd in front of the University of Georgia campus. Why might Arnall have drawn heavy support in Athens?

and colleges. Because the former governor had often blocked changes in the state constitution, the governor's power to veto constitutional amendments was eliminated.

During his term in office, Governor Arnall called for prison reform. The chain gangs, with their striped clothes and their leg irons, were finally abolished.

There were changes in voting, too. A person "old enough to fight is old enough to vote," said the governor. In 1943, Georgia became the first state to lower the voting age from 21 to 18. The General Assembly also abolished the poll tax, which had kept many citizens from voting. Then, in 1944, a federal court ruled that Georgia's "white primary" was unconstitutional. Black citizens could not be excluded from voting in primaries held by the government.

A clamor went up to have the General Assembly change the law so that the party, not the government, would hold the primary. Governor Arnall refused to call a special session of the legislature to do so, asking "good Georgians to let blacks vote in their primary."

The Three Governors Affair

The year 1946 was an election year in Georgia. Under the state constitution, Arnall could not run to succeed himself. Eugene Talmadge returned for another run at the governorship. The issue was white supremacy. "Old Gene" promised to restore the white primary. His opponent for the Democratic nomination was James Carmichael, head of Bell Aircraft at Marietta.

For the first time, thousands of black citizens voted in the primary. When the votes were counted, Carmichael had more than Eugene Talmadge, but Talmadge carried more counties. On the basis of a system called the "county unit vote," Talmadge won the primary.

Eugene Talmadge was unopposed in the general election. (Only the Democratic Party ran candidates in Georgia in 1946. Not until 1966 would the Republican Party seriously try for the office of governor.) However, Talmadge was very ill and died before taking office.

Who was to be governor? The Georgia Constitution provided that the General Assembly would officially count the votes

---

The County Unit System

The county unit system of voting was originally a custom of the Democratic Party in Georgia. In 1917, under an act passed by the General Assembly, it became the official procedure for counting votes in the primary, but not the general, election.

Under the county unit system, a candidate who received the highest number of popular votes in a county won that county's unit votes. Each county in Georgia had two unit votes for each representative it had in the House of Representatives in the General Assembly.

Under the county unit system, small counties had much greater power than the large urban counties. Here is how the system was set up:

The 8 largest counties had 48 unit votes [24 representatives x 2 unit votes]
The next 30 largest counties had 120 unit votes [60 x 2]
The 121 remaining small counties had 242 unit votes [121 x 2]

Thus, even though the 38 largest counties eventually had two-thirds of the state's voters living in them, the 121 other counties had more political power and could nominate [actually elect, since there was only one party] the governor, United States senators, or other state officials elected statewide.

Talmadge vs. Thompson. Citizens in Hartwell follow the local vote count in the race for the governor's office, 1948. How might voters get this information today?

and declare the winner. If no person received a majority of the votes, the legislators would choose from the two candidates with the highest number of votes.

Because Eugene Talmadge was obviously ill, some of his supporters had written in the name of his son, Herman Talmadge, on their ballots. Other candidates had received write-in votes, too. When the ballots were first counted, James Carmichael had the most write-in votes. Then more votes, all from Telfair County—Talmadge's home county—were found. With 675 votes, Herman Talmadge was declared the governor by the General Assembly.

The state was in an uproar. M.E. Thompson, who had been elected Lt. Governor, claimed he should be governor. Governor Arnall refused to give up the office until the issue was settled by the court.

One night, Talmadge forces seized the governor's office in the state capitol and changed the locks. Arnall set up in another office, Thompson in still another. Georgia had three governors! Secretary of State Ben Fortson refused to let any of the three use the official state seal on government documents. Thus, little official action could be taken.

After two months of confusion, the Georgia Supreme Court ruled that Lt. Governor M. E. Thompson should be acting governor until the next general election in 1948. Arnall resigned, Thompson was sworn in, and Herman Talmadge gave up the governor's office.

The Race Issue

In 1948, President Harry Truman, who had become president when President Roosevelt died in 1945, called for measures to protect the civil rights of blacks. The issue split the national Democratic Party.

In Georgia that year, Herman Talmadge defeated M. E. Thompson for the governorship. In the campaign, civil rights emerged as a main issue.

For the next 20 years, Georgia politics would be dominated by questions of race relations and the federal government's role in civil rights. Candidates for office stressed their support of segregation and their opposition to federal intrusion in Georgia affairs. The General Assembly spent much of its time passing laws to block integration and equal treatment of blacks.

Not all Georgians agreed on these matters. In the rapidly growing urban areas, there was considerable support for civil rights. But through the 1950s and into the 1960s, the rural parts of the state controlled politics. Segregation was strongest there.

How did rural voters control government? First, statewide elections were based on the county unit system. Second, the General Assembly membership was based mainly on counties, not population.

Then, in 1962, a federal court made a decision that would greatly affect Georgia politics. The candidates for the Democratic nomination for governor that year were ex-governor Marvin Griffin and Carl Sanders.

Before the primary election was held, the court ruled that Georgia's county unit system was unconstitutional. Why? Under the unit system the vote of a citizen in a rural county carried more weight than the vote of a citizen in an urban county. Later, the U.S. Supreme Court held that political equality in the United States meant one thing—"one person, one vote."

For the first time, Georgia's less-populated counties did not determine the outcome of a governor's race. While Griffin campaigned in the old way, appearing at county courthouses in rural areas, Sanders went on television to appeal to urban voters. The new style of campaigning paid off: Sanders won.

The federal courts also applied the "one person, one vote" rule to apportionment (dividing up of seats) of state legislatures. They ruled that seats had to be apportioned solely on the basis of population. In Georgia, this meant that because population had shifted to urban areas, there would be more urban representatives in the General Assembly.

In the 1960s, the General Assembly ceased to be all male, all white, and all Democratic. In 1962, Atlanta voters elected Leroy Johnson the first black legislator since 1906. In a few more years there were several black legislators, all from urban areas. Women and Republicans would be elected, too.

As governor, Carl Sanders tried to down-play the race issue. He stressed the need for progress in Georgia and worked to get more out-of-state industries to move south.

The governor also worked to improve Georgia's relations with the federal government. But the president, the Congress, and the federal courts were taking actions in support of civil rights that angered many white citizens. In 1966, those actions were on many voters' minds as the campaign for governor got underway.

The main Democratic candidates were ex-governor Ellis Arnall, Atlanta businessman Lester Maddox, and a state legislator from Plains, Jimmy Carter. In the primary, voters chose outspoken segregationist Lester Maddox, who had closed his restaurant rather than serve black customers.

This time, the Republican Party had a candidate for governor—Howard "Bo" Callaway, who in 1964 had been elected Georgia's first Republican congressman since Reconstruction. Like Maddox, he defended segregation and opposed federal civil rights actions.

In the general election, neither candidate had a majority of the votes. About 7 percent of the voters had written in the name of Ellis Arnall on their ballots.

According to the state constitution, the General Assembly would have to choose between the two highest vote-getters. Even though Callaway had received the most votes, the Democratic legislature chose Maddox over Callaway.

Through two decades the civil rights issue had dominated Georgia elections. The next section of this chapter tells about the civil rights movement and what it meant in Georgia.

THE CIVIL RIGHTS MOVEMENT

At the end of World War II, black Americans, and some whites, showed a new determination to break down the barriers to equal opportunity. That determination became the civil rights movement.

THINK ABOUT IT

1. What were some goals of the civil rights movement?
2. How was the *Brown v. Board of Education* ruling important to the movement?
3. In addition to court rulings, what role did the federal government play in the civil rights movement?
4. What kinds of public activities were used to fight for civil rights?

The movement for civil rights grew out of World War II, when blacks fought and died for their country. It was boosted by President Truman's desegregation of military units at the war's end. It came out of the defense plants, where blacks and whites, men and women, worked side by side.

New Deal work programs and war production had brought higher income to many blacks across the land. They were no longer willing to accept lower pay than whites for doing the same jobs. As southern black men and women migrated from farms to cities in the North, they saw possibilities for a more comfortable life. They were no longer willing to accept the status whites had assigned them 50 years before.

School Desegregation

In the late 1940s, lawyers for the National Association for the Advancement of Colored People (NAACP) and other civil rights groups went to court. Their targets were the dual school systems set up by law in Georgia and other states. They pointed out that although black people paid the same taxes that other citizens did, they did not receive the same services from government. In Georgia, for example, government spent over four times as much to educate each white pupil than it did to educate each black pupil. White teachers' salaries were more than double those paid to black teachers.

Here is how one black woman, a former teacher and principal, described her school of the 1940s.

 Rosa Strickland was interviewed at Athens, Georgia, in February 1981.

The particular school where I was, was fair. But getting fuel was bad. We had a pot-bellied stove in each room—we had three rooms, three teachers. In the winter, the boys spent most of the time going to the woods and picking up trash to burn in the stoves. They couldn't study for going to get wood, because the county did not furnish wood to us.

Most of our books was used, second-hand books; some were too old to really be used in school.

We had outdoor toilets—the boys' was pretty bad. The principal was very old and she didn't feel like askin' the superintendent—you know how some black people were afraid to ask white people to do anything—she thought it was an imposition to ask the superintendent to do anything. I would ask her, "Why don't you ask him to fix that floor in the boys' toilet?" But she wouldn't do it.

And we didn't have any water on the place—we had to walk about four blocks or more to a neighbor's house to get water. The children would bring buckets of water from that distance to pour in a big barrel. That's the way they got drinking water.

Then, I became principal and I went to the [main] office more and looked around and saw how we were cheated out of books. I saw the many nice readers that they had on the shelves and I asked the superintendent for them and why he hadn't given us any. He said, "Well, Ah didn't know yuh needed 'um," or something. So, in fact I got the readers, and workbooks along with 'em, and other books—new editions we should have been gettin' all the while.

After that, I asked him about fixing the boys' toilet. He said, "Well, ah am." So, finally, one day, the floor fell through. And that day I got hot. I went by the office and said to the superintendent, "The county could get sued." So, then he sent somebody out to put a new floor in.

Then, after that, I said, "We really need some water on the grounds. It's dangerous; the building could catch on fire. It's not healthy for the children to bring water in the dust all up and down that way, their little dresses getting in the water. It's bad." So, I found somebody to come out and dig a well, and the county paid for it.

Then, after that, I said, "I feel the county should furnish us some fuel." He said, "Well, we just don't have the money for fuel." So, I called the parents together and told 'em the conditions we had and I said if we pledged $2 each, I believe we could buy enough coal and wood to supply us for a time. And we did—enough to keep the boys in the classroom.

Later, I got a blacksmith to make us swings and seesaws for the playground. He came out and put them up.

We even had lights put in the building. I told the superintendent we wanted to have some programs out there at night. He said the county didn't have the money. I asked him if we, the parents, raised $10 would he do it? We raised the money and the county sent the folks out to wire the building. Then we had lights. □

[Of course, many white pupils in Georgia in the 1940s went to one-room schools that had no indoor plumbing.]

With obvious inequalities existing between schools for blacks and those for whites, the legal basis for "separate but equal" began to crumble. Courts began ruling that schools for blacks had to be improved.

Even segregationists began to approve spending more money on black schools. Perhaps in that way, they thought, separate schools could be maintained.

In Georgia, more money was pumped into public education for blacks and whites. In 1947, the General Assembly approved adding a 12th grade to the Georgia system. In 1951, Gov. Herman Talmadge persuaded the legislators to pass a 3 percent sales tax to provide money for upgrading public education.

However, inequalities still existed. In 1954, Georgia spent $190 to educate each white child, $132 on each black child.

On May 17 of that same year, 1954, the United States Supreme Court, in the case *Brown v. Board of Education*, wiped out the legal base for racial segregation in public education. According to the Court, segregation laws were unconstitutional; they violated the 14th Amendment, which guarantees all citizens equal protection (or treatment) under the law. Said the Court, "We conclude that in the field of public education the doctrine of 'separate but equal' has no place. Separate educational facilities are inherently [by nature] unequal." Later on, the Court directed that school systems begin in "good faith" to desegregate (enroll blacks and whites together in the same schools) with "all deliberate speed."

The *Brown* ruling did not bring about the immediate desegregation of schools in Georgia and other states. Most government and school officials opposed it. In Georgia, Governor Talmadge denounced the Court's decision.

The term of Governor Marvin Griffin, 1955-1959, was almost completely taken up with "massive resistance" to desegregation. The General Assembly passed laws to abolish the public schools if need be, to support private schools, to close schools that desegregated, and to prosecute local school officials who permitted desegregation.

Nevertheless, the *Brown* ruling was important because it threw the weight of the nation's highest court behind the effort to give all citizens equal rights. In time, the whole federal government would uphold this principle.

Eventually, change did come. As the 1960s began, some Georgia political leaders, including Gov. Ernest Vandiver, recognized that the schools had to be kept open, even in the face of desegregation. And, in 1961, token integration of Atlanta public schools began. In Athens, the first black students were admitted to the University of Georgia.

Public Facilities Desegregated

The schools were only one example of public, or tax-supported, facilities segregated by law. After the *Brown* ruling, civil rights lawyers challenged segregation in other areas, such as public transportation, libraries, auditoriums, parks, and beaches. In a series of rulings, the Court struck down segregation of these facilities, too.

While the courts were considering these cases, blacks—and whites who supported their cause—began using other methods to arouse public support. In 1955, black residents of Montgomery, Alabama, began boycotting that city's segregated buses. Boycotts followed in other cities. By 1960, the civil rights movement included "sit-ins" at segregated bus station waiting rooms and chain-store lunch counters. Later, "moving sit-ins" were organized with "freedom riders" traveling on interstate buses into segregated bus stations. Civil rights "demonstrations"—such as picketing of segregated businesses, street marches, and protest rallies—followed.

Federal Government Role Changes

The legislative and executive branches of the national government followed the lead of the federal courts. In 1957, Congress passed a law giving the Department of Justice new powers to investigate violations of civil rights. That same year, President Dwight Eisenhower used federal troops to enforce court-ordered school desegregation in Little Rock, Arkansas.

In the early 1960s, President John Kennedy used the power of the federal government to enforce desegregation of schools and colleges in Alabama and Mississippi. After President Kennedy's assassination in 1963, President Lyndon Johnson pushed for passage of more laws to protect civil rights. Then Congress

A Civil Rights Confrontation, July 4, 1962. In front of a segregated Atlanta hotel, one man pickets for an end to discrimination while another hands out KKK leaflets.

passed the Civil Rights Act of 1964. The act prohibited racial discrimination in employment and labor unions and in public facilities, such as swimming pools and playgrounds. It also outlawed discrimination by race in privately owned public accommodations, such as hotels, restaurants, theaters, amusement parks, and sports stadiums. The act allowed the government to withhold federal funds from school systems that refused to desegregate.

In 1968, the Fair Housing Act outlawed racial discrimination in the buying, selling, renting, and leasing of real estate.

Voting Rights

THINK ABOUT IT

1. What was the effect of the Voting Rights Act of 1965 on voter registration in Georgia?
2. What evidence is there that more blacks voted after passage of the act?

Since the early days of "Jim Crow," blacks in Georgia and other states had been denied the right to vote (see page 147). The Civil Rights Act of 1964 required state election officials to treat white and black voting applicants the same way.

Voter registration drives were conducted throughout the South. But some people fiercely opposed registration of black voters. After violence left several civil rights workers dead, Congress passed the Voting Rights Act of 1965. Under this act, the federal government had the power to register voters in certain states. It could also send federal examiners into counties where local election officials might be discriminating against blacks.

Following passage of the Voting Rights Act, hundreds of thousands of black citizens became registered to vote in Georgia and six other southern states. As a result, black candidates began to be elected to public offices.

Continuing Efforts

Despite civil rights laws and court rulings, desegregation proceeded slowly. For

**Hands that pick cotton...
now can pick our public officials**

Register And Vote!

Through the 1970s, efforts to get people to register and vote continued.

example, by 1966, only 6 percent of Georgia's black children went to formerly all-white schools. School desegregation suits dragged on in the courts into the mid-1970s. But 20 years after *Brown*, segregation by law (*de jure*) was a thing of the past.

Black citizens still suffered racial discrimination in jobs and housing. This was *de facto* segregation. It meant that discrimination actually existed, though it was not required by law. Black workers were usually assigned to the lowest paying jobs and had unemployment rates much higher than white workers. In housing, blacks were not allowed to live in certain neigh-

REGISTRATION, BY RACE, IN GEORGIA—1965, 1967, 1972

1965			1967			1972		
White	Black	Gap	White	Black	Gap	White	Black	Gap
62.8%	27.4%	35.2%	80.3%*	52.6%	27.7%	70.6%	67.8%	2.8%

*Race was unknown for 22,776 registered voters in 1967.

ELECTED BLACK OFFICIALS IN GEORGIA

Year	State Offices*	County Offices	Municipal Offices	Total
1968	11	4	6	21
1974	16	43	77	136
1979	23	71	143	237

*All legislators.

Source: U.S. Commission on Civil Rights

borhoods. In both northern and southern states, millions of black people were crowded into urban ghettos. Riots in American cities in the mid- to late-1960s renewed efforts by civil rights leaders to fight unfair treatment and lack of opportunity for blacks. Efforts to solve these problems continued through the 1970s into the 1980s.

Attitudes toward Civil Rights Progress

THINK ABOUT IT

1. What were some of the reactions of whites to the civil rights movement?
2. What did Ralph McGill ask southerners to do? What seemed to be his attitude toward his fellow white southerners?
3. What position did the Augusta newspaper take in 1963 toward integration?

Of course, many white Georgians, as well as other southerners, were outraged that the federal government was tampering with southern customs. Some blamed the racial unrest on outsiders—whites and blacks from the North. Candidates for public office and leaders in state and local governments spoke out against federal government attempts to enforce civil rights laws.

There was violence. Organizations such as the Ku Klux Klan and the White Citizen's Councils arose to battle for segregation. Blacks were threatened, intimidated, and beaten for civil rights activities. Often the police looked the other way or even supported the violence.

Other voices among white southerners attacked the unfair treatment of black southerners. One such voice belonged to Ralph McGill.

Ralph Emerson McGill was born in Tennessee in 1898. In 1929 he went to work for the *Atlanta Constitution* as a sports writer. Later he wrote about politics, economics, and life in the South. He was concerned about the plight of the poor, black and white, and worked to bring help to them.

In his writing, he attacked the white supremacy policies of Gov. Eugene Talmadge. In 1942, he managed Ellis Arnall's successful campaign for governor. That same year he became editor of the *Atlanta Constitution.*

In the 1950s, McGill called on his fellow southerners to pull down the barriers to blacks' full participation in community life. He said not to wait for the federal government to step in. His opinions became known all over the country; by 1958 he was being called the "conscience of the South."

Not all readers liked what Ralph McGill wrote. In some places in Georgia, the *Atlanta Constitution* vanished from newsstands. He was threatened by the Ku Klux Klan and others.

Ralph McGill tried to see all sides of the issues surrounding race relations in the South—and tried to explain what he saw to his readers. He also tried to explain to Americans in other parts of the country what was happening in the South in the 1950s and early 1960s. The following reading is from his book, *The South and the Southerner.*

 Brotherhood in the South

One night I was asked to talk to the men's Bible class of a smalltown church. I tried to speak casually, yet seriously, noting that we Southerners have a reputation for being Bible-oriented, for quoting from it, and for using it in our politics. I said that somehow along the way we had managed to exclude the Negro from our concept of the Fatherhood of God and the brotherhood of man. . . .

Our basic national problem, but more especially ours in the South, was to accept the Negro as one with us in human brotherhood. We need him in the South, and in the nation, as an educated, trained, participating citizen. This did not mean, I insisted, that anyone's privacy would be disturbed. It was only necessary for us to grant the full rights of citizenship and to see the Negro as just another human being. . . .

There was polite applause. Later, when the meeting was concluded, an old man came up to me. "I just want you to know," he said, and there was no heat in his voice, "that I believe in white supremacy. Even the Bible says as much. I hold with our traditions."

I patted him on the shoulder and said, "Well, the Bible is interpreted in many ways."

He was old and troubled and on the defensive. Also, there was a genuine pathos [sorrowful quality] in him. There are many like him, young and old. If they cannot hold on to the concept of their superiority, their small universe will crumble. . . .

There was an impulse to put my arms about his frail shoulders, showing so beneath his worn, clean, church-supper coat, and to say to him, Everything will be all right. Don't you try to change. You go right on clinging to what gives you strength.

I put out my hand and he took it. I went away thinking about all the cynical and bitter men, in politics and out, of this generation and of those of the past who have had a part in making that old man (and the thousands like him) what he was . . . . □

[Adapted from Ralph McGill, *The South and the Southerner* (Boston: Little, Brown and Company, 1959, 1963), pp. 232-34.]

Many newspapers in Georgia took a stand on civil rights questions. They tried to influence the opinions and actions of citizens. At first, most opposed change. Gradually more and more newspaper editors counseled their readers to be reasonable. Here is an example from the *Augusta Chronicle and Herald* in 1963:

 The Time Has Come (An Editorial)

That Augusta has not been subjected to the same degradation that many other cities in the country have experienced in the form of irresponsible race demonstrations is no happenstance.

Augusta is blessed with an abundance of sensible people, men and women of both races. . . .

It is because Augusta has such a healthy atmosphere that this newspaper makes bold to suggest today that the time has come for a reappraisal of our race relations with the view to extending to the responsible Negroes of this community a more equitable share of citizenship.

We see it as a step to be taken in our common interest.

We see it as a step in keeping with the trend of the times.

We see it as being the right thing to do.

Augusta already has witnessed an integration of its buses, its library, its Municipal Auditorium, its variety store lunch counters and at least one of its public parks. The city and county together also have taken steps to remove signs over public facilities in the Municipal Building that have proved offensive to Negroes.

We see integration as being feasible in the field of education, voting, and in job opportunities with either the city or county. In other words, we believe that the Negro should be given equality of opportunity in those areas in which he participates as a taxpayer. . . .

The *Chronicle and Herald* historically have defended many forms of segregation on the bases of constitutionality and tradition. We still hold that the Supreme Court desegregation decisions have contravened [contradicted] the Tenth Amendment to the Constitution. But we recognize the Court's authority, and we see no event short of congressional action as being capable of reversing the current judicial trend.

Insofar as tradition is concerned, this newspaper has maintained that full equality for the Negro can best be achieved by evolutionary rather than revolutionary processes. We see the moves we now suggest as being in harmony with this position. . . . □

[Adapted from *Augusta Chronicle and Herald*, July 14, 1963, p. 1.]

Martin Luther King, Jr.

THINK ABOUT IT

1. What was "non-violence?" Why might Dr. King have chosen it as the proper technique to use in the civil rights struggle?
2. In his writings, what kind of a future was he calling for?
3. Was Dr. King successful in what he was trying to do?

Martin Luther King, Jr., the leading civil rights leader of the 1960s, was born and raised in Atlanta, Georgia.

King, a black Baptist minister, became famous for advancing the cause of civil rights through the use of a technique called "non-violence." His followers might choose to disobey laws they felt unjust, and fill up a community's jails by doing so. They might resist—and take abuse—when ordered to "move on." But, they would be peaceful. There would be no violence.

King, a graduate of Morehouse College, earned a Ph.D. in theology from Boston University in 1955—the same year he became a leader in the civil rights movement. The next year he was arrested for the first time for his civil rights activities. In 1957, Dr. King helped create a new civil rights organization, the Southern Christian Leadership Conference, and became its president. Three years later, he became co-pastor (with his father) of the Ebenezer Baptist Church in Atlanta. That year, he was arrested for trespassing at a sit-in to desegregate the lunch counter at Rich's department store. In 1961 and 1962, King was arrested and jailed in Albany, Georgia, for leading mass demonstrations to desegregate public facilities.

In 1963, he turned his efforts to Birmingham, Alabama. Again he was arrested and jailed. By then King was getting a lot of criticism, not only from segregationists but also from white "moderates," even clergymen. He was causing too much turmoil by trying to move too fast. He should be patient.

In response, Dr. King penned a "Letter from Birmingham Jail," explaining his actions. Here is a part of that letter:

✒ . . . For years now I have heard the word "wait." It rings in the ear of every Negro with piercing familiarity. This "wait" has always meant "never." We must come to see . . . that "justice too long delayed is justice denied."

We have waited for more than 340 years for our constitutional and God-given rights . . . but we still creep at horse-and-buggy pace toward gaining a cup of coffee at a lunch counter. Perhaps it is easy for those who have never felt the stinging darts of segregation to say, "wait." But, when you have seen vicious mobs lynch your mother and father, . . . when you see the vast majority of your twenty million Negro brothers smothering in an air-tight cage of poverty in the midst of an affluent society; when you suddenly find your tongue twisted and your speech stammering as you seek to explain to your six-year old daughter why she can't go to the public amusement park that has just been advertised on television, and see tears welling up in her eyes when she is told Funtown is closed to colored children; . . . when you take a cross-country drive and find it necessary to sleep night after night in the uncomfortable corners of your automobile because no motel will accept you; when you are humiliated day in and day out by nagging signs reading "white" and "colored," . . . then you will understand why it is difficult to wait. . . .

—April 16, 1963 ☐

[Martin Luther King, Jr., *Why We Can't Wait* (New York: Harper & Row Publishers, Inc., 1963), pp. 83-84.]

In August 1967, Dr. Martin Luther King, Jr., was photographed on the steps of his boyhood home in Atlanta. For 10 years, Atlanta was the headquarters for many of America's civil rights efforts.

A few months after his "letter," Dr. King led 250,000 citizens—blacks, whites, Indians, Hispanics, and others—in a "March on Washington" to demonstrate the tremendous support behind the civil rights movement.

The highlight of the gathering was a speech by Martin Luther King, Jr., from the steps of the Lincoln Memorial. "I have a dream," King said.

✒ . . . I have a dream that one day this nation will rise up and live out the true meaning of its creed, "We hold these truths to be self-evident, that all men are created equal." I have a dream that one day on the red hills of Georgia, sons of former slaves and the sons of former slave owners will be able to sit down together at the table of brotherhood. I have a dream that one day even the state of Mississippi, a desert state sweltering with the heat of injustice, sweltering with the heat of oppression, will be transformed into an oasis of freedom and justice. I have a dream that my four little children will one day live in a nation where they will not be judged by the color of their skin, but by the content of their character. . . .

—August 28, 1963 ☐

The March on Washington generated support for civil rights. The next year Congress passed the far-reaching Civil Rights Act of 1964. That year King made headlines all over the world, winning one of the highest international awards—a Nobel Peace Prize.

After the passage of the Voting Rights Act of 1965, Dr. King turned his attention to fighting poverty and discrimination in housing and jobs.

In the spring of 1968, Martin Luther King, Jr., went to Memphis, Tennessee, to lead a protest march in support of striking sanitation workers. There on April 4, 1968, King was assassinated. As the news of the murder spread, riots broke out in Washington, D.C., and dozens of other cities. But Atlanta, Dr. King's home, was relatively quiet as the city prepared for his funeral.

Thousands of mourners poured into Atlanta from all over the country. On their televisions, millions of Americans saw Dr. King's casket borne through the streets on a mule-drawn farm wagon. They also saw the nation's leaders gather in the small Ebenezer Baptist Church to pay tribute to the man who taught non-violence.

ACTIVITIES FOR CHAPTER 14

Discussion

"The biggest change since 1940? Why Georgia definitely became a better place to live—for both black people and white people."

1. What evidence in this chapter supports the statement? What evidence refutes it?

2. What do you think was the greatest influence on change—economic prosperity, law and government actions, or attitudes of the people?

3. Of the specific changes that have occurred, which do you feel are the most important to you?

Writing Project

Four men quoted in this book talked about relations between black people and white people. Two were white: Atticus G. Haygood and Ralph McGill. Two were black: Booker T. Washington and Martin Luther King, Jr.

Write an essay comparing the writings of two of these men from different periods. How are they similar? Different? What was the frame of reference of each writer? How did it influence what each said? What occurred in the intervening (in-between) years that might help explain differences?

Or—list the main ideas in two writings and be prepared to explain orally how they differ.

15 A New Image

At the end of a long campaign, I believe I know our people as well as anyone. Based on this knowledge of Georgians—north and south, rural and urban, liberal and conservative—I say to you quite frankly that the time for racial discrimination is over. Our people have already made this major and difficult decision. . . .

No poor, rural, weak, or black person should ever again have to bear the additional burden of being deprived of the opportunity for an education, a job, or simple justice. . . .
—Governor Jimmy Carter, Inaugural
Address, January 12, 1971

Of course, racial discrimination did not end in 1971. The struggle for civil rights continued. Yet, certain events indicated that times were changing. In 1972, Georgia sent a black man, Andrew Young, to Congress. The next year, voters elected Maynard Jackson as Atlanta's first black mayor. Through the 1970s, many black candidates were elected to state and local offices. During those years many Georgians were turning their attention to other issues.

THE ENVIRONMENT

In the early 1970s, people in Georgia as well as the rest of the nation began talking about "the quality of life." They noted that the quality of life suffered when air and water were polluted by wastes. They regretted the loss of green areas paved over

After serving in the U.S. Congress and as U.S. Ambassador to the United Nations, Andrew Young became mayor of Atlanta in 1982.

The Georgia Agrirama at Tifton. Established by the General Assembly in 1972, this outdoor museum recreates Georgia rural life of the late 1800s.

for more highways or parking lots. They lamented when a 100-year-old house was torn down for yet another gas station. What could be done, they asked, to save the countryside from the blight of garbage dumps, junkyards, and strip mining?

Groups of citizens organized to conserve natural resources, preserve historical places, and generally clean up their environment. They pushed their representatives in government to pass laws to protect the environment.

In Georgia, Governor Carter made protection of natural and historical resources a major part of his administration.

Sometimes, state and federal governments worked together on meeting environmental problems. One focus in Georgia was the coastal islands where uncontrolled development threatened to ruin the balance of nature. Through a combination of laws and citizen concern, the islands have gained protections. The U.S. Congress made Cumberland Island a national seashore and wilderness area for all citizens to enjoy.

State and federal government began spending much public money on protecting the environment in the 1970s. Part of this money was used by citizens' groups working to make their communities more attrac-

tive places to live. Many groups raised their own money to fund environmental projects.

In Savannah, for example, the oldest part of the city was run-down by the 1960s. Then some residents got together to save hundreds of houses, many dating back to the early 1800s. Their effort paid off in several ways. Business in downtown Savannah started thriving. Tourists flocked to Savannah to walk through a bit of the past recaptured. Hundreds of people now live around the beautiful squares laid out by Oglethorpe.

Residents of other cities, from big Columbus and Macon to little Madison and Winder, were busy rescuing old theaters, train depots, courthouses, churches, and residences.

GOVERNMENT SERVICES EXPAND

Another area the people of Georgia gave more attention to, and spent more money on, was social welfare. Better schools and colleges, more facilities for ill and handicapped persons, and an improved prison system resulted.

Of course, government services cost money. Fortunately, the state's economy continued to grow in the 1970s. Business and government leaders from cities and counties across the state kept working to bring still more industry, more jobs, and more tourists to Georgia. Governor Carter and his successor, George Busbee, traveled to South America, Europe, and Asia to attract more business to Georgia. As the economy grew, state and local government took in more tax revenue. More money was available than ever before to spend on government services.

By the mid-1970s, Georgia was getting much national attention. People in other parts of the nation began to see Georgia as an attractive place to live.

George Busbee, elected governor in 1974, stressed efficient business-like government. In 1976, Georgia voters amended the state constitution to allow the governor to run to succeed himself for another term. In 1978, Busbee became the first governor in over 100 years to be elected to eight consecutive years in office.

A GEORGIAN BECOMES PRESIDENT

Jimmy Carter also drew attention to Georgia. Shortly after leaving the governor's office, he began a campaign to become president of the United States.

At that time, many Americans were disgusted with national politics. Caught up in a scandal called "Watergate," a United States president had resigned in 1974. That had never happened before. Some of his closest aides went to prison.

When Jimmy Carter began his campaign, he was almost unknown outside Georgia. He crisscrossed the country in 1975 and 1976, telling Americans that the problem was not with their system of government. He stressed the need for honesty, for leveling with the people, for making government serve the people. In one campaign speech, this is what he said:

I intend to win. Being elected president is very important to me. But it is not the most important thing in my life. I don't have to be president.

There are a lot of things that I would not do to be elected. I would never tell a lie. I would never make a misleading statement. I would never betray your trust in me. And I will never avoid a controversial issue. . . .

If I should ever do any of those things, don't support me. Because I would not be worthy to be president of this country. But I don't intend to do any of them, because . . . people like you . . . want us to have once again a nation with a government that

President and Mrs. Carter, a few minutes after he was sworn into office, Washington, D.C. Breaking with tradition, the Carters walked the mile from the inaugural stand at the Capitol to the White House.

is as honest and decent and fair and competent and truthful and idealistic as are the American people. If we could just have a government once again as good as our people are, that'll be a great achievement. □

What Carter had to say appealed to a majority of the voters. In 1976, he became the first candidate from the Deep South to be elected president of the United States.

Jimmy Carter's presidency, 1977-1981, was beset with difficult domestic and foreign problems. At home, inflation bothered many people. They expected the president's programs to solve these problems. They didn't.

President Carter's foreign policy stressed peace and human rights. While he won praise for working out peace agreements between Israel and Egypt, his general handling of foreign affairs was criticized.

In November 1979, 52 Americans were taken hostage at the U.S. Embassy in Iran. The next month, the USSR invaded its neighbor, Afghanistan.

As the president's attempts to free the hostages or get the USSR to withdraw from Afghanistan failed, his popularity dropped. Many Americans felt their government had become weak. The economy wasn't getting any better. In November 1980, Jimmy Carter was defeated for reelection by Ronald Reagan.

On January 20, 1981, President Carter's negotiations finally got the hostages released from Iran. As those 52 Americans flew home to the U.S., Jimmy Carter flew home to Plains.

NEW GEORGIANS, NEW OPPORTUNITIES

THINK ABOUT IT

1. Which counties of Georgia grew the fastest in the 1970s? In general, where are they located?
2. From where did most of Georgia's new settlers come?

On February 12, 1981, visitors crowded into the state capitol for a special event. It was "Georgia Day"—the 248th anniversary of the landing of Oglethorpe's settlers at Savannah. To mark the occasion, state officials displayed the charter King George II had granted to the trustees.

At the same time, several miles away at the Atlanta International Airport, new "settlers" were arriving in Georgia. Among them was a family from Laos. Like the settlers of 1733, this family came to Georgia "on charity," sponsored by a church organization in Atlanta. Like the settlers of 1733, they came looking for a new start in life, a new opportunity.

A Chance for a Better Life. A church organization helped this girl's family get from Cambodia to Georgia. In 1982, she was learning English while older family members were finding jobs.

The Laotian family was one of thousands that came to the United States that month, fleeing poverty or persecution in other parts of the world. They came from Cuba, Viet Nam, El Salvador, Mexico, and elsewhere. Many of them settled in Georgia.

Although foreign immigration to Georgia was never heavy after the Civil War, some ethnic groups had established communities—Chinese in Augusta, Italians in Elberton, and Greeks in Atlanta. These communities were not very large, however. In 1932, a state government publication had boasted that "Georgia's people are 99½% American born," mainly descended from Anglo-Saxon pioneers, and that "Georgia's people speak no polyglot of languages." Well, in 1981, one might hear people speaking Spanish, Chinese, Arabic, French, and Japanese—among other languages—on the streets of any major Georgia city.

By 1981, Atlanta could boast that it was an "international city," with daily flights from its airport to England, Germany, Belgium, Mexico, and other countries. Foreign governments and companies had offices in the city.

But most of the new Georgians arriving in February 1981 were not from other countries. They came from Michigan, Illinois, Pennsylvania, New York, and other states of the northeast and midwest. Their move to Georgia was part of the large migration of Americans from the "Snowbelt" to the "Sunbelt."

Although some of Georgia's newcomers settled in rural areas, most were attracted to metropolitan urban communi-

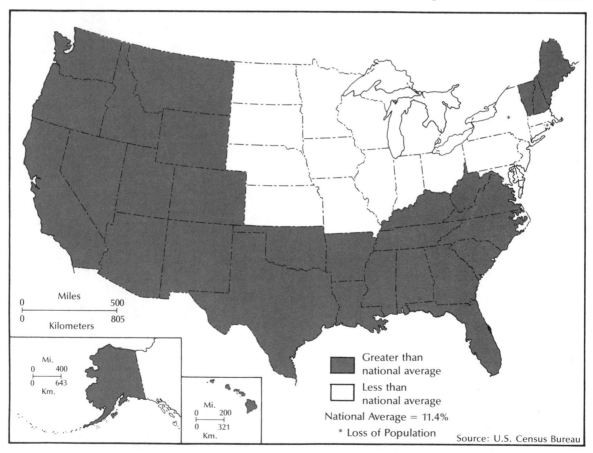

Greater than national average

Less than national average

National Average = 11.4%

* Loss of Population

Source: U.S. Census Bureau

MAP 26. *From the Snowbelt to the Sunbelt. Except for New England "vacation" states, the U.S. population shift in the 1970s was to the South and West. What factors might account for this shift?*

ties.* However, unlike the farm-to-city migration of Georgians in the 1920s and 1930s, recent settlement has been mainly around large cities, not in them. These surrounding areas, once countryside, are the suburbs. Not only newcomers to the state but also Georgians from the farms and city centers have been attracted to suburban areas. From 1960 to 1980, Georgia's suburban counties generally grew the fastest in population.

As the result of this growth, the character of suburban counties has changed drastically. Air-conditioned shopping malls replaced dairy farms. Office parks replaced piney woods, condominiums replaced cotton fields, and expressways replaced dirt roads. Along with growth in the suburbs have come "city" problems: pollution, traffic, noise, and crime.

Rural life in Georgia has changed, too. Although many Georgians still live in rural areas, only a small number of them are actually farmers. Like the suburban residents, they often work at jobs "in town."

*The U.S. Census Bureau sets up "Standard Metropolitan Statistical Areas" (SMSAs) to make it easier to collect information about urban areas. They are often referred to as metropolitan, or metro, areas. The Census Bureau recognized that people living outside the official "city limits" are very important to the life of a city. An SMSA can be made up of a county or group of counties which contain at least one city of 50,000 or two cities close to each other with a combined population of 50,000 or more. The county or counties must have a close connection with the city to be included in the SMSA. Residents of the county probably work, shop, and play in the city. So, the population of the counties and city are socially and economically integrated into one big urban community.

An SMSA can grow in area as well as population. In 1960, the Atlanta SMSA included only five counties; in 1980 it included fifteen counties. People living farther from the city of Atlanta had become part of the urban community.

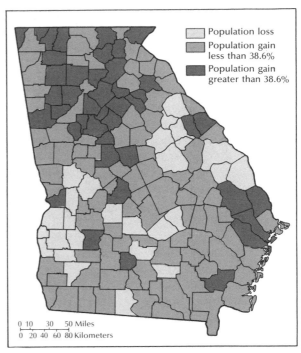

Population loss

Population gain less than 38.6%

Population gain greater than 38.6%

0 10   30   50 Miles
0 20 40 60 80 Kilometers

MAP 27. *Population Change, 1960-1980. The state's population grew by an average of 38.6 percent. Which parts of the state grew at a greater rate?*

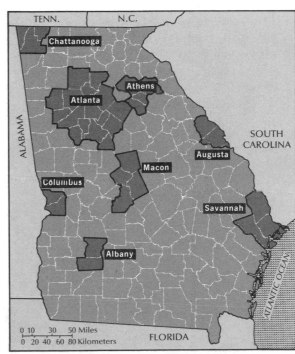

0 10   30   50 Miles
0 20 40 60 80 Kilometers

MAP 28. *Georgia SMSAs, 1980. Some metro areas spill over state boundaries.*

Figure 5 shows that since the 1790 census, the movement to urban life has been steady.

Metro Atlanta

By far the largest of Georgia's urban-suburban areas is Metro Atlanta. Its recent population growth, too, has been in surrounding counties, not in the City of Atlanta.

However, in the 1960s and 1970s, the city itself has grown in other ways. From the political and business capital of Georgia, Atlanta has grown up as a social, economic, and cultural center.

What accounts for Metro Atlanta's growth? Don't look for a simple answer to that question. The following story may provide some clues.

THINK ABOUT IT

1. What are some reasons Mr. DeMarco's company chose to expand in Georgia?
2. How did Mr. DeMarco explain Atlanta's growth to his children?

Welcome to Georgia: A Story

Joe DeMarco hurried home early from his office in downtown Cleveland, Ohio. His wife had just arrived home and was unpacking some groceries.

"Louise, I'll help you with those later. Sit down a minute. I've got big news."

"What's wrong, Joe?" she asked anxiously.

"Nothing's wrong. How'd you like to move to Georgia?"

"Georgia? What are you talking about?" Mrs. DeMarco looked puzzled.

"Remember, I told you the company might open a regional distribution center? Well, we're going to do it. Near Atlanta. A place called Norcross. And, I've been asked to head the new operation there."

"But Georgia! That's in the South. Why there?"

Mr. DeMarco began talking excitedly. "The South is where it's happening, Louise. Last year our sales tripled in the South.

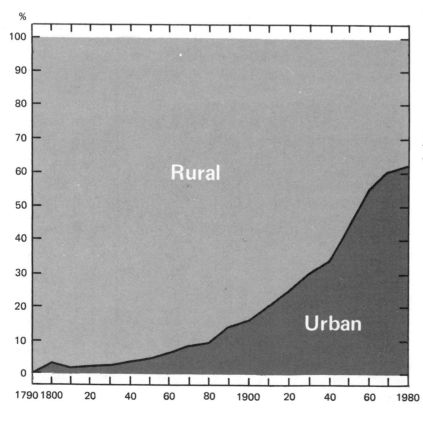

FIGURE 5. Georgia's Population: The Shift from Rural to Urban Life, 1790-1980

That's not the case with our sales anywhere else in the country. The board of directors decided it was high time we had our own operation down there."

"I guess you're right about the South, Mrs. DeMarco said slowly. "Judy Benson moved to Albany last year—she used to be in my office carpool. Her husband lost his job and he went down there to work for a tire company. And the Kelly's oldest daughter is studying engineering at Georgia Tech. Oh, and remember the Marcus family? Their son Steve works with the national park system on Cumberland Island."

"I guess Georgia is attracting a lot of northerners," Joe commented.

"How do you think the kids will take the news?" Mrs. DeMarco was concerned.

"They'll love it—I hope. I'll tell them after supper—before Gina starts practicing her trumpet and Tony goes to baseball practice."

*   *   *

"Oh, Daddy, no!" Gina wailed as she heard the news. "You can't mean it. Is this a joke? You know I just won first chair in the all-city band. And all my friends are here, I can't leave."

Mr. DeMarco gulped. "I, uh, thought you'd like Georgia. It's a. . . ."

Tony turned off the TV. "Why did the company pick Atlanta?"

Mr. DeMarco sighed. "That's tough to answer. I've been reading about it. I'd say it's a combination of location and people. Here, look at this map." Mr. DeMarco picked up an atlas. "Location was first. Atlanta, you know, is the capital of Georgia. See, it sits at the southern end of the Appalachians. Over a hundred years ago it was right in the path of migration to the West. Early on, it became a railroad hub. Later it developed air transport and a good interstate highway system. That's one reason the company is going there. Good transportation has attracted many kinds of businesses there—businesses that our company can sell to."

Mrs. DeMarco's face perked up. "With all those companies I ought to be able to find a good job."

"Right. There are more than 2,000 manufacturers there, from Coca-Cola to cargo planes. There must be plenty of jobs for a good computer programmer."

Mr. DeMarco looked around, pleased that his family was listening intently. "Another thing that the company directors liked was that Atlanta is the financial center of the South. To grow, a business needs money to invest. Recently, the banks have done for Atlanta's growth what the railroads did 100 years ago—attract more businesses."

"So, it's all location?" Tony asked.

"Well, its people, too—people who helped the city grow. They built a big convention center and airport. They have plenty of sports—the Falcons and the Braves play in the stadium there, and they

"Hammering Hank." Hank Aaron's 715th home-run breaks Babe Ruth's long-standing record. Atlanta-Fulton County Stadium, April 8, 1974.

built the Omni where the Hawks play. I think they perform a lot of plays and concerts at that Memorial Arts Center, too. The directors considered these things, too, before choosing where to locate in the South."

"Hey, I just remembered, Eric and his parents visited Atlanta last summer," said Tony. "His dad had to go to some convention there. Eric had a pretty good time. They went to some super amusement park called Six Flags Over Georgia. I think they went to the Georgia mountains, too, and hiked at the beginning of the Appalachian Trail. I'll have to ask him about that at baseball practice tonight—which reminds me—I better get going or I'll be late. Hmmmmm. Guess I'll have to give up the Cleveland Indians and become a Braves fan now. That's not going to be easy." Tony picked up his glove from the sofa and headed out the door.

"Looks like we're leaving Cleveland for Atlanta," Gina said glumly.

Mrs. DeMarco grinned. "Gina, remember the record we bought your father for his birthday? Robert Shaw and the Atlanta Symphony? You thought it was great. Do you know where Shaw was before he went to Atlanta?"

"Don't tell me. Cleveland? OK, you win. If Shaw can move to Georgia, I guess I can."

*   *   *

After school was out for the summer, the DeMarcos packed up and moved to their new house. They were sitting on the front steps, watching the movers unload the van.

"I can't believe we're really here!" Tony said.

"Uh oh. Looks like our neighbors are here, too." Gina pointed out a man and woman coming across the lawn. The man carried a picnic jug.

"Y'all look like you could use a cold drink. I'm James Young and this is my wife Ellen. Welcome to Georgia."

Robert Shaw conducts the Atlanta Symphony.

ACTIVITIES FOR CHAPTER 15

Discussion

What is history? Some historians have emphasized the role of great persons in shaping events. Others have concentrated on ordinary people and everyday life.

A. Take some time to think about all the persons in Georgia's history whom you have read about.

   1. If you could personally meet one person from Georgia's past, who would it be?

   2. Why did you choose that person?

B. Now think about all the periods of Georgia history you have studied.

   1. Which period do you think presented the biggest challenge to ordinary people?

   2. How did they respond to the challenge?

   3. Would you like to have been part of that response? Why?

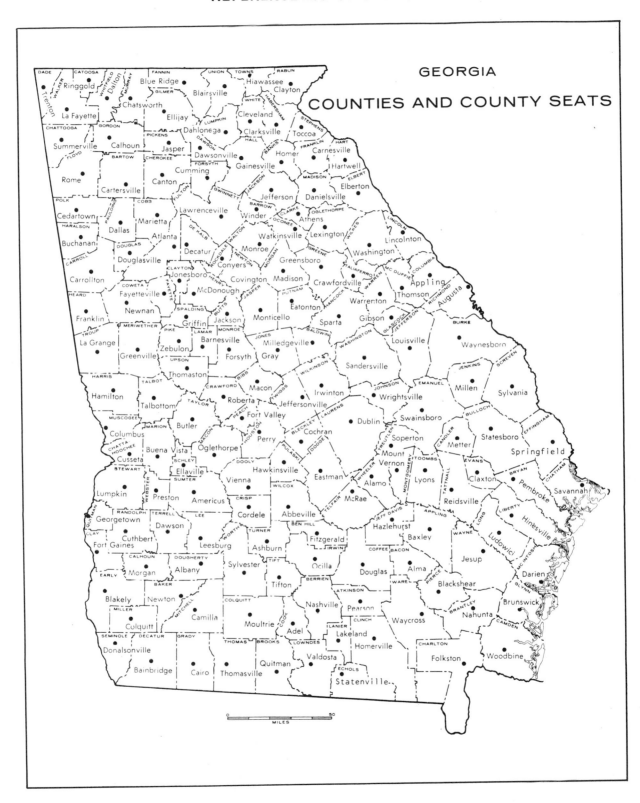

GEORGIA

COUNTIES AND COUNTY SEATS

INDEX